SAGE TALES

Wisdom and Wonder from the Rabbis of the Talmud

Rabbi Burton L. Visotzky

For People of All Faiths, All Backgrounds

JEWISH LIGHTS Publishing

Woodstock, Vermont

Sage Tales:
Wisdom and Wonder from the Rabbis of the Talmud

2011 Hardcover Edition, First Printing
© 2011 by Burton L. Visotzky

Grateful acknowledgment is given for use of the following: p. 22, Roman scale illustration, © 2011 Leora Visotzky; p. 177, the Iudea Capta coin, Classical Numismatic Group, Inc., http://cngcoins.com (en.wikipedia.org/wiki/File:Sestertius_-_Vespasiano_-_Iudaea_Capta-RIC_0424.jpg); p. 183, Roman matron with palla (en.wikipedia.org/wiki/File:Matron_palla2a.jpg).

Library of Congress Cataloging-in-Publication Data
Visotzky, Burton L.
Sage tales : wisdom and wonder from the rabbis of the Talmud / Burton L. Visotzky. — 2011 hardcover ed.
p. cm.
Includes bibliographical references.
ISBN 978-1-58023-456-6 (hardcover)
1. Rabbis—Legends. 2. Jewish legends. 3. Talmud—Legends. 4. Talmud—Criticism, interpretation, etc. I. Title.
BM530.V57 2011
296.1'27607—dc22

2010053964

10 9 8 7 6 5 4 3 2 1
Manufactured in the United States
Jacket design: Tim Holtz
Jacket art: Image—*Ezra Reads the Law.* Synagogue interior wood panel, Dura-Europos synagogue, Syria. Gill/Gillerman slide collection, adapted from Yale Divinity Digital Image and Text (commons.wikimedia.org/wiki/File: Ezra_Reads_the_Law_1.jpg). Curtains—©iStockphoto.com/Billyfoto. Audience—©Max Blain/Fotalia, modified by Tim Holtz.

For People of All Faiths, All Backgrounds
Published by Jewish Lights Publishing
A Division of Longhill Partners, Inc.
Sunset Farm Offices, Route 4, P.O. Box 237
Woodstock, VT 05091
Tel: (802) 457-4000   Fax: (802) 457-4004
www.jewishlights.com

For
David Daily
with love
Welcome to the family

Contents

1 / א

Elijah
the Prophet

A third of a century ago, on the day I was ordained a rabbi, I went on a journey to save Jews from an oppressive government. I traveled to the city of Bukhara in the country of Uzbekistan, then part of the USSR. We had the name of a family there—let's call them "the Goldbergs"—who had applied for visas to depart the Soviet Union so they could move to Israel. But the Russian government refused them their visas and fired them from their jobs. My mission was to bring them blue jeans to trade on the black market so they could put food on their table, let them know they were not forgotten, and gather what information I could to help make their plight known to the Western world.

We had been carefully briefed before our trip not to get into a cab in front of our hotel. The intelligence was that the cabbies reported directly to the KGB and they would blow our cover. Instead, we set out on foot from our six-story hotel, which seemed to be the largest building in town, slowly sounding out the street names in Cyrillic script, looking for Ulitsa Zagorodnaya 8. Bukhara is an old silk-route town; it's been around more than a millennium, so its streets are not exactly on a grid. And although it was only the end of May, the temperature was 43 degrees Celsius (that's 110 degrees Fahrenheit)! To make matters worse, I was "undercover," which meant I was without my yarmulke—my version of going commando. We got

1

profoundly lost, wandering through the warren of winding lanes for an hour and more.

I was hot and thirsty, and my bald spot was bright pink. I gave up finding the address I was sent to visit and instead approached any and every passerby, asking in broken Russian where the hotel was. No reply. I showed them the hotel's card, conveniently given out at the front desk so a non-Russian or Uzbek speaker might stand a chance of finding his way home. No luck. It slowly dawned on me that no one would speak to me because I looked so conspicuously Western, maybe even Jewish. While I was on that trip, I was actually accosted in a posh St. Petersburg hotel by an old, hook-nosed Jew, who asked me in loud, shrill Yiddish, "*Du bist a Yid?*" (Are you a Jew?). I'm ashamed to say that after a terse reply, "*Wu den?*" (What else?) I turned tail and fled. Maybe my Bukharan nightmare was comeuppance for my loss of nerve.

And then I saw a wizened old man dressed in a long, dusty, black caftan, carrying what looked to be a shepherd's crook. Gray beard down to his chest, he seemed as old as Bukhara itself. I approached him with the hotel card in my hand, but as I drew near to him found myself saying, "Ulitsa Zagorodnaya?" I didn't say the house number for two reasons. First, I couldn't count that high in Russian. Second, we were told to be vague about our destinations, lest we compromise the families we were trying to visit. With a brief nod, the old man signaled that we should follow him. In and out of the maze we went. He spoke now and then in what I assume was Uzbek, and I dutifully replied, ever so sagely in my limited Russian, "*Da, da, xorosho*" (Yes, yes, okay). I felt very James Bond, albeit the heat had left me feeling shaken, not stirred.

The old man stopped and with his staff, rapped on an arched wooden door. There, outlined faintly in chalk was the number 8. Was this the house we were looking for? Using mime, we gestured for the old man to stay put while we knocked on the door and stuck our heads in to ascertain that this was Ulitsa Zagorodnaya 8 and that the Goldbergs lived there. We stepped from the street into a scene right out of the Talmud: chickens pecking at the dust, children playing, a water pump, and a half-dozen shacks, which were the dwellings of the residents who shared the courtyard. We asked for "Goldberg" and were immediately informed, "*Da, da, xorosho.*" We had found the right place. The entire conversation took no more than twenty seconds. We popped back out into the street to thank our elderly guide; but he had vanished into the shimmering hot air! We looked down the street the way we had come. Not there. We looked the other way. Not there either. But we noticed that the street took a short dog's-leg bend, so we scurried down the road to see if our nice old man was yet there, just out of our sight lines. But he was gone, gone.

Perplexed, we went back to the arched doorway and peeked back inside. Through a bit more mime, a smattering of Russian, and a dash of dictionary work, we were made to understand that while the Goldbergs did live in the courtyard, they weren't there just at that moment. We were told to return in a few hours. I offered the hotel card in the hopes of getting directions back to the hotel, but the residents looked at me as if I were an idiot. I asked in bad Russian, "Where Hotel X?" At this point one of the children in the courtyard took me by the hand and led me down to the bend in the road. When we got to the exact place where we had sought in vain for the old man, the child pointed upward. There right in front of us was our hotel, not fifty yards away! We were dumbfounded. How was it possible that we had missed the street earlier? We were so close, and we were certain that we had read every street sign. We had. The small bend in the road had its own name, not Ulitsa Zagorodnaya. So we sounded out the Cyrillic script once more, this time in full, to be sure we would be able to find our way back to the Goldbergs later that day. The street was named "Shchalomo Aleikhema," or as we would say in Hebrew or Yiddish, "Shalom Aleichem"! Welcome to the Jewish neighborhood, coincidently right next door to our hotel.

As for our elderly guide, we were left wondering how he knew we were seeking door number 8. Perhaps it was obvious that the Western Jews were in Bukhara to visit the Goldbergs, who were already infamous for trying to leave for Israel and became refuseniks. Perhaps we were one of a stream of young Jewish visitors who made our way to that very street in Bukhara to offer assistance and hope. But, schooled in the stories of the ancient rabbis as I was, another possibility entered my head. Perhaps that old man was the biblical prophet Elijah, who much later in the Talmud appears to rabbis to help them perform good deeds and commandments. Maybe on my first week as a rabbi, I, too, had merited a visit from the legendary world traveler. It fit the pattern. Rabbi, on a mission to save Jews, seems doomed to failure. Elijah appears and leads him to the proper result. *Shalom aleichem.* Peace.

Elijah Stories

I am, of course, what my old English professor would have called "an unreliable narrator." Although I will insist to you that I've told the story exactly the way it happened, there are clues in the telling to let the careful reader know my memory is, shall we say, selective. First, it should set you on edge that I am the hero of my own narrative. I just can't be very reliable about that now, can I? And, I've been conditioned to certain patterns of narrative, types of tales, modes of discourse. My story just might wink at you like a neon sign declaring that what you have read is didactic literature, either edifying fiction or a crafted fable with a moral to the story. And then there's the rabbi bit. Rabbis love to tell stories. We've been doing it for almost two thousand years.

Even as it was happening to me, I experienced the story through two distinct narrative lenses. The first was vintage 1960s, and there I was playing James Bond, spying (as it were) in an exotic foreign clime. True, I lacked a tuxedo, fancy car, and gadgets crafted by Q. But for a boy who grew up reading Ian Fleming, the pocket Hebrew-Russian dictionaries and Star of David necklaces that I had secreted in my luggage would just have to do.

When that old man appeared on the scene to guide us to our destination, though, my door of perception opened to a particularly rabbinic view of the scene. With all the hubris of a newly minted twentysomething rabbi, I found myself living out an Elijah tale. It seemed like that as it was happening, and I grew ever more certain with every telling and retelling of the tale. Since my narrative world was biblical, why not become a character in my own rabbinic interpretation? After all, it's what my rabbinic forebears did all the time. I was enough enamored of the quirky stories of the sages to return to seminary to do a doctorate in the literature, so my experience of the situation through that peculiar lens was a foregone conclusion.

Here's an Elijah story from the ancient rabbis found in the Babylonian Talmud, so you can see how my experience stacks up. By the way, all of the translations in this book are mine.

> Rav Kahana was reduced by poverty to selling wicker baskets in the women's marketplace. There, a matron importuned him for sexual favors. He said, "Wait, while I go make myself pretty for you." He went up to the roof and flung himself to the ground, rather than succumb to his libidinous urges. Elijah came and caught him. Elijah said to Rav Kahana, "You've troubled me to travel four hundred miles to catch you." Kahana replied, "And what caused me to be sitting here in the marketplace open to temptation? Was it not my poverty?" So Elijah gave him a jar of gold coins.
>
> (BABYLONIAN TALMUD, KIDDUSHIN 40A)

Well, it's not exactly the same story, I admit. It does have Elijah helping out a rabbi, though. Maybe if we try another Elijah-saves-a-rabbi story you'll get the idea:

> Once upon a time the Jews wished to send a bribe to the court of Caesar. They wondered who to send and settled on Nahum of Gimzo, who was experienced in miracles. They sent him with a sack of precious gems and pearls in hand. On the way he stayed at an inn. During the night the innkeepers took what was in his bag and filled it instead with dust. When Nahum got to the court of Caesar and they opened the sack and saw it was full of dust, they wanted to kill everyone, for Caesar said, "The Jews are mocking me!"
>
> Elijah appeared to them in the guise of one of their royal courtiers and suggested, "Perhaps that dust is the dust of their ancestor Abraham, who when he threw dust, it turned into

swords, and when he threw straw, it turned into arrows, as it is written in Scripture, 'His sword is like the dust, his bow like the wind-driven straw' [Isaiah 41:2]."

There was a city that Caesar had been unable to conquer. He tried the dust and captured the city! So he took Nahum into his treasury, filled the sack with precious gems and pearls, and sent him home with great honors.

When Nahum returned to the inn, the innkeepers asked, "What did you bring him that you are given such honor?" Nahum replied, "What I took from here, I brought there." They demolished the inn and brought it to the court of Caesar. They said, "That dust that he brought you, it was ours!" They tried the dust, but of course it didn't work. So they executed those innkeepers.

(BABYLONIAN TALMUD, *TAANIT* 21A)

That's more like it. We've got the biblical Elijah, a rabbinic character on a journey to save Jews and deliver a bribe, a miraculous salvation, and while we're at it, comeuppance for the bad guys. Nice. Still, these Elijah stories are odd. The guy seems a bit like Superman and Clark Kent all rolled into one. And both of the Elijah stories from the Talmud end with a bundle of *Gelt* in the rabbi's possession. Ain't that a rabbinic fantasy!

Elijah is a character in the Hebrew Bible, an Israelite prophet, a consummate showman (he calls down fire from heaven more than once) who challenges authority. Like the stories the rabbis told about him so many centuries later, Elijah is not beyond taking to the sky to get from one place to another. In fact, our final view of Elijah in the Bible has him departing from his disciple in a flourish: "And as they were walking and talking, behold! A fiery chariot with fiery horses separated them; and Elijah ascended to heaven in the whirlwind" (2 Kings 2:11).

This dramatic disappearance gave rise to centuries of Elijah legends. The Bible does not record his death. Further, the biblical prophet Malachi cryptically ends his work with the line, "Behold! I will send

Elijah the Prophet to you before the coming of God's awesome, great day" (Malachi 3:23). This double whammy, that he didn't die and that he will return, leads many to imagine Elijah as the harbinger of the One. Very Neo. As the rabbis and their Jews play out the legend, they imagine that Elijah appears at every circumcision ceremony and Seder table, like a Jewish version of Santa. It's a very short leap from there to suppose that Elijah would appear to individual rabbis to help them out of a pickle.

I've taken some time to give you the Elijah tour so you can get a taste of the sheer weirdness of these rabbi stories, or sage tales, as I like to call them. I can still recall the days of my childhood when Ronald Reagan introduced *Death Valley Days* on television. All those glorious TV Westerns, stories of sagebrush and cowboys. Well before I knew anything about rabbis, I was imbibing sage tales. Maybe that's why I'm so susceptible to these quirky narratives.

The Elijah stories teach us something else, as well. Folktales and religious anecdotes share something in common with cowboy yarns. They follow predictable patterns. Readers and listeners, once they've learned the formula, more or less know what to expect. Clued into the conventions of the telling, we anticipate plot devices and even character types. The lives of the saints, be they Christian, Jewish, or Muslim, follow predictable patterns, and these patterns afford a certain pleasure. Once you know the rules, as it were, you get it. Novelist Arundhati Roy captured this well when she wrote in her book *The God of Small Things*, "The Great Stories are the ones you have heard and want to hear again. The ones you can enter anywhere and inhabit comfortably.... They are as familiar as the house you live in." Our sage tales are "Great Stories," lives of Jewish saints.

We might like to think that the gossip we all tell about our clergy—admit it, when we're not totally ignoring them, we gossip or tell jokes about them—if we take that gossip and add five hundred years, we'll have sacred literature! Unfortunately, it doesn't actually work like that. Like Jesus's parables, or the short stories of Franz Kafka or Robert Coover, the stories of the rabbis require some background knowledge to penetrate their often opaque shell.

Why bother? Well, great stories have the power to draw the heart. But certain stories have the power to draw the heart to God and to awaken the better angels of our nature. The earliest rabbinic commentary on the biblical book of Deuteronomy (*Sifre Ekev*) teaches, "Do you want to know your Creator? Learn stories; that's how you'll know the One who spoke the world into being." *Sage Tales* collects stories of the rabbis of old and unlocks them. In learning how and why these oft-told tales were spun, we can learn how they continue to hold value for the fabric of our lives.

Let's let one last Elijah legend, easier than most to appreciate, show us the poignant power of these stories to tug at our heartstrings and teach us lessons ever fresh.

> Rabbi Akiva, a poor shepherd, betrothed the daughter of Ben Kalba Savua, a very rich man. When he heard about their impending marriage, her father vowed to disinherit her. It was winter when they married, and they had nothing but straw for their bedding. Rabbi Akiva said to his bride, "If I could, I would adorn you with a tiara of gold, shaped like the skyline of Jerusalem."
>
> Elijah came to them in the guise of a poor man. He begged them for a bit of straw, "My wife is about to give birth and she has nothing to rest upon."
>
> Said Akiva to his wife, "See, here is a man who doesn't even have straw …"
>
> (Babylonian Talmud, Nedarim 50a)

There is always someone who has less than we do (and it's a wonder she didn't sell her hair and he buy her a comb). In this case, Elijah shows up not only to teach that lesson, but the implied one as well: no matter how poor you may be, you can gain dignity through helping others. Even if your satisfied son-of-a-bitch of a father disowns you. And if you think I'm being a tad harsh in my characterization of the rich father, well he shows up again and again whenever these stories require a rich guy. We'll meet him later in the pages of this book, along with Rabbi Akiva and his disciples (and Elijah, too). I'm not actually sure that Rabbi Akiva's father-in-law's name really was Ben Kalba Savua. You see, these stories have a way of connecting the characters one to another, so that there is a consistent cast of characters for our entertainment. And, not so coincidently, if we translate that rich SOB's nickname into English, it means "satisfied son of a [female] dog"—really!

Not all of these sage tales are straightforward. Many come at their Torah, the lessons they impart, somewhat obliquely. Most are, in fact, somewhat open-ended, so that the story serves as a template for readers to test their own values, ethics, and morality. These narratives all qualify as what the late Belgian Jesuit, Bollandist monk Hippolyte Delehaye called "legends." I, a rabbi, am quoting a venerable monk because Father Delehaye explained that legends were stories told about people who really lived, but the events may not have happened as described in the narrative. In fact, the ancient legends were often moralizing fiction, stories made up in order to teach a point. Delehaye taught us the difference between biography and hagiography. In biography, we attempt to capture an actual life, as lived. Good biography shows the ups and downs, the warts and wrinkles. Hagiography, on the other hand, is the life of a saint. Delehaye and his Bollandist brothers researched the lives of the saints of the church. Those lives, arranged around the church calendar, were recounted to teach spiritual and moral truths.

The sage tales of this book are the rabbis' version of lives of the saints. But being Jewish, these particular saints observe rabbinic law, love to engage in dialectic (a nice way to say they argue with one another), and are often depicted like the quirky fellows we just encountered with Elijah. After four decades of studying and teaching these sage tales, I remain convinced that they have something to teach us, a millennium and a half or more after their first telling. There is an urgency to their wisdom that speaks to the contemporary heart. As a professor of Jewish literature, I firmly believe that the way to a person's heart is through his or her intellect. So in this book we will read the stories within their historical background and with an eye for their literary art.

From the marriage of history and art, life's truths are born. We do not worry if it really happened, but we care passionately that it whispers truth to our souls.

Rabbinic Lit. 101

All of the tales we've encountered so far are found in one grand collection of rabbinic literature called the Babylonian Talmud. I'm going to spend a few paragraphs now describing the Talmud and the other rabbinic literature that our sage tales are drawn from. If you don't want the nitty-gritty, just skip right on down to the last paragraph of this chapter.

The Talmud is a decorator's dream, as it comes in oversize leatherette bindings and is twenty volumes in most modern editions. Within these tomes is a motley collection of rabbinic law and lore, compiled in Hebrew and Aramaic, and edited in sixth-century Jewish Babylonia (modern-day Iraq). Nowadays it's a little jarring to realize that Iraq was home to one of the greatest and longest-flourishing Jewish communities in history. Jews were exiled there from the biblical Land of Israel by the Babylonian Empire back in 587 BCE (Before the Common Era). The Jewish population lived there quite comfortably through the Persians and the Medes, the Sassanid-Zoroastrian conquests, and successive Muslim governments, right up to modernity.

We're talking about a Jewish community that survived, even thrived, in Mesopotamia for twenty-five hundred years! The Talmud is the product of their rabbinic academies that flourished there from about 220 CE (Common Era) into the mid-sixth century, when the unwieldy work got edited. Since that time the Talmud has been studied in Mediterranean and European rabbinic academies, commented upon, copied in manuscripts, and later printed with many of those classic commentaries. That's how the Talmud became the twenty volumes we have today. They say if you study a folio page (two sides) each day, it will take seven years to complete the work.

The Talmud is a compendium of many earlier works of rabbinic literature. It is organized as a commentary, not on the Bible, but on the first work of rabbinic literature, the Mishnah. The Mishnah is a collection of mostly legal opinions. It's not exactly a law code, as it regularly offers multiple (and often conflicting) opinions on any given issue. The Mishnah is organized around broad socio-anthropological categories of rabbinic Jewish law. For example, one entire section is dedicated to the ins and outs of the Jewish holidays, another to rabbinic courts and torts. The Mishnah was compiled in the Land of Israel around the year 200 CE, when it was under Roman occupation. Most of the Mishnah's sensibilities reflect later interpretations of biblical laws, as would be expected. The rabbis had to adapt a good deal of this legislation in light of the destruction of the Jerusalem Temple and its priestly cult by the Romans in 70 CE. Even so, some of the Mishnah reflects Roman law, which, on reflection, might also be expected.

The Babylonian Talmud also quotes from rabbinic traditions of Mishnah study and interpretation done in the Land of Israel up to and including the shift of the Roman Empire to Christianity. There actually was an earlier Talmud, this one of the Land of Israel, edited in the late fourth to early fifth century CE. In addition to this Palestinian Talmud (and here I should note that the term "Palestinian" is one the Romans used to describe the province under their rule—it does not reflect in any way modern political considerations about Israel and/or Palestine), there were also Bible commentaries (midrash) composed by rabbis early and late. Some date from the time of the Mishnah (composed in the first two centuries and edited in the third), others from the time of the Talmud (third through sixth centuries), still others in the Muslim period (from approximately 612 to 1000).

Sage Tales will retell and analyze stories from all these works and eras. We will try to focus on a loose cast of characters to help you follow the flow of the centuries and the narratives. We'll be flying on a magic carpet of stories told from the shores of the Tigris River, on the east, to the countries of the Mediterranean, on the west. Our earliest tales will date from just after the destruction of Jerusalem in the first century CE. Our latest stories were told sometime in the ninth or tenth century. That's a lot of years and plenty of real estate to cover. We have stories from A to Z—well, actually from א to ת, through all twenty-two letters of the Hebrew alphabet. At the end of the book there's a glossary, a who's who of rabbis mentioned, the complete texts and the original sources of our sage tales, and suggestions for further reading. But now, let's meet the cast of characters in our next chapter.

A Happy Ending

One last thing, for those of you who still are wondering. Back in Bukhara all those years ago, we eventually did meet "the Goldbergs." Within a year of our visit, they were granted visas to emigrate. They moved to Israel and might still live there—maybe even happily ever after.

2 / ב

The Cast
of Characters

*P*laybill in hand, you enter the theater, find your seat, and settle in to wait for the curtain to rise. After reading the synopsis, you turn to the page that lists the "Cast of Characters (in order of appearance)." A familiar performance for those familiar with performance. There's a good bit we can learn from observing this scene as we wait for the overture to begin: the whole ritual of theater, both onstage and off. We, the audience, are an integral part of the evening. Whether it is our familiar custom of wiggling out of our coats, trying not to block the aisle, turning off our electronic devices (good citizens that we are, we do so before the recorded announcement chides us), or squinting through the tiny print to see if we know any of the listed donors. Or whether it is our unintended challenges to the performers with our coughs, candy wrappers, rushing out at the end to catch the 10:52 to Ronkonkoma. Of course, we all recognize the value of our applause—as the star enters for the first time, after a wonderful song or soliloquy, and the requisite standing ovation (so we feel we've gotten our money's worth) at the end.

The performers for their part depend on our applause, "the roar of the crowd." Every show is affected by the mood of the audience, the conditions in the theater, costumes, pay scale, and other intangibles invisible to the reader of the script or libretto. The cast, of course, is essential to the play, their performance to our appreciation of it. And yet the stories of old that we tell and retell are often but words on the page. The entire audience is one person, curled on a couch or sitting on a subway. And that lone individual actually has the task of being performer and audience as one. How sad for the lone listener, the isolated reader. So few cues or clues to reconstruct the experience of a really great story. These limitations will haunt us as we try to re-create the settings of these stories and the tellings of these tales. To start with only a listing of the cast of characters, without any accompanying list of the performers of those roles, is as much to say: It's up to you. This is now a one-woman show.

Along the way I'll offer you, dear reader, some clues, thumbnail sketches for each character and his or her motivation. That way you will know what voice to assume and how to read your lines properly (even if you are only reading them in the privacy of your own head). One of the signatures of sage tales is the relative consistency of characters across centuries of telling. Indeed, with but the addition of some local color and perhaps a slight shift in cultural ideology, Rabbi X will speak in pretty much the same voice, be he in Baghdad or Cairo, Jerusalem or Rome. Which is to say, once we know who's who, we can begin to predict his or her role in our drama.

The Cast (in Order of Appearance)

One family of leading rabbis, the Gamalielites, traced its proud lineage back to Temple times. They successively led the Jewish community as patriarch, in a dynastic office passed from father to son, much as was the case among the priests or kings of Israel. The patriarchate persisted for centuries following the destruction of Jerusalem as a political office under the aegis of Rome.

At the outset, however, there was Jewish opposition to this form of leadership. Rather than re-create a dynastic office, some rabbis wanted an academic meritocracy. Although they might not have been able to trace their bloodlines back for generations, they had intellectual patrimony. Let rabbis and their disciples rule the community! These academic rabbis styled themselves as though they were the heads of Greek philosophical schools. Among the pagans, when a new philosopher took over a school, he presented his intellectual lineage, tracing it back to the founder of the school. For example, the new head of the Stoic school would trace himself back to Zeno, or the new head of the Platonic school would trace his lineage back to Plato. In the 70–90s of the first century CE, the erstwhile head of the rabbis who opposed the Gamalielite dynasty offered his own chain of tradition, tracing his lineage back to God, through Moses at Mount Sinai:

> Moses received the Torah at Sinai and transmitted it to Joshua. From Joshua to the Elders; from the Elders to the Prophets; and the Prophets transmitted it to the Men of the Great Assembly.... Shimeon the Righteous was among the remnant of the Great Assembly.... Antigonus of Sokho received the tradition from Shimeon.... Yosé ben Yoezer of Tzeraidah and Yosé ben Yohanan of Jerusalem received the tradition from them.... Hillel and Shammai received the tradition from them.... Rabbi Yohanan ben Zakkai received the tradition from Hillel and Shammai. He used to say, "If you have studied much Torah, don't claim merit for yourself, for you were created to do so." Rabbi Yohanan ben Zakkai had five disciples. These are they: Rabbi Eliezer ben Hyrcanus, Rabbi Yehoshua ben Hananiah, Rabbi José the Priest, Rabbi Shimeon ben Netanel, and Rabbi Elazar ben Arakh.
>
> (*PIRKE AVOT* 1–2)

In this rabbinic chain of tradition, leading from God and Moses at Mount Sinai, Torah was faithfully transmitted and received through fourteen generations (I've omitted some above) until it reached Rabbi Yohanan ben Zakkai and his five famous disciples. And now, ladies and gentlemen, I present to you our cast of characters (in order of appearance): "Rabbi Yohanan ben Zakkai had five disciples. These are they: Rabbi Eliezer ben Hyrcanus, Rabbi Yehoshua ben Hananiah, Rabbi José the Priest, Rabbi Shimeon ben Netanel, and Rabbi Elazar ben Arakh."

In a few moments, we'll read the earliest report of the fabulous five and their teachings. But let's stop and savor this statement we just read, for it will command so much of our subsequent rabbinic storytelling. I know it sounds overly determined, even mechanical, but once we've memorized the cast in order of appearance, it seems fated that thus shall they ever after appear. These rabbis will be the characters of most, but not all, of the sage tales in this book.

First among equals comes Rabbi Eliezer ben Hyrcanus. At opening glance, it's a name like any other. Eliezer is a good Hebrew name, found in the Bible. Abraham had a servant with that name, and Moses named one of his sons Eliezer. Yet many folks jump on his father's Greek name (the *ben* means "son of") as proof that Eliezer came from an assimilated Hellenistic family, with little Jewish background. Indeed, later rabbinic texts assume that Hyrcanus had very little rabbinic knowledge—although at the time there wasn't all that much rabbinic knowledge to be had, so what did they expect? Now it is true that Hyrcanus is a Greek name, but a Greek name need not a pagan make! After all, think of people with classical German names like Goldberg or Goldstein. These are, it is true, German names. But most folks who hear those monikers think "Jewish" and are more often than not correct in their assumption. Hyrcanus was a name of Jewish kings and high priests from the family of the Maccabees. Yes, it was Greek, but when you heard it you would have thought "Jewish." As it turns out, Eliezer ben Hyrcanus went on to become one of the most famous characters in rabbinic literature. He's quoted so often that he is frequently referred to as Rabbi Eliezer the Great.

Next on our list is Rabbi Yehoshua ben Hananiah. His name, too, is good biblical Hebrew. Moses's successor was named Yehoshua, or in King James English, Joshua. Rabbi Yehoshua is a good example of how the rabbis, like the Stoics, cut across class lines in their circles. He earned his daily bread as a charcoal maker. This was a dirty job that required Yehoshua to dig peat moss and burn it until it was reduced to briquettes. Once, when visiting his home, one of the patrician Gamaliel family (mentioned above) archly observed, no doubt as he gingerly ran his finger over the surface, "From the walls of your home one can see that you are a charcoal maker." It would take another eighteen hundred years for the wealthy to appreciate that burning peat could be used to make an excellent single malt scotch.

Then there's Rabbi José the Priest. Despite his name, he's not Hispanic. I could have as easily transliterated his name as Yossi but chose José precisely because the Spanish form is so clearly a diminutive of Joseph. The same is true in Hebrew, Yossi/José being a nickname for Yosef/Joseph. What's really interesting about this disciple, though, is his lineage. He comes from priestly roots, which is to say he's a *kohen*. The priests, who had controlled the Jerusalem Temple, were decimated by the Romans as the Jewish revolt against the empire (66–70 CE) was so brutally suppressed—battered and banned from Temple and power, but not wholly obliterated. So here's a priest among the faithful remnant, as it were, and he's thrown his lot in among the rabbis and their disciples. No more dynastic bragging rights for José, just discipleship and study. On Rabbi Yohanan's side of the equation, the master gets to co-opt one of the former ruling class into his close circle. Or at least claim to for posterity.

Rabbi Shimeon ben Netanel is the odd man out. He just doesn't fit well with the other characters. We don't know much about him, aside from his distinction of having been Rabbi Yohanan ben Zakkai's disciple. Throughout rabbinic literature, from the second century through the twentieth, he's only mentioned in lists containing the names of the other disciples listed here or in expansions of the texts that will unfold before us. Still, he's a member of the entourage, which I suppose is an achievement.

Finally, there's everybody's favorite, Rabbi Elazar ben Arakh. Elazar is also a biblical Hebrew name. Moses had a nephew, his brother Aaron's son, named Elazar. He surely suffered from the continual annoyance of being confused with Eliezer (it's not just we who get those two confused). In Hebrew pronunciation of the times, which we know from early manuscripts, as well as transliterations of Hebrew words and names into Greek letters, both Elazar and Eliezer were pronounced Lazar (like Lazarus in the Gospels or like Lazar Wolf the butcher). We'll worry more about this name later, when folks in the very stories we are reading start confusing it. But know this: for a guy whom everyone seems to think is hot stuff, Elazar quickly cools and vanishes from sight in later rabbinic literature.

About the Cast

Now that we've met our cast of characters, let's read on in our imaginary *Playbill*, "About the Cast." The passage we're reading comes from one of the earliest documents of rabbinic literature, the Mishnah. And the part of the Mishnah we are reading is that collection of pithy wisdom called the Chapters of the Fathers. In Hebrew it's *Pirke Avot*, sometimes translated as Ethics of the Fathers. Immediately following the chain of tradition, which traces the transmission of Torah from God to Moses at Sinai all the way down to Yohanan ben Zakkai, the good rabbi is quoted speaking about his fab five:

> He recounted their virtues: "Eliezer ben Hyrcanus is a lime-plastered cistern that doesn't lose a drop; Yehoshua ben Hananiah: happy is she who bore him! José the Priest is pious; and Shimeon ben Netanel fears sin; while Elazar ben Arakh is an overflowing wellspring.
>
> (*PIRKE AVOT* 2)

Nice compliments I guess, even if some are opaque and others seem rather generic. How would *you* like to be called a "lime-plastered cistern"? Actually, it's a telling piece of praise. The rabbis taught and transmitted their traditions by memory. Books were scarce and expensive. They did write the Five Books of Moses onto Torah scrolls; but the rabbinic interpretations and the Mishnah, those were recited by memory and repeated face to face. In a social setting where oral transmission is the norm, a steel-trap memory is a great virtue. Or, as they would say, a "lime-plastered cistern." In southern Palestine, storage of the winter rains was a must if people were to survive. The worst imaginable thing would be to have stored water in a cistern only to see it slowly seep into the ground. So, like Huck Finn painting his picket fence, they daubed their cisterns with lime until they were sealed water-tight. Eliezer's memory was so good, he didn't lose a drop. Of course, a cistern only holds water; it has no source beyond what is diverted to it through rain. No wellspring, no underground sources. You only get out what you put in. Elsewhere in rabbinic literature Eliezer gets what sounds to our ears like a dubious compliment: "He never said an original word in his life." We might find Eliezer a very dull boy, but in a setting where accurate oral transmission was highly valued, original thinking runs the risk of contaminating tradition. Being a lime-plastered cistern was really pretty good after all.

As for Yehoshua, his mother would be so proud! Rabbi Yohanan's compliment makes him sound like a sweet Jewish mama's boy. But the comment echoes Proverbs 23:24–25, "The one who begets a wise son will rejoice in him ... she who bore you will delight." I suppose that just confirms that he was a sweet mama's boy—a virtue in the Jewish community from the time of the Bible until today.

That Rabbi Shimeon fears sin speaks for itself. In the rabbinic world, there were two overlapping paths toward relationship with God (and maybe toward parents, too): one was to serve God out of love, and the other was to obey God out of fear. Shimeon was of the latter school, but I'd like to think that he had a fair salting of love in his devotion to God, too.

I skipped over José the Priest because the compliment his teacher gave him takes a bit of unpacking. If he were listed in a *Playbill*, either he'd have a longer listing or we would need to propose alternate squibs for his bio. Rabbi Yohanan describes him as pious, my translation for the Hebrew word *hasid*. Both Wikipedia and the dictionary define "Hasid" as relating to Orthodox Judaism and Eastern European piety. I assure you, José the Priest was neither an Orthodox Jew nor one of those guys running around in tights and wearing earlocks; both notions are modern (to use the term very loosely). The term *hasid* might mean that José was simply pious—nothing wrong with that, unless you're one of those folks who use the term "pious" as a put-down.

But, the term *hasid* also might refer to a first-century sect, a group of separatist ascetics. The ancient historian Josephus wrote about them, and his Greek term is usually transliterated into English as Essene. Some scholars think those *hasid*s were associated with the folks who lived at Khirbet Qumran, the ones who gave us the Dead Sea Scrolls. They were priests who rejected the Jerusalem Temple and what they perceived to be its corrupt priesthood. So when we say José the Priest was a *hasid*, who knows?

Which brings us to Elazar ben Arakh. Not only does he metaphorically have his own source of water, but he's also an over-flowing wellspring. Wisdom and Torah are regularly compared to water for the thirsty. The biblical book of Proverbs advises, "Drink water from your cistern, rivulets from your well. Your springs will gush outward, streams of water in the streets.... May your water sources be blessed" (Proverbs 5:15–18). Yohanan has given Elazar a dandy compliment.

Weighty Characters

We've met our cast of characters and read what their teacher thought of their, well, characters. Eliezer and Elazar seem to have gotten compliments that had some oomph to them. In fact, we have a couple of traditions that Rabbi Yohanan had even nicer things to say about our friend Lazar than how well he held water. The trouble is that the tradition has been transmitted to us in two different flavors, one favoring Elazar and one favoring Eliezer. In Hebrew, the difference in spelling those two names is the teeniest letter of the alphabet, *yod* (ʼ), so it would be really hard to know for sure which student was meant unless their fathers' names were mentioned. And, as we've already noted, both names were pronounced pretty much the same way, as Lazar, so there are oral and written grounds for confusion. Let's listen to what Rabbi Yohanan said:

> He used to say, "If all of the sages of Israel were on one scale of the balance and Eliezer ben Hyrcanus were on the other scale, he would outweigh them all."
>
> But Abba Saul quoted in his name, "If all of the sages of Israel were on one scale of the balance, and even if Eliezer ben Hyrcanus were among them, Elazar ben Arakh would out-weigh them all."

> (PIRKE AVOT 2)

Before we even think about which student Rabbi Yohanan actually was speaking of, we need to wonder about those scales. Surely this is metaphor, but even a metaphor needs to make some sense. What was Yohanan seeing in his mind's eye? Did he think Lazar (let's embrace the confusion of names for the moment) could outweigh everyone because he was really dense? Or did he imagine a hugely fat Lazar outweighing all of his colleagues? We can stipulate that he metaphorically referred to Lazar's prodigious intellect and critical acumen, but still, I cannot shake the desire to have a clear image of Yohanan's reference.

Because this is "oral literature," imagery will tend to be concrete rather than abstract. Abstract thought (such as higher math or physics) requires written notation. That's why at universities and research labs, scientists speak with one another chalk in hand. The physical notation of abstract formulas helps scientists understand one another. When a group eschews writing and chooses to do its business orally, the imagery becomes much more solid. Abstract ideas, like numbers, don't travel as well orally. So, a theologian like Rudolph Otto might *write* about a "transcendent, numinous deity," while the rabbis would *speak* by comparing God to a king of flesh and blood.

Which brings us back to Yohanan's compliment of Lazar. If you still aren't sure what Yohanan is seeing, allow me to take you on a tour of the Mediterranean world in the first century. Let's travel to southern Italy (always a nice place to visit), to the town of Pompeii. I choose that site because Pompeii sat in the shadow of Mount Vesuvius and in 79 CE, the volcano erupted, burying the town under almost twelve feet of ash. Pompeii was immured there, frozen in time, until it was excavated in the nineteenth and twentieth centuries. Among the interesting things we learned from what was dug up by archaeologists is that Pompeii apparently exported kosher food; most likely to the Jews of Roman Palestine. I note this because it means that there was contact between the lost city of Pompeii and the world of the rabbis at precisely the time that Rabbi Yohanan was speaking about his student Lazar.

Pompeii had a market that was regulated by an imperial appointee, called an *agoranomos*; he was literally the law (*nomos*) of the marketplace (*agora*). He ensured the honesty of the weights and measures (unless, of course, he was taking bribes). Modern butchers have electronic scales, but they still have some sign on them or even a lead seal to show they were inspected for accuracy. How did the *agoranomos* of Pompeii ensure the weights were accurate? This is relevant to our discussion because we are talking about weights put on one scale of the balance, just like in our Lazar imagery. In Pompeii, the market supervisor ensured accurate weights by making those weights mini-busts of himself! Here's a picture of a scale excavated from Pompeii.

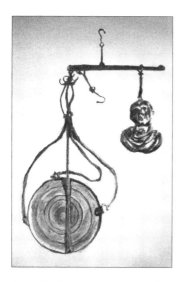

If we assume that such weights were common across the Mediterranean basin, we now know what Rabbi Yohanan had in mind when he complimented Lazar. We also have some insight into the concreteness of rabbinic metaphor. It is anything but abstract, but instead revels in stuff; the real, rather than the ideal.

Back to our two rabbis and the confusion between them. The first tradition, apparently quoting Rabbi Yohanan directly, praises Eliezer ben Hyrcanus. The second tradition, in which Abba Saul quotes Eliezer, offers regard to Elazar ben Arakh. So which is correct? Perhaps the first tradition is more original. It is reported without any intermediaries, so shouldn't it be more accurate? Or should we worry about the precision of an editor reporting a tradition over a century old without any reliable authority intervening to transmit it?

Is Abba Saul's tradition more reliable then? And what about the name Abba? To avoid a musical segue into "Mamma Mia" and the inevitable chorus of "Dancing Queen," let me point out that *Abba* was a title of respect in the first century. *Abba* means "father." The great leaders of the Jewish world, Hillel and Shammai (mentioned in our chain of tradition at the outset of this chapter), are called "Fathers of the World." Catholic priests are still called Father, and the monks who head monasteries are called *abbot*, a word that comes from *abba*. More than fifty rabbis in classical rabbinic literature share *Abba* as a title or proper name. Our Abba Saul is often invoked as a reliable transmitter of early traditions.

It may be a good idea to have an intervening link in a chain of oral tradition. Perhaps Abba Saul heard it from Yohanan or a contemporary and in turn told it to the editor of our text. We're trying to get a handle on traditions that are almost two thousand years old that by their own description are oral. This is slippery stuff, but the Abba Saul tradition has a tell, the twitch that gives the hand away. Note that he says, "If all of the sages of Israel were on one scale of the balance, *and even if Eliezer ben Hyrcanus were among them....*" He shows us that he already knows the Eliezer ben Hyrcanus tradition! With all due deference to Elazar ben Arakh, I think Eliezer gets the benefit of being first on this one. But, we still might wonder, did Rabbi Yohanan say "Lazar" and each rabbi's friends jumped to conclude it was *their* Lazar of whom he spoke?

The Good Way

Our cast of characters now introduced, Rabbi Yohanan's reviews of them heard, some confusion about who's who sorted out as best we can, it's time for the play to begin. Rabbi Yohanan sets the scene in motion with an interrogation that would warm the heart of any Stoic philosopher. He asked his disciples:

> "Go forth and see: what is the good way that a man should adhere to?"
>
> Rabbi Eliezer said, "A good eye."
>
> Rabbi Yehoshua said, "A good colleague."
>
> Rabbi José said, "A good neighbor."
>
> Rabbi Shimeon said, "The one who sees that which is born."
>
> Rabbi Elazar said, "A good heart."
>
> He said to them, "I prefer the words of Elazar ben Arakh, for his words include your words."
>
> (*PIRKE AVOT* 2)

Before we consider the views of Yohanan's five disciples, let's take a moment to answer his question for ourselves. What *is* the good way a person should cling to? These are ancient texts, to be sure, but their wisdom might offer us a path in life. If the rabbis' answers in this passage are somewhat opaque or untimely, the question Rabbi Yohanan poses is surely worthy of our consideration. How might you answer his philosophical query? It does not matter whether you share a worldview that embraces "the good" as your own organizing principle. What matters is that you set a way to follow. A conscious choice of path helps give life meaning and a goal, and allows you to realize when you've strayed as well.

As for Yohanan's students and their opinions, let's begin with Rabbi Eliezer's "good eye." I do not think that he was referring to Derek Jeter at bat for the Yankees. In fact, for rabbinic Hebrew of that period, a "good eye" meant one who saw broadly and therefore was generous to others. Rabbi Yehoshua's offering, a "good colleague" is a bit harder to crack. The obvious definition of the term is that having a good colleague or friend leads to other Goods. But the Hebrew term I've translated as "colleague," *haver*, has a broader range of meaning beyond friendship. A *haver* may be a study partner. In the context of the first century, a *haver* is also a technical term meaning a person who is trustworthy about tithing grain and observing rules of Jewish ritual purity. In other words, a *haver* is someone at whose table you would eat, a table companion. In modern parlance, we might say it is someone who keeps kosher the same ways you do (if you observe Jewish food law). This was a bit of a political distinction back then, even as it is now. I like to joke that for some people the whole point of keeping kosher is so that there can be someone else's kitchen you won't eat in!

Rabbi Shimeon is the odd man out. I have literally translated what is most likely an idiom meaning someone who can foresee the consequences of his or her actions. I very much doubt that Shimeon's "one who sees that which is born" refers to an ob-gyn. Still, the idiom breaks the pattern of "A good X." He must have been a nonconformist or perhaps came late to class and didn't get how to play this particular game.

And then there is Elazar. At least for his champion Rabbi Yohanan, Elazar's suggestion of a "good heart" is all-inclusive. In modern English, the heart is the seat of our emotions; so we can be brokenhearted, or to complicate the metaphor, our heart "sings" when we are happy or in love. There are certainly those in the ancient world who thought that the heart was the place from which emotions emanated. But others thought that the heart was the source of the mind or intellect. This debate over heart and head is found as early as Plato and Aristotle. We simply cannot know whether Elazar thought that good intellect or good emotional balance was the key to a good life. I am also sorely suspicious that were Elazar to have answered the question by saying, "Good oobleck," his teacher Yohanan would have beamed and preferred his teaching over the statements of the others.

Once the students reply to Yohanan's philosophical inquiry on "the Good," he rephrases it negatively to complete the lesson:

> "Go forth and see: what is the bad way from which a man should distance himself?"
>
> Rabbi Eliezer said, "A bad eye."
>
> Rabbi Yehoshua said, "A bad colleague."
>
> Rabbi José said, "A bad neighbor."
>
> Rabbi Shimeon said, "The one who borrows and does not repay." One who borrows from a human is like one who borrows from the Omnipresent, as it is said, "The wicked borrows and does not repay, while the righteous gives generously" (Psalm 37:21).
>
> Rabbi Elazar said, "A bad heart."
>
> He said to them, "I prefer the words of Elazar ben Arakh, for his words include your words."
>
> (PIRKE AVOT 2)

Again, ask yourself Rabbi Yohanan's question. What is it you must avoid to keep your life from being "bad"? Might you agree with the rabbis and Stoics that anger should be avoided? What about accumulation of money and material possessions? *Pirke Avot* actually quotes a rabbi saying, "More stuff, more worry." What about avoiding threats to family stability? This can range as broadly as never being home for dinner or helping your kids with their homework to avoiding office flirtations. There are so many temptations that avoiding junk food and empty calories seems like a minor annoyance.

We can turn back to the rabbis' discussion of the *via negativa*. Eliezer's "bad eye," we now know, is the opposite of "good eye." In later Hebrew we might have to translate the term "evil eye," for it would mean to avoid getting hexed. But in Eliezer's day, having a "bad eye" meant you were stingy, miserly, tightfisted. It should be clear from this that the term in Hebrew (*ra*) means "bad, wicked, evil." That also means that were George W. Bush the one translating the verse of Psalms just quoted, he'd have said, "Evildoers don't repay."

Which brings us around to Shimeon, again the outlier. Is what he says the opposite of "the one who sees that which is born"? I would argue that if you cannot foresee the consequences of your actions, you well might borrow without being able to repay. As evidence, consider the recent housing bubble and the financial disaster that ensued. I am not suggesting that those benighted borrowers were evil or even bad, but their debts sure were for them and everyone else.

In this round of answers, Shimeon appears prolix. I do not think he was the author of all the words attributed to him here, however much he didn't get the rhythm of "good X/bad X." It is likely that one and maybe even two scribes offered their own commentary on his statement. Maybe it began as a marginal note and worked its way into the body of the text, as often happens in manuscripts. In the end there was a gloss on Shimeon's words, equating borrowing from a human to borrowing from God (who most assuredly collects debts for sins—at least in the rabbis' theology). Along came the next scribe who thought, "I know the perfect verse to illustrate this remark," and so, our clunky passage was created. We need not comment further on Rabbi Yohanan's preference for Rabbi Elazar's "bad heart." We can all agree that a bad heart is a bad thing and that we should avoid cholesterol and evil thoughts.

Sage Advice

So far, all the dialogue has been rather formulaic. We might take Rabbi Yohanan's compliments and add them to those "goods" and "bads" to start to get a bit of a feel for our characters. But wouldn't it be good to hear them speak, as it were, each in his own voice? Before we bend our ears to listen in, a reminder: this is drama, not biography. We cannot guarantee that any of our rabbis actually said the lines attributed to him. Yet, they each spoke truth.

> They each said three things.
>
> Rabbi Eliezer said, "Let your friend's honor be as dear to you as your own. Do not easily anger. Repent one day before your death. Warm yourself at the hearth of the sages, but be wary not to get scorched by their coals; for their bite is the bite of a fox, their sting is the sting of a scorpion, and their hiss is the hiss of an asp. All of their words are like fiery coals!"
>
> Rabbi Yehoshua said, "A bad eye, a bad libido, and misanthropy remove a person from the world."
>
> Rabbi José said, "Let your friend's money be as dear to you as your own. Prepare yourself to study Torah, for it is not automatically bequeathed to you. Let all your doings be in God's name."
>
> Rabbi Shimeon said, "Be punctilious in the recitation of the *Shema* and in the Prayer. When you pray, do not pray by rote, but address God in supplication and desire for mercy; as it is said, 'For God is gracious and compassionate, slow to anger, abounding in kindness, and renouncing punishment' [Joel 2:13]. Do not consider yourself evil."
>
> Rabbi Elazar said, "Be diligent to study Torah. Know what to reply to Epicurus. Know before whom you labor, who is the Master of your labors who will reward you for your deeds."
>
> (*Pirke Avot* 2)

Our passage opens with a mnemonic device. The oral reciter reminds himself (and us) that each of the rabbis said three things. One can almost see him count off on his fingers to be sure of the accuracy of his memory as he performs the text. To state the obvious, Rabbi Eliezer seems to have trouble counting to three. It might be the case, as we saw above, that Eliezer really did have three sayings attached to his name at the outset, and then later editors, knowing he was the great Rabbi Eliezer, added further observations that they attributed to him.

Eliezer begins with honor, a social construct broadly embraced in Mediterranean societies. The sheer ubiquity of honor as a motivator of society demands that you consider it within a wide circle of friends. But honor has a soft underbelly—shame. It is easy to take umbrage if you think your honor or your friend's honor has been impugned. So it's good advice to be slow to anger; otherwise, feuds abound. Eliezer's point about repentance is sweet piety, if somewhat paradoxical. Elsewhere, one of Eliezer's students asks him, "But rabbi, how do you know when you shall die?" You can almost see Eliezer smack his forehead and say, "That's the whole point! You can't know; so you have to repent daily!" Such good advice, and delivered with such wry subtlety.

Our text imagines Eliezer shoehorning even more pithy advice into his rule-of-three allotment: "Warm yourself at the hearth of the sages, but be wary not to get scorched by their coals; for their bite is the bite of a fox, their sting is the sting of a scorpion, and their hiss is the hiss of an asp. All of their words are like fiery coals!" As a rabbi-academic I particularly like this advice. I could imagine a colleague who is all warm and fuzzy, full of homey wisdom, who then turns pissy toward his student and stings her with criticism or reproach. Sadly, this is true of "friends," too.

We should also note the importance of historical context. When Eliezer warns of the potential irascibility of his rabbi colleagues, it sounds like sage advice. Yet when Jesus (a first-century rabbi, after all) says to his fellow Jews, the Pharisees, "You brood of vipers ..." (Matthew 12:34), virtually every Jew I know quivers with outrage. Now maybe when Jesus said it, and even when Matthew wrote it (around the time of Rabbi Eliezer), it also was sage advice. Two thousand years later, too much bad blood has spilled between Christians and Jews to hear these words comfortably. It's good for both Jews and Christians to see that some statements, restored to their original context or compared with one another, might have been less inflammatory when first uttered, even as we recognize their inappropriateness today.

Yehoshua also utters sage advice. We already know that his "bad eye" refers to a lack of generosity. I confess I tilted toward Freud in translating his next statement. Literally what he said was "a bad inclination." The book of Genesis (8:21) imagines God wistfully commenting after Noah's flood, "The inclination of a human's heart is evil from his infancy." From this biblical phrase the rabbis develop a concept of the duality that resides in each human: the inclination to good (Hebrew: *yetzer tov*) and the inclination to evil (*yetzer ra*). Later rabbinic interpreters explain that this inclination to evil can be channeled to good. For instance, sexual urges can lead to promiscuity, but properly directed they also can lead to marriage and children. So I translate "inclination to evil" as "libido," supposing that the Torah serves as Freud's superego. Yehoshua is, of course, quite correct: stinginess, a rampant libido, and misanthropy are a pernicious combination. You and everyone around you lose. Such a person is removed from civilized society. No one wants anything to do with someone that boorish.

Rabbi José's words remind us of the virtues of mammon. Above I translated it as money, but the Hebrew word that José uses is precisely *mammon*. The good rabbi disagrees with his older contemporary Jesus, who says in Matthew (6:24), "You cannot serve God and mammon." José demurs, but with a caveat: If you care as much about your neighbor's cash as your own, if you are as protective of his or her resources as you would be of yours, then you actually can serve God by caring about mammon. Indeed, as later commentators to the passage note, you then will have fulfilled the commandment to "love your neighbor as yourself" (Leviticus 19:18).

The truly poignant thing that José the Priest says is, "Prepare yourself to study Torah, for it is not automatically bequeathed to you." José's priesthood was, indeed, bequeathed to him, passed down patrilineally, from father to son. With the ruins of the Jerusalem Temple as a depressing reminder, José embraces what is eternal, if spiritual. Learn

Torah, he says, and you can almost hear him whisper, "That, they can't destroy."

Once again, Shimeon stands outside of the circle. If we translate José's "Torah" a bit more generically as "philosophy," then everything our sages have taught here is within the comfortable orbit of Roman Stoicism. Shimeon seems parochially Jewish. He reminds us to punctiliously recite the *Shema* (a prayer made up of three biblical passages, from Deuteronomy 6 and 11 and Numbers 15). He goes on to say the same for "the Prayer"—he does not mean generic prayer, but rather specifically the prayers the rabbis themselves authored. He adds a warning against fixed formula. While it is helpful to have the words to say it, there is a danger of mindless rote recitation when praying daily. Shimeon tells us to really speak from our hearts, supplicating God's mercy. Finally and perhaps related to a tendency when praying to be self-denigrating, he reminds us not to have a negative self-image. Too many Jewish prayers tend to be of the I-am-a-worm-step-on-me variety. Shimeon counsels prayer with dignity and self-respect.

There is one statement of Elazar's I want to look at because I've suggested that much of the teaching we find here is Stoicism, the general ethos of the Roman Empire. Like a good Stoic, Elazar reminds us to know how to reply to Epicurus. He and his disciples were opposed to Epicurean teachings primarily over whether the gods paid any attention to human goings-on. Epicureans did not believe in divine providence. This denial of God's reward and punishment was anathema to the rabbis. They accepted the theology of Deuteronomy and all the retributive justice it implied. For the rabbis, God surely cared what humans did, and rewarded and punished accordingly. So Rabbi Elazar's warning was well sounded. In later Hebrew, the term *epicurus* came to mean a heretic or anyone who denied rabbinic teachings.

I cannot complete this chapter without quoting one final passage from the Mishnah text we have been studying together. Right after we have met our cast of characters and heard their words, one other early sage, Rabbi Tarphon, says, "It is not yours to complete the task, but neither are you free to abandon it" (*Pirke Avot* 2).

3 / ג

A Story Well Told Is Worth Retelling

R abbis write commentary. This seems to need no further elabora-
tion, as it captures an essential truism about rabbis and their literature. The commentary-like nature of rabbinic writing is captured in a
famous tale about the founding fathers of the rabbinic movement,
Hillel and Shammai.

> A story is told about a gentile who came to Shammai and said
> to him, "Convert me, but on the condition that you can teach
> me the entire Torah while I stand on one foot."
>
> Shammai repelled him with the builder's cubit in his
> hand.
>
> He came to Hillel, who converted him. Hillel said to him,
> "Don't do anything to a friend that you hate yourself. This is
> the entire Torah. The rest is commentary. Go study."
>
> (BABYLONIAN TALMUD, SHABBAT 31A)

This oft-told tale puts into Hillel's mouth a negative form of the Golden
Rule ("Do unto others as you would have them do unto you"; see
Matthew 7:12). This poignant fiction is part of a cycle of Hillel and
Shammai stories that circulated in the Jewish world and made its way
into the Babylonian Talmud (five stories on the same page, in fact). In
each of these tales, Shammai plays the curmudgeon and Hillel is the

nice guy. The narratives serve to help define the essentials of Judaism to curious outsiders, and so, to Jewish readers, too. What's intriguing is the matter-of-fact way Hillel says, "The rest is commentary" and assumes that this is so self-evident it will be immediately understood.

In fact, what may seem obvious in hindsight need not have been the case in the first century, when Hillel lived. I've been careful to only attribute the adage "The rest is commentary" to a story about Hillel. It's not that I think he didn't say it—he certainly might have—but Hillel is a character here in a story told centuries later. By then, it was a given that rabbis write commentary, so why not have Hillel assume it, too?

But ask yourself, of all the styles and types of literature the rabbis decided to write, must commentary have been one of them? Those old rabbis knew how to tell a short story. That type of narration, where a rabbi is a character in the story and he or another character makes a pronouncement about life, was well-known in the broader Greco-Roman world in which they lived. This style of storytelling was taught to advanced Greek grammar school and rhetoric students. Narration was part of the training for public speakers, so they were well rehearsed at telling long, middling, or short versions of the same story. A good story got your point across. It was as true then as it is today.

The rabbis knew how to tell the kind of stories that were familiar in style and content to their pagan and Christian peers. In fact, another of the Hillel stories on that same page of Talmud tells us of a would-be convert who wants to convert in order to become the high priest in Jerusalem. Saint Jerome, a famous fifth-century father of the church, tells a very similar story about a pagan who says he's ready to convert to Christianity, if only they would make him pope! Jerome, too, was trained in rhetoric and knew how to spin a good story with a religious moral to it.

But commentary was also a well-known genre among the same rhetoric schools that taught Romans how to recount their stories for effective public speaking. Since every literate Greek speaker knew huge sections of Homer by memory, pagans in the Eastern Empire shared a common "sacred scripture" in the *Iliad* and *Odyssey*. Not only could they recite the words of the blind bard, but they could also comment on every detail. If Nestor said something that bothered them, they would interpret it to mean something less troubling. Pagan grammarians of the great city Alexandria even suggested changing Homer's text now and then, to make it read more smoothly with their sensibilities. When the story's ethics really bothered them, they would allegorize it, finding the presumed hidden meaning by assuming that the surface narrative alluded to something else entirely. And pagan lawyers, then as now, knew how to read between the lines of any law on the books in an effort to benefit their clients.

The rabbis who commented on the Bible made full use of the interpretive techniques *en vogue* throughout the Greco-Roman world. We might be justified in suggesting that the very fact that rabbis write commentary is testimony to their comfort in the surrounding pagan culture. Like the Greek speakers who formed their culture around the twenty-four books of the *Iliad* and of the *Odyssey*, the rabbis created their community around their own canon of Scripture. With a bit of creative arithmetic, the rabbis insisted that the Hebrew Bible was also made up of twenty-four books (this required, among other things, that they count all twelve of the Minor Prophets as one book). As Jewish civilization shifted from Temple cult to Torah canon, commentary on the Book seemed as natural for Jews as it was for those under Homer's aegis.

But this oversimplifies the inherent messiness of history. After all, in addition to their role as members of Hellenistic civilization, the rabbis were inheritors of a Semitic biblical tradition. Commentary was in their blood, not just in the air they breathed. The Torah itself has a running interior commentary. For instance, Adam and Eve get names early on in Genesis. When each is named, an explanation for the name is offered. So Adam was named that because he was taken from the earth (in Hebrew: *adamah*). Eve (in Hebrew: *Havvah*) was dubbed mother of all living things (*hay*). Bad puns, yes, but commentary! Elsewhere in Genesis, readers are given information along the way, such as the place Jacob named Bethel "used to be called Luz" (Genesis 28:19) or that when Abraham first went to the Promised Land, "the Canaanites were then in the land" (Genesis 12:6).

As this latter example shows us, commentary can be quite disturbing. In the case I just quoted, one medieval rabbi surmised that if the Torah says the Canaanites were *then* in the land, it implies that they no longer were in the land at the time of the book's writing. This led that medieval rabbi to leap to a startling conclusion: Moses was not the author of the Torah! For if he were, then when he was writing the book, the Canaanites should still be in the land. Oops. Sometimes commentary gives away too much.

This leads us to our second commentary conundrum. If commentary is what later folks wrote on an earlier book, then how is it that there are dozens, if not hundreds of internal comments like the ones above, already found in the Torah? This means that the biblical text we have underwent many, many changes during the centuries of its transmission as sacred text of the Jewish community. Over time, obscure references (like the original name of Bethel) got added to the text, and observations (like that thorny one about the Canaanites) were inserted into the telling. Finally, though, at some point we declared the text closed. And then it truly became open season on commentary. But from that moment onward, Jews were a people of the Book, and it was a book that begged for commentary.

So rabbis wrote commentary. And it wasn't just the Bible that they commented upon. We actually can infer just how important a book was in the Jewish community by the amount of commentary it attracted. The more important the work, the more central it was to core Jewish identity, then the more commentaries it attracted. So there are hundreds, even thousands of commentaries on the Bible. But other works were also important and attracted their own commentaries. Almost as soon as it was published at the end of the second century in the Galilee, the Mishnah, that compendium of Jewish law that we've already quoted from, also attracted commentary. The largest commentary on the Mishnah was done in Jewish Babylonia. Its dialectical commentary stretched for more than three centuries before being compiled into the vast unwieldy work we call the Talmud. Many of the stories we've shared thus far are from the Babylonian Talmud (like the ones about Hillel and his hopping-on-one-foot friend, or Elijah and his rabbis).

The Mishnah actually garnered even more commentaries (as if the Talmud wouldn't have been commentary enough). There's a second- to third-century companion piece to the Mishnah called the *Tosefta*, and there's a fourth- to fifth-century Talmud commentary from the Land of Israel (Roman Palestine), too. Enough already! Well, almost, but not quite.

The Commentary

The rabbis clearly loved the Mishnah, but they viewed the tractate *Pirke Avot* as somehow different from the rest of the work, which delves into the intricacies of Jewish law. *Pirke Avot*, on the other hand, teaches us ethics, wisdom, and character. We've already studied a bit of *Pirke Avot* back in chapter 2 when we read about our cast and their characters. It got its very own special commentary called *Avot DeRabbi Nathan*, which means that it's a commentary on Mishnah tractate *Pirke Avot*, according to Rabbi Nathan (a prominent second-century rabbi). No one actually thinks that Rabbi Nathan authored the work, which most scholars assume was edited in the eighth to ninth century. But his name appears early on in the commentary, so he gets posthumous pseudonymous credit as "author."

This is more than enough detail; let's move on to the commentary. Like the biblical texts just quoted, *Avot DeRabbi Nathan* seems to add "internal" commentary. I reproduce segments below, which "retell" *Pirke Avot*. *Avot DeRabbi Nathan's* "comments" appear in italics, so you can see what the original *Pirke Avot* text is and what's been added or changed.

> Rabbi Yohanan ben Zakkai had five disciples. He *gave them each nicknames.* He called Eliezer ben Hyrcanus a limed cistern that does not lose a drop, *a pitch-coated amphora that preserves its wine.* He called Yehoshua ben Hananiah *"a threefold cord not easily broken"* (Ecclesiastes 4:12). José the Priest he called a pious one *of his generation.* Shimeon ben Netanel he called a *succulent plant in the wilderness that holds fast to its water. Blessed is the disciple whose master compliments him and testifies about*

him. He called Elazar ben Arakh *a flowing stream and* an over-flowing wellspring *whose waters overflow outside, to fulfill that which is written, "Your wellsprings will gush forth in streams in the public squares" (Proverbs 5:16)*.

(AVOT DERABBI NATHAN A, CHAP. 14)

Avot DeRabbi Nathan 14 recapitulates *Pirke Avot* 2, with a number of interesting additions and changes. First, it doesn't bother listing the fab five as a group. Instead, and perhaps presuming that we already know the cast in order of appearance, it plunges right into Rabbi Yohanan's praises. In the earlier text, Yohanan lists their "virtues." Here, he gives them "nicknames" (the Hebrew literally says, "He called them each names," but that seems derogatory in common English). Eliezer is still plastered, but now he has a wine flask to help him get that way.

In the ancient world they did not age wine in wooden barrels; instead, they used earthenware amphorae. Each vessel was large and could hold many gallons of wine. The trouble with earthenware is that it sweats. If you simply put wine in a clay vessel to age, when you returned to drink it you'd find vinegar! So throughout the Roman Mediterranean world they lined the clay amphorae with pitch or with pine resin to make it watertight. The good news was that the wine did not sour. The bad news was that the wine tasted like pitch or resin. Greek wine still has that resiny flavor to this very day. It's called Retsina precisely for the resin that was used in sealing the amphorae. Let us toast Eliezer and his Retsina-fueled memory!

In *Pirke Avot* Rabbi Yehoshua was characterized with a biblical allusion (to Proverbs 23:25), "happy is she who bore him." In the new, improved version we've switched one biblical text for another—this one from Ecclesiastes 4:12. Yehoshua is now like the sturdy lanyards we used to weave in camp arts and crafts. It's true; the threefold cord is not easily broken.

Rabbi José has an interesting addition to his earlier compliment. He had been called pious. Now, he is "a pious one of his generation." Is this better or worse? I suppose it depends on who else was in his generation. Since we know the cast of characters, being the pious guy among them makes José out to be pretty pious. This is not unlike the biblical notice that "Noah was a righteous man, blameless in his generation" (Genesis 6:9). In the fifth century in the Galilee, it was reported that two rabbis disagreed about how to read this verse. Rabbi Judah said, "Sure he was righteous in his generation. But had he lived in the generation of Moses or Samuel, he wouldn't have been thought righteous. In the marketplace of the blind, the one-eyed man is called great." His colleague Rabbi Nehemiah disagreed, "If he was righteous in his own generation, surely he'd be righteous in Moses's generation" (*Genesis Rabbah* 30:9).

Our friend Rabbi Shimeon's compliment has transformed from "fears sin" to a metaphor that seems more apposite for Eliezer: he holds on to his learning like a succulent plant, which opens its fleshy leaves in the night to capture any moisture that the evening dew may bring. During the heat of the day, the plant snaps shut, holding fast to precious water. This compliment is followed by a generalization of how happy the master's praise makes a disciple. I am certain this would have been true for Shimeon. But it is true of any student who thirsts for some recognition from his or her teacher, my own students included.

Finally, there is Elazar. As in the earlier text, he is likened to an overflowing wellspring. But *Avot DeRabbi Nathan* waxes poetic, layering on another flowing water metaphor and then literally taking it over the top, by applying a verse of Scripture to Elazar. This is more than simply quoting a verse. Our text imagines Rabbi Yohanan praising his favorite by asserting that Elazar fulfills a verse of the Bible. It is as though the verse prophesies Elazar. In Christian Scripture we frequently find the same formula: "in order to fulfill that which is written" in the Hebrew Bible. There, of course, the fulfillment of those verses is applied to Jesus. Once again, it appears that Rabbi Elazar takes home the gold.

This last instance, where an extra metaphor and an apposite verse of the Bible are applied to Elazar, looks like a clear case of commentary. But what if this isn't commentary at all? Since I've been making a case that these traditions were transmitted orally—indeed, the rabbis refer to their teaching as Oral Torah—maybe what we are looking at is simply two performances of the same basic *Pirke Avot* text. Perhaps we shouldn't be thinking so much of a script or libretto and instead think of both *Pirke Avot* and *Avot DeRabbi Nathan* as forms of improvisation—like the performances at Second City, in my native Chicago. Or, it might help to think of Rabbi Yohanan's compliments for his students as a form of Mad Libs. When we come to Rabbi Yehoshua, we need to fill in the box with a biblical verse extolling some personal virtue. What that virtue may be is more or less fungible. In the cases of Eliezer, Elazar, and now, Shimeon, the compliment should be a water metaphor. This is wholly appropriate, since Torah and God's wisdom are so often likened to water for the thirsty, like the prophet Isaiah says, "Yo! All who are thirsty, come for water.... Hear Me ... declares the Lord" (Isaiah 55:1, 55:3, 55:8).

Let's also recall the tendency we have already observed for scribes to insert their own biblical references into the transmitted text. Now we may have to rethink whether *Avot DeRabbi Nathan* is a commentary on an earlier text or simply a different improv performance of that text. To test whether we are looking at a retold story or a commentary on it, let's see how *Avot DeRabbi Nathan* handles what the students said in reply to Rabbi Yohanan's assignment about "the good way" (*Pirke Avot* 2:13). You will recall, that he asked them:

> "Go forth and see: what is the good way that a man should adhere to *so that he might enter the World to Come?*"
>
> Rabbi Eliezer said, "A good eye."
>
> Rabbi Yehoshua said, "A good colleague."
>
> Rabbi José said, "A good neighbor, *a good inclination, and a good wife.*"
>
> Rabbi Shimeon said, "The one who sees that which is born."
>
> Rabbi Elazar said, "A good heart *toward heaven and a good heart toward one's fellow creatures.*"
>
> He said to them, "I prefer the words of Elazar ben Arakh, for his words include your words."
>
> (*Avot DeRabbi Nathan* A, chap. 14)

I will avoid the urge to make Henny Youngman jokes about Rabbi José's "take my wife, please" addition. But I've indicated in italics what is clearly extraneous material, which stands out because it breaks up the terseness of the oral formula. Still, we cannot be sure whether the addition of "good inclination" and "good wife" is really commentary or just a different telling. But when we come to Yohanan's question, and for that matter, Elazar's good-hearted reply, we can discern a reformulation of the original text with an ideological twist. The addition of "the World to Come" (a rabbinic messianic concept), as well as having "a good heart toward heaven," seems to me to be a reaction to the almost secular Stoicism of the earlier text. *Avot DeRabbi Nathan* is commenting by making the text more pious, more Jewish, if you will. God and ultimate reward are schlepped into the text because in its retelling half a millennium after the first performances, the editor felt he needed to inculcate listeners/readers with a bit more rabbinic religiosity. As Hillel might have said, "The rest is commentary."

4 / ד

On Loan

Commentary, of course, can take many forms. Sometimes a comment on a verse of Scripture or even an earlier rabbinic statement takes on a life of its own. The bare bones of a comment will take on the sinew of plot and the flesh of character development. Suddenly, what began as an observation about a text becomes a story. This is exactly what happens in *Avot DeRabbi Nathan*'s "commentary" on *Pirke Avot*. Before I offer up the next bit of text, I want to remind you of Rabbi Shimeon's odd answers to the "good/bad" questions his teacher had asked:

- The good way: Rabbi Shimeon said, "The one who sees that which is born."
- The bad way: Rabbi Shimeon said, "The one who borrows and does not repay." One who borrows from a human is like one who borrows from the Omnipresent, as it is said, "The wicked borrows and does not repay, while the righteous gives generously" (Psalm 37:21).

Now, let's turn to *Avot DeRabbi Nathan* to see how these not so apparent opposites play out. Immediately following its expansion of the discussion about the good way and the bad way that we read in chapter 3, *Avot DeRabbi Nathan* waxes into unexpected narrative:

40

When Rabbi Yohanan ben Zakkai's son died, his students came to comfort him. Rabbi Eliezer entered and sat before him, saying, "Rabbi, may I say something to you?" Rabbi Yohanan replied, "Speak."

He told him, "Adam had a son who died and he accepted comfort. Where does Scripture speak of his accepting comfort? As it is said, 'Adam again knew his wife' [Genesis 4:25]. So too, you should find comfort."

He replied, "Is it not enough that I have my own troubles that you remind me of the sorrows of Adam?"

Rabbi Yehoshua entered and said to him, "May I say something to you?" He said, "Speak."

He told him, "Job's sons and daughters all perished on the same day, and yet he was comforted for his loss of them. You, too, should find comfort. Where does Scripture speak of his accepting comfort? As it is said, 'The Lord gives and the Lord takes away, blessed be the name of the Lord' [Job 1:21]."

He replied, "Is it not enough that I have my own troubles that you remind me of the sorrows of Job?"

Rabbi José entered and sat before him, saying, "Rabbi, may I say something to you?" Rabbi Yohanan replied, "Speak."

He told him, "Aaron had two adult sons who both died on the same day. Yet he was comforted, as it is said, 'Aaron was silent' [Leviticus 10:3]. Silence here means comfort, so you, too, should be comforted."

He replied, "Is it not enough that I have my own troubles that you remind me of the sorrows of Aaron?"

Rabbi Shimeon entered and said to him, "May I say something to you?" He said, "Speak."

He said, "King David had a son who died and he was comforted, so you, too, should be comforted. Where does Scripture speak of David receiving comfort? As it is said, 'David comforted his wife Bat Sheva, he came unto her and lay with her. She gave birth and called the child Solomon' [2 Samuel 12:24]. So you, Rabbi, should accept comfort."

He replied, "Is it not enough that I have my own troubles that you remind me of the sorrows of King David?"

(*AVOT DERABBI NATHAN* A, CHAP. 14)

Suddenly, *Avot DeRabbi Nathan* has shifted from retelling and commenting upon the earlier text into inventing its own narrative. We have precious little historical evidence about Rabbi Yohanan's son or his purported death, so I will treat this story as didactic narrative—a tale told to make a moral or an educational point. There is so much going on in the telling, however, that we have to pause and watch how the storyteller unfolds his tale.

The formulaic nature of the narrative makes it fairly clear that we are not dealing with a firsthand account of Yohanan's prolonged mourning; it's highly unlikely that each student came in and said virtually the same words. In fact, mindful of the eighth- to ninth-century dating most scholars assign to *Avot DeRabbi Nathan*, we may be getting this sad report as much as 750 years after the purported fact. Our storyteller is constructing his narrative using basic building blocks that he repeats over and over. The students appear—surprise, surprise—in the precise order that they appeared when we first met them in *Pirke Avot*. Then, the narrator plugs in the name of a biblical character who lost a child as each successive student's example for Rabbi Yohanan to take comfort from.

We might wonder how our performer chooses those biblical characters. There are a limited number of individuals in the Hebrew Bible who lost children. If the storyteller chose from among those names at random, he might offer them up in the order they appear in Scripture, if for no other reason than ease of memory. In fact, it is most often the case that when a string of biblical examples are offered in rabbinic literature, they appear precisely in the order of Scripture. Once an order has been fixed in a reciter's mind, it seems hard to change it, whether it's a Bible text or a Mishnah text like the *Pirke Avot* tradition we are involved with here.

But wait—while the order of Scripture would surely bring us Adam as the first example, what is Job doing next up? His book actually comes quite late in the Hebrew Bible, among the final section called Writings (*Ketuvim*). And while we're speculating about what order the narrator is using to produce his biblical examples, should we wonder whether there is any connection between each rabbi and the Scripture put into his mouth? I ask this because we can immediately see how appropriate it is for Rabbi José *the priest* to offer Aaron *the priest* as his example. Is there a connection we're missing between Eliezer and Adam or between Shimeon and King David?

In the end, I think not. Rather, the characters from the Bible are chosen in what the rabbis imagined to be their *historical* order. Again, Adam comes first. As for Job, most rabbis believed that he was a contemporary of Abraham. According to that view, Job should be listed between Adam and Aaron, just the way he is in our text. But you should know that there are some rabbis who wonder about Job altogether. They say, "Job never existed; he wasn't created." For those rabbis, Job was a fictional character. This seems to imply that at least one of the books of the Bible might itself be didactic fiction. I guess the idea of telling such a narrative to teach a point has its origins in Jewish literature (the Bible) centuries before the rabbis came along.

Returning to our story of Yohanan and his students offering him comfort on the loss of his son, we should point out something that is not in the narrative but that must be assumed if we are to understand the unfolding of the story. Traditionally, Jewish observance calls for a seven-day mourning period. During the first half of that period, those who come to visit the mourners do not initiate conversation, but instead wait until the mourner chooses whether to do so or not. Further, during the seven-day period, the mourner is enjoined not to bathe, change clothing, or indulge in other bodily luxuries. Finally, it is presumed that at the end of seven days, most, if not all, of daily life is resumed. Yet as will be made clear from the continuation to our story, Rabbi Yohanan's grief (or possibly his feelings of parental guilt) over his lost son is so great that he remains in mourning even after the seven-day period. Hence his students' exhortations to him to accept comfort.

Our narrator somewhat mechanically, then, imagines a situation in which four of Yohanan's students come to offer him comfort by mentioning biblical characters who have also lost children. Presumably Yohanan is meant to take some solace that he is not alone and learn from the example of others that life can go on. But he is having none of it. He just isn't ready yet to snap out of it. Instead, he snaps at them that's he's got his own *tzuris* (the Yiddish term is the same as the word used in the Hebrew text, translated above as "troubles"). Each student's attempt to offer comfort is pushed away.

Enter Elazar

Then, Elazar appears.

> Rabbi Elazar ben Arakh entered. When Yohanan saw him he told his servant, "Gather my clothing and prepare to follow me to the bathhouse; for Rabbi Elazar is a great man and I shall not withstand him."
>
> Elazar came in and sat down before Yohanan. He said to him, "I will give you an analogy. This is like a man with whom the king has entrusted a deposit of some value. Each and every day that man would wail and moan, 'Oy for the time that I will return this deposit in peace and fullness!' So you, Rabbi, had a son. He studied Torah: Pentateuch, Prophets, Writings, Mishnah, Laws, and Narrative. And he departed this world without sin. You should take comfort that you have returned your deposit in peace and fullness."
>
> Rabbi Yohanan said to him, "Elazar, my son, you have comforted me like a Mensch."
>
> (*Avot DeRabbi Nathan* A, chap. 14)

No sooner does Yohanan see his favorite student than he is ready to get up, change his clothes, take a bath, end his mourning. It is as though he was just waiting for Elazar to show up to finally find comfort. Elazar, for his part, knows just what to say. He does not mention bibli-

cal characters, nor does he refer to others' losses. Instead he percep-
tively concentrates on Yohanan's fathering. Elazar seems to be saying to
him: Do not feel guilty. You did everything that you could have. Look
at the wonderful son you raised. He embodied rabbinic values and
learning. More so, he died without sin. No sin, no guilt. Do not take
this upon yourself. You and your son are both innocent. You returned
to God what God had given you. It was yours only for a short while,
and that, on loan. You returned it whole, in peace.

There is a pun here for "peace and fullness," hard to capture in
translation. The term he uses is *shalem* (complete or whole), which is
the same as *shalom* (peace, but also hello and, poignantly in our case,
goodbye). These are words of comfort Yohanan needs to hear. He is
released from his feelings of guilt and now is ready to move on with his
life. He literally tells Elazar, "You have comforted me in the way that
men comfort one another," which is what I've translated above as "like
a Mensch."

We would be remiss if we did not notice one more thing about
the exchange. It is a small aside, one that teachers often invoke when
speaking to their students, but here it takes on added valence. Yohanan
refers to his favorite disciple as "Elazar, my son." It is as much as to say,
"Now that my surrogate son, my student Elazar, has arrived, now I can
let go of my mourning and guilt for my natural son who has died."

Although Elazar is the focus of Rabbi Yohanan's attention, I have
not lost sight of the odd statements of Rabbi Shimeon. He had said that
the good way is "the one who sees that which is born," or foresight;
and the bad way is "the one who borrows and does not repay." In the
story of Yohanan's dead son, each of Rabbi Shimeon's observations is in
play, driving the narrative. The good way is quite literally imagined as
that which is born, a son who is raised to be the epitome of rabbinic
teaching. And the bad way is to not want to repay that which has been
loaned to you. In this case, Yohanan is called upon to give back the
soul of his son to God, who loaned it to him. This metaphor forces
Rabbi Yohanan to dwell not on his loss, but on the enormous value and
responsibility of what he had—a dutiful son. His responsibility to God
repaid, Yohanan can take comfort.

Hot Springs / Cold Comfort

There is a curious coda to the story. It appears to be a quasi-historical note on the ultimate disposition of the famous five students. It is our narrator's way of accounting for the odd fact that Elazar, for all that he was Yohanan's clear favorite, virtually disappeared from subsequent rabbinic literature.

> When they left Yohanan, Elazar said, "I will go to Damasit, a place of beauty with pleasant and beautiful waters."
>
> The other four disciples said, "We will go to Yavneh, a place where so many disciples of the sages love the Torah."
>
> He who went to Damasit, the place of beauty with pleasant and beautiful waters, his name diminished in Torah. They who went to Yavneh, the place where so many disciples of the sages love the Torah, their names were exalted in Torah.
>
> (*AVOT DERABBI NATHAN* A, CHAP. 14)

Location, location, location. Apparently Elazar, in choosing a Palm Beach–like locale, found himself isolated from his colleagues and his reputation soon diminished. The other disciples chose to go where the action was—well, the Torah action anyway. There at Yavneh, surrounded by other rabbinic sages, they made their names and their status grew. Rabbi Yehoshua, who we will recall was a peat-moss digger, became the putative vice president of the rabbinic council. And Rabbi Eliezer became one of the most frequently quoted of all the sages.

What was so bad about moving to Damasit? And where or what was Damasit? Other versions of this story have an entirely different name for the place where Elazar ben Arakh moved. In those traditions he is said to have moved to Emmaus. The name is a Greek transliteration of the Hebrew term *hammam*, or hot springs. In that town were baths that capitalized on naturally flowing hot springs. In fact, the name Damasit also alludes to those hot springs, for they were a public convenience. They were designated in Greek as "public" (*demosia*, like in *demo*cracy). The Greek, in turn, was transliterated into Hebrew as Damasit.

But was there anything wrong with moving to Damasit/Emmaus? It might have raised an eyebrow, as Emmaus was a town associated with early Christianity (see the Gospel of Luke 24:13ff.). Is it possible that Elazar, from the rabbis' perspective, fell in with the wrong crowd? I actually doubt it. More likely we have here a lesson in propinquity. Stay close to your colleagues and you will flourish. Abandon them for the hedonism of the beach life and your rabbinic career may wash away like sand as the tide goes by.

5 / ה

The Woman
of Valor

The story of the death of Rabbi Yohanan's son confronts the issue
of theodicy in a profound way. Can we justify God—for that is
literally what "theodicy" means—when innocent children die? Early
rabbis, following the book of Deuteronomy, suggested that "there is
no death without sin." Yet we have just read a narrative in which
Rabbi Elazar consoles his teacher by assuring him that his son
"departed this world *without* sin." In much, if not all, of earlier rabbinic thought, theodicy was of paramount importance. Those rabbis
seem to have thought that showing that God did justice yet
remained somehow beneficent brought order and meaning to the
bereaved at a time of emotional chaos. But the downside of this rabbinic justification of God's decree was the rabbis' tendency to blame
the victim of tragedy for sinning and so to deprive the bereaved of
consolation.

In the story we just read about Yohanan and his disciple, Elazar
comforts him like a Mensch. This new leaf in rabbinic literature essentially avoids asking why a tragedy occurs and instead jumps directly to
consoling the grieving mourner. It seems to say, never mind who is to
blame or if there even is blame—our job is to comfort those who are
hurting. This worldview is echoed in another contemporary rabbinic
tale. Again, it is a story about the loss of children and how such a
tragedy tests the mettle of the parents involved. Here, too, the father is

a prominent rabbi. What makes this account distinctive is that his wife is also very much part of the story.

"A woman of valor, who can find?" (Proverbs 31:10). They told a tale of Rabbi Meir who was sitting and expounding in the study house one Shabbat afternoon when his two sons died. What did their mother do? She rested the two of them upon the bed and spread a sheet over them. When Shabbat had ended, Rabbi Meir returned home from the study house. He asked, "Where are my two sons?"

She told him, "They went to the study house."

He replied, "I looked for them at the study house, but I didn't see them."

She gave him a cup of wine to pronounce the blessings for ending Shabbat, and he recited them. He asked again, "Where are my two sons?"

She said, "Sometimes they go to some Place; they're on their way now." She put dinner before him and he ate. After he had recited the blessings following the meal, she said to him, "Rabbi, I have a question to ask."

He said to her, "Ask your question."

She asked, "Rabbi, earlier a man came and left me something on deposit. Now he has come to collect that deposit. Shall we return it or not?"

He said, "My daughter, is it not clear that one who is entrusted with a deposit must return it to its master!"

She said, "I wouldn't have returned it without your consent." What did she do? She took him by his hand, led him up to that room, brought him close to the bed, and removed the sheet from them. He saw the two of them lying dead upon the bed and began to weep.

He said, "My sons, my sons, my rabbis, my rabbis! My sons by nature, but my rabbis in that they enlightened me with their Torah."

At that time she said to Rabbi Meir, "Rabbi, did you not tell me that we must return the deposit to its Master? Thus it says, 'The Lord gives and the Lord takes away. Blessed be the name of the Lord' [Job 1:21]."

Rabbi Hannina said, "With these words she comforted him and settled his mind. That is why it says, 'A woman of valor, who can find?' [Proverbs 31:10]."

(*MIDRASH MISHLE* 31)

Everywoman?

I've told the entire sad story at one go to allow its poignancy to wash over us. As a tale it is tightly constructed, opening and closing with the same verse of Proverbs 31, the famous biblical paean to idealized woman. There are essentially two main characters in our narrative, the rabbi and his valorous wife. Rabbi Meir was another of the famous rabbis of the Mishnah. He was the disciple of Rabbi Akiva (we heard a story about him, his wife, and their encounter with the prophet Elijah in chapter 1). Meir's student, in turn, was the editor-compiler of the Mishnah. Meir's wife was the extraordinary woman Beruriah. She is one of the very few women mentioned by name in the male-dominated rabbinic literature, although notably in our story, her name has been effaced.

It behooves us to ask about this. Why isn't her name mentioned? The story I've quoted is from a ninth-century source, the midrash to the book of Proverbs. This text knew the Babylonian Talmud stories and so knew perfectly well that Meir had a wife named Beruriah. So why not mention her name here? Is this just one more instance of rabbinic unfriendliness to women? That even a well-known woman might have her identity suppressed? Given that Beruriah is quoted in the Talmud as correcting her husband (and it turns out she is right and he is wrong), was there perhaps a desire, post-facto, to get even, as it were? Or, more generously to the rabbinic storytellers, in the case of the death of children—a much more common occurrence then than now—maybe there is benefit to casting this famous mother as "Everywoman."

Another possible answer has to do with the enormity of the death of children. At the moment a parent grasps the tragedy, it seems that his or her entire identity is focused on that loss. So it is an accurate representation when our narrator refers to her not by her own name, but simply as "their mother." Or again, this is a story about Rabbi Meir and how he bears his loss. A story by rabbis about a rabbi. So the wife, even as she is framed by the verse of Proverbs, recedes into the shadows as we tell Rabbi Meir's story. All of these are possible readings to account for Beruriah's nameless status.

One final possibility must be mentioned—for it cuts to the heart of rabbinic storytelling and how the ancient rabbis thought. Meir's wife, the boys' mother, has a famous name, Beruriah. Yet her name is not a Hebrew name. Beruriah actually is a Latin name. By means of a linguistic shift, the first *r* in her name represents the letter *l* in Latin—not unlike the shift that would take place were a Japanese speaker to try and say the word *shalom*. And the letter *B* at the outset of the name is readily softened in Hebrew pronunciation to a *V* sound. Beruriah then, in Hebrew, is actually the Latin name Valeria. Beruriah is quite literally the "woman of valor." Given the verse at the start and end of the story, the rabbis may have been quite content that they had identified our heroine rather clearly.

Role Reversals

I mentioned above that the story is reported in a ninth-century source. Like the story of Yohanan's son's death, this is a tale told centuries after the events it purports to relate. Again, we are faced with a tragedy that is not historical, but performed to teach a point about theodicy and parental grief. As if to make the point as clearly as possible, not one but two sons die in one fell swoop. Given the history of diseases decimating communities in the Middle Ages, there is a certain verisimilitude here. It could have happened to Meir and his wife, and no doubt happened to others. The point here is not historical accuracy, but spiritual truth. Whether it happened or not, the story rings true.

Meir is in the study house, teaching Torah on Shabbat afternoon. The scene is set to make it clear that he is doing what he is supposed to—no sin on his part to account for blame. The very setup of the story precludes the "no death without sin" theodicy. Further, there is Meir's expectation that his boys would be there in the study house with him. They are good boys; neither he nor they are the sinners of the tale. Nor, in fact, is their mother. She faces the tragedy stoically, deferring or suppressing her own mourning so that her husband may weep instead. This dynamic is not unknown even among modern couples, who take turns falling apart, as it were. One spouse must see to the family and the funeral arrangements, while the other wails. Later, perhaps, they will exchange roles, so that each will have a turn to mourn.

There is another type of role changing taking place in this story. Meir, the prominent rabbi, is minimally rabbinic, while his famous wife plays that role throughout the tale. Role reversal is a universal sign that mortality is upon us. Think of adult children who find themselves suddenly thrust into the role of caring for their aging parents for the first time ever. Now look who is writing the checks, or worse, who is diapering whom. When these role changes occur, the terrible knowledge is upon us that the angel of death is nigh.

Beruriah acts in a rabbinically proper fashion. Since it is still the Sabbath when the boys die, there is no formal mourning or preparation for burial that can take place. She does exactly what Jewish law demands under the circumstance: rests the corpses upon a bed or bier and covers them with a sheet pending the Sabbath's end. Further, she asks Meir a simple query regarding the return of a loaned object to its master. The answer is obvious to her, to Meir, and to us, the listeners. Why then does she ask it? She not only manipulates him into saying the words of theodicy that will allow him to "return the deposit to its master," which is to say, accept the death of his sons and their return to God. She also briefly empowers him by allowing him his rabbinic expertise in the moment before he perhaps will feel more impotent than at any time in his adult life. His sons are dead, and there is nothing he can do about it but accept the reality of it. "The Lord gives and the Lord takes away" are words of theodicy that still are recited at

Jewish gravesides. In this story and the Rabbi Yohanan narrative that preceded it, we are offered consolation to comfort the mourner for his or her loss. No sin needs to be assigned, no blame established. Instead the storyteller seems to take up the words of Isaiah, "Take comfort, take comfort, O My people, says your God" (Isaiah 40:1).

Like Rabbi Yohanan who spoke of Elazar as his surrogate son, Beruriah in some ways treats Meir as her surrogate child. When he asks too many questions, she stops answering and feeds him. When he returns to questioning, she places a cup of wine in his hand. She treats him like one would treat an easily distracted child. Maybe this is her way of managing her own grief, even as she prepares him for the awful news.

Note, too, that when Meir asks after his boys, she actually lies to him, saying, "They went to the study house." In rabbinic thought, truth telling is not an absolute virtue. Sometimes what we might call a "white lie" is considered permissible for the sake of familial peace. The classic example of this is actually comical, as the rabbis quote Scripture as their proof of the principle. In the book of Genesis, when the angels announce to Sarah that she will have a child, she laughs, saying that she longer menstruates and "my husband is so old" (Genesis 18:12). Yet when God repeats this to Abraham, God discretely omits mentioning the part about her "old husband."

Beruriah, for her part, first puts Meir off by saying the boys were on their way to the study house. This seems to be a falsehood, although I suppose we could rationalize it by suggesting that she meant the Study House on High. When he presses her again, she lies again—and here, too, there might just be some wiggle room. She says, "Sometimes they go to some Place," which I've capitalized. This is because in Rabbinic Hebrew the word "Place" is also an epithet for God, the Omnipresent being the "Place of the universe." So while he heard that "sometimes they go someplace," she meant that "they are on their way to God."

Finally, the awful moment dawns, and at that point our narrator, and so Beruriah, runs out of words. There is nothing that can be said at this terrible moment. Verb after verb unfolds in the absence of dialogue: "She took him by his hand, led him up to that room, brought him close to the bed, and removed the sheet from them." When he is confronted with his dead sons, Meir weeps and stutters out, "My sons, my sons, my rabbis, my rabbis!" This doubling of nouns is common in the Bible when tragedy strikes. Think of King David mourning, "My son, Absalom, my son, my son, Absalom!... Absalom, my son, my son!" (2 Samuel 19:1).

Meir, as it were, adds nuance, in that he calls his sons his rabbis. Why his rabbis? "They enlightened me with their Torah," he tells us, and here, too, we lose a precious pun in translating the Hebrew. For the word for "enlighten" in Hebrew is *meir*. The boys were quite literally mini-"me"*irs* who lit their father up with the pleasure of their questions and their study with him.

When the Rabbi Weeps

We are left with a valorous, stoic wife and a weeping rabbi. We need to wonder about the rabbinic storyteller's gender notions. Are we meant to understand Meir's weeping as yet another role reversal? Is it the case that among the rabbis, as the movie title would have it, that "boys don't cry" (and is it mere coincidence that a screenwriter of that film worked at the Jewish Theological Seminary)? Is Beruriah the "man" here and Meir being "feminized" in his grief? Or is this story meant to teach us a different construction of masculinity, one in which a rabbi can be comfortable with a strong and knowledgeable wife, a gender role where rabbis can cry in the face of loss and still be real men? Meir was certainly a famous (and manly) rabbi. Perhaps we need to rethink what it means when a rabbi cries. Our next story, of how Yohanan's disciple Eliezer ben Hyrcanus came to study Torah, will allow us to examine that very question from another perspective.

6 / ו

How a Boy
Became a Rabbi

Eliezer ben Hyrcanus had, by any measure, an extraordinary career—
which is to say that the traditional stories about him report an
extraordinary career; we cannot really recover much of his factual
biography. But as a character in sage tales, Eliezer is reported to have
begun his studies somewhat late in life (as we will see, the reports
vary), continued on to a brilliant legal career as a rabbi, even had God
come to his defense in an argument with his colleagues ("What have
you against Rabbi Eliezer?" thunders the Almighty in this rabbinic fantasy. "The law is always according to his opinion!" [Babylonian Talmud,
Bava Metzia 59b]), and ended his rabbinic days excommunicated from
his colleagues, following his stubborn resistance to a legal decision of
the majority. A tragic character, actually.

It's hard to know whether later stories about Eliezer take this basic
narrative arc into account as they tell the tale of his beginnings. It's
harder still to know just what these stories are trying to tell us about
Eliezer, his teacher Rabbi Yohanan ben Zakkai, and the study of Torah
in general. Let's hear how a medieval narrator tells the tale, eight hundred years after the fact:

> A tale is told of Rabbi Eliezer ben Hyrcanus, whose father had
> plowmen who would plow the furrow, while Eliezer plowed
> the stony hillocks. He sat and wept. His father asked him,

"Why do you cry? Perhaps you are upset that you are plowing the stony hillocks? Now, go plow the furrow."

Eliezer sat upon the furrow and wept. His father asked him, "Now why do you cry? Are you upset at having to plow the furrow?" He replied, "No."

He asked, "So why do you cry?"

Eliezer said, "Because I want to learn Torah."

His father replied, "Look, you are twenty-eight years old! *Now* you want to study Torah? Get yourself a wife, have kids, take *them* to school!"

Eliezer went for two weeks without eating a thing, until Elijah—may he be remembered for good—appeared to him. He said, "Son of Hyrcanus, why do you cry?"

Eliezer said, "Because I want to learn Torah."

Elijah said, "If you wish to study Torah, go up to Jerusalem to Rabbi Yohanan ben Zakkai."

(*PIRKE RABBI ELIEZER* 1)

This is a good place to interrupt the story because I am sure you are surprised at the so-called "facts" of this telling. Our hero seems to be a crybaby, his father a bit of an unsympathetic boor, and the prophet Elijah an enabler who is encouraging the boy to run away from home! Eliezer not only cries at the drop of a hat, but he also refuses to eat until he gets his way. And sure enough, after two weeks of starving himself, Elijah appears to him and tells him exactly what he wants to hear. I suspect that this method is pretty reliable; after two weeks of starving yourself, Elijah will appear to you, too, and tell you whatever you want to hear (kids, don't try this at home)! It is hard for me to read this dispassionately when I think of how so many folks, young women in particular, are afflicted with eating disorders. And lest you think that eating disorders are a particularly modern middle-class affliction, note well that the Mishnah (second- to third-century Palestine) mentions "bulimia" by name. In a discussion of the laws of fasting on Yom Kippur, the Mishnah states that someone who is smitten with bulimia (and is obsessively gorging) may even be fed nonkosher food on Yom Kippur, "until their eyes clear," that is, restored to full health (*Yoma* 8). Even eighteen hundred years ago, this eating disorder was taken so seriously that it overturned the law of refraining from food on Judaism's holiest day of the year.

It's Never Too Late to Learn Torah

If not eating and constant crying weren't shocking enough for our apparently dysfunctional would-be Torah scholar, it turns out he is twenty-eight! It's one thing if young Eliezer were a wee lad of seven or eight (I always think of Timmy in the *Lassie* television series), but twenty-eight? Really? Well, maybe not. It seems there are variant tellings of the tale. In another text, Eliezer is reported to be only twenty-two. That's somewhat better, but still, Eliezer seems less than stable to the modern eye. But wait, there's an even earlier tradition of this story from fifth-century Galilee in which Eliezer's age remains unmentioned, so perhaps we can preserve our idyllic version of a mere boy, beaten down by the sorrow of pushing the plow.

But if that's so, how did he get to be twenty-eight in our version? Here I think the concept of performance of these stories is helpful. Eliezer's age was changed from telling to telling to account for the audience. If the listeners were, say, undergraduates, then the storyteller might make Eliezer twenty-two. Message: it's never too late to learn Torah. And if the listeners were graduate students, as it were, then Eliezer became twenty-eight—which was (perhaps not coincidentally for the Muslim milieu in which our story was told) the same age as the prophet Muhammad when he first got married. But in seeking to add a new moral to the story about when it is appropriate to begin Torah study, our narrator inadvertently added a character flaw to Eliezer's personality. At an age when he should have been a fully functioning adult, he now seems to be a crybaby.

This merits some further consideration, especially in light of Rabbi Meir's weeping, which we witnessed in the previous chapter. It is certainly possible that all this crying indicates a weakness of character—as much as to say that Eliezer is not a real man until he masters

Torah, for it is then that his weeping finally stops. But when Rabbi Meir cried, he was already a master of Torah. Yes, but Meir wept at the death of his sons, and that is appropriate in almost any society. Perhaps we need to rethink weeping altogether. Maybe weeping could be construed as a good thing? A sign that young (okay, not so young) Eliezer is, in fact, an appropriate candidate for the rabbinate? Maybe it indicates that he is empathetic, the kind of man who has the emotional connectedness it takes to be a good pastor.

My colleague in Jerusalem, professor of Jewish mysticism, Moshe Idel, once suggested to me that Eliezer's weeping is a sign of his spiritual state. The constant crying may indicate that he is adept at bringing on visions. Professor Idel pointed to the mystical circle in twelfth- to thirteenth-century Germany called *Hasidei Ashkenaz* (the Pious of Franco-Germany), who learned to cry so that they could bring on mystical revelations. While Idel's example is from three to four centuries later than our story and from much farther west on the Jewish map, it should give us pause. Perhaps Eliezer is demonstrating signs of his pneumatic talents. After all, he does conjure a vision of Elijah the prophet, and elsewhere (as mentioned above) Eliezer calls down God's voice from heaven to support his legal arguments.

But perhaps we should not get carried away. Maybe all this crying is just the common motif of the farm boy who yearns for the intellectual life of the big city. Here's the biblical apocryphal work, the Wisdom of Ben Sira, speaking in the second century BCE of the conflict between these two lives:

> How can the plowman become wise, whose sole ambition is to wield the goad; driving his oxen, engrossed in his work, his conversation is of nothing but cattle? His mind is fixed on the furrows he traces, and his evenings pass in fattening his heifers....
>
> It is otherwise with the man who devotes his soul to reflecting on the Law of the Most High.
>
> (*Ecclesiasticus* 38:25–27, 39:1)

Study in Jerusalem

No matter how we construe Eliezer's tears, he has heard what the prophet Elijah has counseled. It's time for a road trip!

Eliezer arose and went up to Jerusalem to Rabbi Yohanan ben Zakkai. He sat and wept.

Yohanan asked him, "Why do you cry?"

He replied, "Because I want to learn Torah!"

Yohanan asked him, "Whose son are you?" But he did not tell him. Yohanan then asked, "In all your days have you not learned to recite the *Shema*, or the Prayer, or the Blessing after Meals?"

He replied, "No."

Yohanan said, "Arise and I will teach you all three."

He sat and wept.

He asked him, "My son, why do you cry?"

He answered, "Because I want to learn Torah!"

So Yohanan recited two laws of Mishnah each day of the week, and Eliezer would review them until they stuck. Eliezer went eight days without eating a thing, until the smell from his mouth came to Rabbi Yohanan ben Zakkai's attention. Then he stood away from him. Eliezer sat and wept.

Yohanan asked him, "Why do you cry?"

He replied, "Because you stood away from me as though I were covered in boils!"

Yohanan said, "My son, just as the scent of your breath has come to my notice, so may the savor of the laws of the Torah ascend from your mouth to Heaven."

(*Pirke Rabbi Eliezer* 1)

Let's give Rabbi Yohanan the award for most diplomatic way to tell a student that his breath reeks! Eliezer makes his way to Yohanan in Jerusalem—apparently well before the Jewish revolt against Rome. So, we can set the scene as taking place in the early 60s of the first century CE. As soon as Yohanan encounters his newest student—surprise, surprise—Eliezer begins to cry. While Yohanan seeks to determine the cause of all this weeping, we readers learn a few things about the great rabbi. He seems at first like your typical university registrar, seeking to determine the student's name and appropriate placement in the correct classes. But as we will see later in this book, Yohanan takes an undue interest in parentage; this is a character trait by which he is depicted, almost in thumbnail sketch, throughout rabbinic legends. Much like a short-story writer awards each character a tic that makes him or her quickly recognizable, our sage tales do the same for their characters.

A good example of this phenomenon may be seen in the depictions of another famous rabbi, Shimeon ben Yohai. Throughout classical rabbinic literature he is described as being haughtily arrogant. One text imagines (we do not know if this is what Rabbi Shimeon really was like; it's just the imaginary character who is shown this way) that Rabbi Shimeon proclaims, "My teacher Rabbi Akiva said four things with which I disagree. And I am right and my teacher Akiva is wrong" (*Sifre Deuteronomy* 31). In rabbinic circles, it simply was not done to publicly disagree with your teacher. Yet another text has Shimeon declare, "If there are ten righteous men in the world, I and my son are among them. If there are but two righteous men in the world, they are my son and I. And if there be but one righteous man, it is I" (*Genesis Rabbah* 35:2). A final story that conforms to this thumbnail of conceit has Rabbi Shimeon announce, "There are four things that God hates; and I'm not crazy about them either" (*Leviticus Rabbah* 21:8). You get the point about Rabbi Shimeon; he's one arrogant dude!

In our text, Rabbi Yohanan ben Zakkai asks after Eliezer's parentage but receives no reply. It is startling to imagine a student go mum in the face of his new mentor. But we might speculate that Eliezer did not wish to be caught out as a runaway nor returned to his home. Further, we might also imagine what it is like to be the child of a wealthy man—and wish, just once, to be judged for yourself, rather than for your father's wealth. One of my students once suggested that

Eliezer was embarrassed at being an ignoramus and so stayed silent to protect his father from the shame of not having properly educated him. In any case, Eliezer does not reply to Yohanan's seemingly innocuous query.

But Rabbi Yohanan, nonetheless, quizzes Eliezer on his previous education. We already saw in our reading of *Pirke Avot* earlier in this book that students are admonished to "be punctilious in the recitation of the *Shema* and in the Prayer [or *Amidah*]" (*Pirke Avot* 2). Here, Yohanan inquires whether Eliezer has ever learned these two rabbinic liturgies and adds a third, the "Blessing after Meals." This prayer is recited by observant Jews to this very day to thank God for the food we eat. What fascinates me about this story is the assumption that minimally, Eliezer should have known these three basic prayers. Even Eliezer himself doesn't consider learning these anything but rudimentary. He cries yet again because he wants to learn "real" Torah, Jewish law.

When they finally do settle down to study, Yohanan transmits two sections of Mishnah daily. Of course, the Mishnah as it is known today and throughout the Talmudic period was only edited at the very end of the second century. So we must presume that what they are memorizing was proto-Mishnah, not unlike the *Pirke Avot* texts we studied back in chapter 2. I suppose if the course of study required us to memorize two bits of oral text daily, we also could do so. Think, for a moment, of all the song lyrics you might be able to recite. Each day of the week Yohanan taught Eliezer two texts, so that by Shabbat he would have mastered a dozen sections of Jewish law. On Shabbat, he had the luxury of reviewing, reciting until the texts were well "stuck" in his lime-plastered cistern of a memory.

Let's Do Lunch!

But once more Eliezer is not eating. We are left with the impression that this time it is not in a fit of pique, but because he has run away from home and is penniless—Eliezer is starving. In the fifth-century account of this legend, the narrator imagines Eliezer was eating clods of dirt to keep his belly feeling full. Either way, the malnutrition leaves his breath, shall we say, somewhat noticeable to Rabbi Yohanan. It's easy to imagine them studying face to face, and each day Rabbi Yohanan inching further and further away. Following Eliezer's now predictable tears and the ensuing contretemps, this dialogue is related:

Rabbi Yohanan asked, "My son, whose son are you?"

Eliezer confessed, "I am the son of Hyrcanus."

Yohanan exclaimed, "Are you not the son of one of the great men of the world! By your life, today you will dine with me!"

Eliezer replied, "I already ate at my hostel."

Yohanan asked, "And who, then, are your hosts?"

He said, "Rabbi Yehoshua ben Hananiah and Rabbi José the Priest."

Rabbi Yohanan sent a messenger and asked the hosts, "Did Eliezer eat with you today?"

They replied, "No. It's been eight days since he tasted anything."

After that, Rabbi Yehoshua ben Hananiah and Rabbi José the Priest went themselves to tell Rabbi Yohanan ben Zakkai, "It's been eight days since he tasted anything."

(PIRKE RABBI ELIEZER 1)

The tender moment having passed between them, Rabbi Yohanan returns to the equally tender subject of Eliezer's parentage. To mitigate the return to an edgy subject, Yohanan summons an affectionate expression, which gives rise to an awkward query, "My son, whose son are you?" Well, if Eliezer is "my son," then we know the answer to the latter question. Of course, we can take the "my son" as no more than a random sobriquet, much like when Rabbi Meir referred to his wife as "my daughter." But still, we cannot overlook our storyteller's technique at delivering the hidden curriculum of his tale. Earlier in our story, Eliezer's father Hyrcanus is depicted as talking with him. There (go

ahead, flip back and look), Hyrcanus does not refer to Eliezer by name
at all. Given the tensions in their exchange, he may as well have said,
"Hey, you." And when the prophet Elijah appears on the scene, he
refers to Eliezer as "son of Hyrcanus." Now that Yohanan is teaching
Eliezer rabbinic Torah, he rightfully refers to him as "my son." The no
longer hidden curriculum is simply this: your "true father" is the one
who teaches you Torah.

But no sooner is that lesson taught to us than Rabbi Yohanan ben
Zakkai fails us. When he learns who Eliezer's natural father is, we can
practically see the dollar signs, cartoon-like, light up his eyes: Yo'
daddy's rich! By God, let's have lunch together! We, dear readers, might
just wonder, why didn't Rabbi Yohanan invite the stranger to lunch
eight days earlier? This moral failing helps explain Eliezer's obstinate
reply, Thanks, but no thanks—I ate already. In fairness to Rabbi
Yohanan, I should quote a performance of this story contemporary to
the one we've just read (from *Avot DeRabbi Nathan* B). In this version,
when Rabbi Yohanan learns that Eliezer has gone eight days without
eating, "he stood and rent his garments, and said to him, 'Woe for you,
Rabbi Eliezer, who has been abandoned among us!'" This shows us a
more sympathetic Rabbi Yohanan, looking out for Eliezer and confess-
ing to his dereliction of duty. But is it too jaundiced of me with the
hindsight of centuries to wonder which version of the story came first?
Is our B version merely apologetic after the fact?

Since I've mentioned that other telling of the story, I should point
out one other peculiarity of it. In that performance, the narrator lists
Eliezer's hosts as "Rabbi Yehoshua ben Hananiah, Rabbi José the Priest,
and Rabbi Shimeon ben Netanel." That's right! We're back at mechanically filling in "the cast in order of appearance," so much so that our
narrator has failed to appreciate a faux pas in the story. If the Jerusalem
Temple was still standing at the time, as it should have been in a story
set in the 60s CE, then Rabbi José the Priest would not have been shar-
ing lodging with non-priests. You see, priests were entitled to eat free
food that came to them as an emolument from the Temple offerings.
But the rules were strict: they could not risk rendering their priestly
portion ritually unfit by contact with non-priests. Just another small

inconsistency in the narrative introduced by playing Mad Libs and filling in names centuries after the fact.

And let us finally wonder, while the spotlight is focused on Eliezer
in Jerusalem, what's going on with his family down on the farm?

7 / ז

Meanwhile Back at the Ranch

Hyrcanus's sons said to their father, "Go up to Jerusalem and disown your son Eliezer from your properties."

When he went up to Jerusalem to disown him, he found a festive banquet taking place honoring Rabbi Yohanan ben Zakkai. All the powerful men of the city were banqueting there: Ben Tzitzit HaKeset, Nicodemus ben Gurion, and Ben Kalba Savua.

Why was he called Ben Tzitzit HaKeset? Because he reclined at banquet above the powerful men of Jerusalem. They said of Nicodemus ben Gurion that he had three bushels of flour to feed each and every inhabitant of Jerusalem. About Ben Kalba Savua they said that he had a house of four acres of gardens overlaid with gold.

(PIRKE RABBI ELIEZER 2)

This introduction to "the three rich men of Jerusalem" obscures much more than it reveals; not the least of which is that these three wealthy birds are trotted out almost any time the rabbis need to tell a tale about rabbis interacting with the well-to-do. We already met Ben Kalba Savua back in chapter 1. He is reputedly Rabbi Akiva's father-in-law, although I am suspicious that what we are seeing is nothing more than the folklore motif of a very rich man's daughter wedded to a very poor rabbi. And I take pleasure in reminding you that Ben Kalba Savua means "satisfied son of a bitch," which is not a bad nickname for a very rich man. *Ben* means "son of." *Kalba* is a female dog. *Savua* translates as "satisfied." It's not so surprising that he was called that name, but that he seems to have accepted it as an appropriate sobriquet is somewhere between refreshingly honest and downright perverse.

Since the founding of the State of Israel, everyone thinks Ben-Gurion is a nice Jewish name. But that founding father was born as David Grün, and he changed it to Ben-Gurion when he moved to Israel. Our guy obviously came first. What was so attractive about this name is that it means "son of the lion"—a good name for a business-man or statesman. The interesting part is the first name, Nicodemus (transmitted in Hebrew as Nakdimon). Later on in the book we will see the rabbis try to offer an etymology for this patently Greek name. Maybe they were disturbed by the fact that another famous first-century rabbi had a wealthy and powerful supporter named Nicodemus. Hint: his story is told in the Gospel of John! We'll come back to crack this nut a little later on.

Finally, there's my favorite name of the three rich men: Ben Tzitzit HaKeset. Literally translated the name means "son of the fringed pil-low"! It is tempting to imagine that his father (Mr. Fringed Pillow) made his fortune in home decorating. There is no gainsaying the fact that these guys have weird names. But we should emphatically note that the comments on these rich men, while interesting, in no way explain how they got their names. And while Ben Kalba Savua may be as rich (and tacky) as Midas, we don't learn how he got his name, either. Further, the "fact" we are told regarding Nicodemus's ability to feed the Jerusalemites is only a relevant piece of information during the Roman siege of the city—which took place after the supposed time of our story—so its mention here is an anachronism. Just as the three rich men will return as recurrent characters, later on in this book we will learn more about how they got their bizarre nicknames.

And let us not forget Eliezer's darling brothers back at the ranch. Nice guys, hey? I can imagine them cast in the role of Cinderella's wicked stepsisters. That said, an attractive theory to explain their nasty role here is to invoke folklore once again. There are many motifs at play in this brief tale. I headed the chapter "Meanwhile Back at the Ranch" in homage to those cowboy sage tales I used to watch on TV as a kid. We all know that scene very well. And we all know equally well from both literature and life the role of jealous, scheming siblings. So it shouldn't be totally surprising that Eliezer has spiteful brothers who make this cameo appearance.

But let's try to see it from their point of view. Eliezer ran away from home and left them holding the plow. Why should he get any share of profit from their hard work? Further, if he were the eldest of the brothers, he would be entitled to a double portion according to the biblical law of primogeniture. So why shouldn't they be completely annoyed with their spoiled brother who would rather cry than plow and then leaves them in the lurch? Obviously our story is told from the point of view of the rabbis, and so Eliezer is meant to be the hero. But the opposition to study among working families is an old story, one we still hear today—especially when someone decides that he or she is abandoning the family business to go to rabbinical school!

The Dinner Speech

So Hyrcanus heads up to Jerusalem to confront his errant son and instead finds himself among his wealthy colleagues—at what apparently is a fund-raising dinner for Rabbi Yohanan ben Zakkai's academy (some things never change).

> They said to Rabbi Yohanan, "Look, here comes Rabbi Eliezer's father."
>
> He said, "Make a place for him"; so they made a place, sitting him next to Rabbi Yohanan. Yohanan looked over at Rabbi Eliezer and asked him, "Say a word of Torah for us."
>
> He replied, "Rabbi, let me give you an analogy for what this is like. It's like a cistern from which one cannot draw more water than what has been put into it. So I cannot say any more Torah but that which I have learned from you."

Rabbi Yohanan replied, "Let me give *you* an analogy for what this is like. It's like a wellspring that gushes water and has the power to give forth more than has been stored in the well. So you can say more Torah than what they received at Sinai."

(*PIRKE RABBI ELIEZER* 2)

What a golden opportunity. Not only has the wealthy landowner showed up at a propitious moment, but now Rabbi Yohanan has the chance to develop a relationship with him for the sake of "institutional advancement." How convenient it is to seat Hyrcanus next to the leader of the school. And Rabbi Yohanan, no fool he, gives the nod to Eliezer to hold forth—no doubt to impress poppa and perhaps set him thinking about donating the "Hyrcanus dormitories." But perhaps this is more my rabbinic fantasy than Rabbi Yohanan's. Maybe he just wants his boy to show off for his dad.

Note that Eliezer is now called Rabbi Eliezer. Apparently some time has passed since the initial flight from home to Jerusalem. And how sweet that there, seated among the rich and powerful, Hyrcanus is now called "Eliezer's father." It reminds me of that transition point in my own life when I went from being a rabbi/professor to being "Leora's father" when I dropped off my daughter at day care. My, how Rabbi Eliezer has grown up. When asked to speak, he demurs, modestly swapping analogies with his teacher about what he might say—and in so doing gains himself a few precious moments to organize his thoughts. We should not lose sight of the analogies the two rabbis trade—right from the pages of *Pirke Avot*. You will recall in that early text Eliezer was called the lime-plastered cistern. You may also recall that it was Elazar ben Arakh who was the overflowing wellspring. Once again, centuries later, the compliments about the two rabbis are confused, or at least freely transported so that they both alight on Rabbi Eliezer.

Rabbi Yohanan's analogy is curious, because it does not quite parallel the one that Eliezer offers. Each rabbi proposes a parable and then explicates what it signifies. In Eliezer's case, he tells Rabbi Yohanan that he is like the cistern who cannot give back more than what "I have learned from you." But when Yohanan offers his analogy in turn, he likens Eliezer to the wellspring who can "say more Torah than what they received at Sinai." We might have expected Rabbi Yohanan to say that Eliezer can "say more Torah than what you received from *me*." The mention of Sinai here breaks the parallelism between the two sets of analogies.

The great rationalist Rabbi Elijah Gaon of Vilna (1720–1797) was disturbed by this passage. He felt it contradicted another piece of rabbinic teaching: the rabbis often suggest that Moses received *all* Torah at Sinai, "even what a senior student of the sages offers as a novel interpretation." This paradox is meant to buttress the authority of the rabbis, for it implies that what they say has the force of God's word to Moses at Mount Sinai. But if we accept this piece of rabbinic ideology, how can it be, asks the Gaon of Vilna, that Eliezer could know *more* than was given to Moses at Sinai? Indeed, that great eighteenth-century rabbi suggests we emend the text so that Rabbi Yohanan tells Eliezer that he "can say more Torah than what you received from *me*."

There is a simple explanation for how Mount Sinai was schlepped into our story. It requires some Hebrew—but not to worry, you only have to look at the shapes of the letters involved; you need not actually read Hebrew. Rabbi Eliezer says to Rabbi Yohanan, "I cannot say any more Torah but that which I have learned from you." And in turn, Rabbi Yohanan tells him, "You can say more Torah than what they received *at Sinai*." The words "at Sinai" which we are troubled by, are written in Hebrew as one word, מסיני. But we expected it to say, "You can say more Torah than what you received from *me*." That final clause, "from me," would be written in Hebrew as ממני. Here, then, is our point of confusion: מסיני looks a lot like ממני, the letters סי easily confused for the letter מ. The puzzle might readily be explained away by understanding this as a simple copyist's error. If that were the case, our original text would be nicely parallel (from you ‖ from me), and the Gaon of Vilna's concerns about Torah at Sinai allayed. Alas, no manuscript has ממני; they all read מסיני, so we will just have to live with the conundrum of how much Torah Rabbi Eliezer could say.

Cue the Violins

Instead of niggling over quantity, let's turn our eyes to see the quality of his teaching. How good were Rabbi Eliezer's words of Torah?

> Rabbi Yohanan said to Eliezer, "Maybe you are shy in my presence? Allow me to stand away from you."
>
> Rabbi Yohanan stood and went outside, so that Rabbi Eliezer could sit and expound. His face beamed like sunlight, rays of light emanating like those that shone from Moses's face, until one could not tell if it were day or night. Rabbi Yohanan came back in behind Eliezer and kissed him on the head. He said, "Happy are you Abraham, Isaac, and Jacob, that this one is your offspring!"
>
> Hyrcanus asked, "To whom do you say this?"
>
> They told him, "To Eliezer, your son!"
>
> He replied, "He should not have said this...."
>
> (*PIRKE RABBI ELIEZER* 2)

Oh, the drama! If this story were a television series, we would break for a commercial here and leave viewers hanging to learn what comes next. Will Hyrcanus disinherit Eliezer? Will he shame him in front of his teacher and colleagues? Don't go away; we'll be right back after these messages.

This segment of our story also shows us Rabbi Yohanan as an experienced teacher who understands the power of his position. When I was a student, I certainly would have been too shy to offer a sermon or a lecture in the presence of my teachers. So Yohanan withdraws to give Eliezer the mental and emotional space to say his piece. This also is a clever bit of storytelling. Earlier, Rabbi Yohanan had stood away from Eliezer because he had bad breath. When Eliezer protested, Yohanan suggested that just as Eliezer's bad breath had caused him to stand away; so might "the savor of the laws of the Torah ascend from your mouth to Heaven." Now, finally, Rabbi Yohanan stands back once more, that Eliezer's words may, indeed, issue forth heavenward. A very writerly symmetry is achieved here.

I imagine Rabbi Yohanan patiently waiting outside, eavesdropping on his disciple's homily, noticing the unearthly glow seeping under the door. Curious, he reenters the room, is amazed at the brilliance, the brightness, the illumination (note how well this metaphor works in English as well as the original Hebrew). Overwhelmed with teacherly pride, he kisses his student on the head and exclaims his delight, invoking the biblical patriarchs. He may as well have said, "Happy is she who bore him!" Of course, that would echo the text in *Pirke Avot* (2), where we were first introduced to Rabbi Yohanan and his disciples. And, to save you the trouble of remembering just who got that compliment way back when, this is another example of translating traditions from one rabbi to another. Rabbi Yehoshua's mother was the one who was so blessed, and now it is Abraham and company who should rejoice at Eliezer's birth. Same template, different characters.

Enough suspense, let's find out how Hyrcanus completed his remarks about his son Eliezer:

> Hyrcanus replied, "He should not have said this; but happy am I that he is my offspring!"
>
> Rabbi Eliezer was sitting and expounding while his father was standing. When Eliezer noticed his father there, he was nonplussed. He said, "Father, sit, for I cannot speak words of Torah while you are standing!"
>
> Hyrcanus replied, "Son, I did not come to hear you preach, but to disown you from my properties. But now that I've come to see you and observed all this praise, your brothers are disowned from the property, and they are given over to you as a gift!"
>
> Eliezer said, "But I am not as worthy as they are. Furthermore, if I were to desire real estate, it would be up to God to provide me, as it is said, 'The earth is the Lord's, and all the fullness thereof, the world and all who dwell there' [Psalm 24:1]. And were I to desire silver and gold, it would be up to

God to provide me, as it is said, 'Mine is the silver and the gold, declares the Lord of Hosts' [Haggai 2:8]. All I wish from God is Torah, as it is said, 'Thus I love Your commandments more than gold, even fine gold' [Psalm 119:127]."

(PIRKE RABBI ELIEZER 2)

Cue the violins! Set the birds a-chirping. Our story has a happy ending—maybe. As always, a lot depends on how we perform this scene. While there is no question that Hyrcanus seems proud of his son—and let us note that for the first time in our story he actually acknowledges Eliezer as his son—how the scene devolves depends upon the reading. I always put my students on the spot when they recite this passage in class. I tell them, "Once more, with feeling." How would you read, "Father, sit, for I cannot speak words of Torah while you are standing"? Is Eliezer speaking in utter annoyance that Hyrcanus doesn't realize the most basic etiquette of the rabbinic academy? Or is Eliezer being utterly deferential to his dad, virtually leaping from his seat to perform the commandment of "honor your father"? For those who wish to think the latter, there is support in the strength of rabbinic deference to parents and teachers. Surely Rabbi Eliezer would wish to show that honor to his father. On the other hand, Hyrcanus's reply to Eliezer, I've come "to disown you," seems an abrupt about-face from his delight at being Eliezer's father. Eliezer must have said something to irk him, something to remind him of his original purpose in coming to Jerusalem.

I cannot satisfactorily decide which way is better to parse this passage. I invite you, dear reader, to try reading the passage aloud; first one way, then the other. Does your own performance of the libretto give you a clue to the original intention of the storyteller? If nothing else, it should give you a clue to your own preference of how to play the scene. Assuming you are not a professional actor, where does your preference stem from? Are you an objective reader, or are your own personal parent-issues affecting your performance? Enough psychology—let's return to the safe ground of our characters and their neuroses.

I'm [Not] Worthy

Hyrcanus clearly still doesn't get the whole Torah thing. He is impressed by the praise of Eliezer, not the content of his teaching. And he remains volatile, now shifting allegiance once more back to Eliezer and away from his brothers. Eliezer demurs, claiming he is not worthy. One manuscript has a small change, omitting one letter from Eliezer's pronouncement. In dropping the letter *yod*, the smallest letter of the Hebrew alphabet, Eliezer goes from saying, "I am not as worthy as they are" to saying, "I am as worthy as one of them." In other words, he only wants his share of the inheritance, no more. It is very hard to tell what we are meant to make of Eliezer. Is he a modest Torah scholar who wishes nothing for himself, or is he a strong son who stands up to his conniving brothers, ensuring his share of the inheritance even as he studies in Jerusalem?

The ending of our tale is, I fear, pure treacle. I half expect Eliezer to start singing, "Wouldn't it be loverly?" He pedantically lectures his father that if he were to desire real estate or even cash, God would provide. All he needs is Torah, sweet Torah. And he even has a verse of Psalms to prove it! A happy ending to a point, except that I cheated and changed the verse of Psalms so it fit our story's ending a tad better than the one the books quote. There, Eliezer ends his speech with Psalm 119:128, "Thus I direct my steps by Your precepts; I hate every false way." Same sentiment, one verse later. Since the two verses begin with the exact same words, I tweaked our text a bit and allowed Eliezer to say outright that he prefers Torah to gold.

Either way, Rabbi Eliezer ben Hyrcanus and his teacher Rabbi Yohanan ben Zakkai appear to live happily ever after. But what about those other students? What happened to Rabbi Elazar ben Arakh and Rabbi Yehoshua ben Hananiah, Rabbi José the Priest and Rabbi Shimeon ben Netanel? What became of them? We saw them briefly as roommates to Eliezer. Did they get to teach and preach? Stay tuned for our next exciting episode!

8 / ח

Road Trip
with Fireworks

L et us squint past Rabbi Eliezer's brilliance to refocus on Rabbi
Yohanan ben Zakkai and his other disciples. Recall that it was Elazar
ben Arakh, and not our boy Eliezer ben Hyrcanus, who had the master's favor. The rapport that Elazar ben Arakh had with Yohanan
allowed for certain liberties to be taken in the strict rules of rabbinic
etiquette. The Mishnah invokes such a rule when it comes to the study
of Jewish mysticism. There has been a long tradition of Jewish speculation about God. Much of the earliest mystical investigation centered on
biblical texts describing God, God's throne, and perhaps most mysteri-
ous of all biblical passages, God's angelic Chariot, described in the biblical book of the prophet Ezekiel, chapter 1. The premiere modern
scholar of Ezekiel, the late Professor Moshe Greenberg, once characterized the first chapter of the prophetic book to me (I quote him verba-
tim), "It's a doozy." But why take his word for it? Let's peruse a brief
section of the prophet Ezekiel's famous vision:

> I beheld a storm wind coming from the north: a huge cloud
> and flickering fire with a radiance surrounding it; and from
> within something like electrum in the midst of the flames. In
> its midst was the appearance of four animals, which looked
> human. Each had four faces and four wings. They had straight
> legs with calf-like hooves, sparkling like burnished bronze....

Their faces resembled that of a human, then a lion to the right, an ox to the left, and an eagle.... Their faces were like glowing coals, with flames of torches flickering between them, with lightning issuing forth from the fire.... When I looked at the creatures there was a wheel touching the ground ... like a wheel within a wheel ... and the rims of the wheels were filled with eyes.... When they moved, the sound of their wings was like that of mighty waters or the din of an army camp.... And upon the expanse above their heads was a throne that looked like sapphire, and upon the throne was what appeared to be a human form, gleaming like electrum, encased in fire ... appearing like a rainbow in the clouds on a rainy day ... thus was the appearance of the form of the glory of God.

(EZEKIEL 1:4–28)

Like Professor Greenberg said, "It's a doozy." And because this vision is so bizarre, the rabbis offer the rule in the Mishnah that one may not explore "the works of the Chariot" with any other person unless he is "a sage who can understand it through his own knowledge." The Babylonian Talmud (sixth century) quotes an early story from the Land of Israel (second to third century) about this ruling:

The story is told that Rabbi Yohanan ben Zakkai was riding his donkey on a journey. Rabbi Elazar was driving the donkey, walking behind it. Elazar asked, "Rabbi, would you recite a chapter of the works of the Chariot for me?"

Yohanan replied, "Did I not teach you the mishnah that 'one may not explore the works of the Chariot with any other person, unless he is a sage who can understand it through his own knowledge'?"

Elazar countered, "Rabbi, permit me to say one thing that you taught me."

Rabbi Yohanan replied, "Speak." At that, Rabbi Yohanan immediately got down off the donkey, wrapped himself in his cloak, and sat upon a rock beneath an olive tree.

Elazar asked him, "Rabbi, why did you get off of your donkey?"

Yohanan replied, "Is it right that I should remain on my donkey while you explore the works of the Chariot? God's Presence will be among us, and the ministering angels will accompany us!"

Elazar immediately opened the works of the Chariot and expounded. Fire came down from heaven and surrounded all of the trees in the field. They all burst into song. What did they sing? "Praise God from the earth, sea monsters and all the depths ... fruit trees and all the cedars say ... 'Hallelujah!' (Psalm 148)."

An angel answered from amidst the flames, "These, yes, yes, these are the works of the Chariot!"

(BABYLONIAN TALMUD, HAGIGAH 14B)

Quite the pyrotechnic display! But now that we are finished ooohing and aaahing at the fireworks, let's go back and figure out just what happened. Like many good stories, this one is about a "road trip." Our two male characters take their places, one driving, the other comfortably seated, riding shotgun, as it were. Elazar is displaying the courtesy disciples show their masters, offering Yohanan his service as donkey driver—presumably whacking the donkey now and then on its rump with a stick that is long enough to avoid getting kicked in return. Why does Elazar perform this lowly function for his master? First, he gets the satisfaction of doing the right thing and helping his teacher make his journey. Second, and not to be slighted, is the one-on-one face time that comes with serving the sage.

This ethos of "serving the sage" was a part of the fabric of rabbinic society. It was so for Yohanan and his disciples. It was so for Jesus and his disciples before that. It also was so for Aristotle and his disciples before that. "Serving the sage" allowed disciples to learn by observing their teachers in everyday situations. Elsewhere in the Talmud (Berakhot 62a) there is a series of stories about the lengths to which students would follow their teachers to learn Torah. Rabbi Akiva claims to have followed Rabbi Yehoshua into the bathroom and learned three things, "for this is Torah, and I needed to learn." And the Babylonian Rabbi Kahana once hid beneath the bed of his teacher Rav, while, as the Talmud delicately reports, he was "conversing and doing his needs with his wife." When Rav realized they were not alone, he hauled the disciple out and said, "Kahana, leave, this is not proper!" Kahana's explanation for his ill-conceived behavior? "This is Torah, and I needed to learn."

Great Balls of Fire

Let's look away from this awkward scene and return to our rabbis on the road with a fresh appreciation that donkey driving is among the least of the things students will do to learn from their masters. Elazar, given his chance, asks right off to learn the secrets of the Chariot. Much has been made of the way the Talmud tells the story, for Elazar asks Rabbi Yohanan to "recite a chapter of the works of the Chariot." This reference to chapters prompted the great scholar of Jewish mysticism Gershom Scholem to infer that as early as the first century there was an edited corpus of mystical literature being passed down orally, like the Mishnah, from teacher to student. While other scholars debate this conclusion, there is no question that there were esoteric teachings and that those who were initiated into the mysteries passed them on with great caution.

Rabbi Elazar proves himself adept. Characteristically, before he even opens his mouth, Rabbi Yohanan expresses his confidence in his favorite student by preparing himself for the effects of Elazar's discourse: God and the ministering angels will come to hear Elazar expound! Yohanan grounds himself firmly on stone beneath an olive tree (I have absolutely no idea why), wraps himself in his cloak in anticipation of what will follow, and Elazar holds forth. Yet again, one of Rabbi Yohanan's students shows his brilliance, this time by bringing fire down from heaven to illuminate the surroundings. The trees are aflame, perhaps like Moses's burning bush was aflame with God's Presence. But I should point out that one version of the Talmud text imagines the trees getting singed by the fire—unlike Moses, who noted that "the bush was not consumed" (Exodus 3:2).

The fire sets the wood crackling and popping or, as it is poetically expressed, "singing." The Talmud pedantically inquires as to the lyrics of the song. With ease, a section of Psalm 148 is trotted out, suggesting that the trees and all God's creatures sing "Hallelujah." In the Palestinian Talmud, *Hagigah* 2:1 (77a), when this story is told, they offer another lyric, this time from Psalm 96:12, "Then shall all the trees sing their joy." To accompany the psalm, an angelic voice offers verification of Rabbi Elazar's prowess. Since we've read the wacky passage from Ezekiel, we know that God's Chariot actually is composed of angelic beings, so they ought to know what's what. Looks like Elazar hit the ball out of the park on his first at bat! How did Rabbi Yohanan react?

> Rabbi Yohanan stood and kissed Elazar on the head. Yohanan said, "Blessed is God, the Lord of Israel, who gave such a son to Abraham our father; for he knows how to understand, and investigate, and expound upon the works of the Chariot. There are those who preach well, yet they do not practice. There are those who practice well, but they cannot preach. You practice what you preach! Happy are you, Abraham our father, that Elazar ben Arakh is your offspring!"
>
> (BABYLONIAN TALMUD, *HAGIGAH* 14B)

Well, we've heard this before, haven't we? In Jerusalem, Yohanan kissed Eliezer ben Hyrcanus on the head. On the road, he gives Elazar ben Arakh the head-kiss. Is this another instance of confusing traditions about the two colleagues and transferring what was said of one to the other? Or did Rabbi Yohanan just make a habit of showing his approval with a kiss on the head of the student who pleased him at any given moment? We have also heard Yohanan say of Eliezer ben Hyrcanus in Jerusalem, "Happy are you, Abraham, Isaac, and Jacob, that this one is your offspring!" (see chapter 7). That is obviously not too different from the compliment delivered to Elazar above, although it neglects Isaac and Jacob. As I said when we encountered it earlier, it is a riff on *Pirke Avot's* (2) paraphrase of Scripture, "Blessed is she who bore you." Either Yohanan was not very original when it came to complimenting his students or perhaps our storytellers include this compliment as part of their thumbnail description of Rabbi Yohanan ben Zakkai in their performance repertoire.

Doing Mysticism

Two other aspects of this story bear our notice. Nowhere are we actually told what Rabbi Elazar said when he expounded on the Chariot. This is in keeping with the general rabbinic attitude that it is okay to talk about mysticism, but not to publicly reveal the contents of the teaching ("One may not explore the works of the Chariot with any other person, unless he is a sage who can understand it through his own knowledge" [*Mishnah Hagigah* 2]). It's almost a tease: we'll tell you that it happened, but not what happened! I would note that the same thing was true of Eliezer ben Hyrcanus's brilliant and illuminating exposition back in Jerusalem. We weren't told what he said there, either. This has led some scholars to speculate that he, too, gave a mystical discourse. In the story in this chapter, Rabbi Yohanan compliments his student Elazar ben Arakh by saying he "knows how to understand, and investigate, and expound upon the works of the Chariot." This string of three verbs (where one would do perfectly well) is another tease about rabbinic mysticism.

In the first millennium of the Common Era, Jewish mysticism was theurgic, which is a nice way of saying "magical." When you "did Jewish mysticism," it was not so much a subject of study as actually something you *did*. The esoteric knowledge allowed the practitioner to be godlike and manipulate the universe. So, one of the great medieval rabbinic mystical works (*Merkaba Shelaymah*), which literally measured God's body (yikes!), used the measurements like a magic formula. If you got the combinations right, you could change the world. As it happens, that mystical work recommends these manipulations for the purpose of warding off mosquitoes! Now that sounds faintly ridiculous to us. But let us not forget that mosquitoes bring malaria, so the ability to keep them at bay could be a matter affecting life and death. Furthermore, in rabbinic natural science, the mosquito is thought of as the smallest of God's creatures. So if the mystic could control the smallest of God's creations, he was learning to manipulate the universe that God created. In essence, the mystic was seeking to emulate the Creator. This is assuredly more noble than a fourth-century rabbinic mystical text (*Sefer HaRazim*) that teaches its practitioners how to win at the racetrack!

In our Talmudic tale, Rabbi Yohanan alludes to the fact that the rabbinic mystics loved to string together verbs that mostly mean the same thing ("understand, and investigate, and expound") as a type of mantra. In reciting these strings of verbs, the mystic moved into a trancelike state, ready to enter the Divine Presence. Even now, the Jewish prayer book has many sections that include such strings of verbs, an indication of the "normal mysticism" of daily prayer in rabbinic Judaism. These segments of the prayer book originated in mystical circles but made their way into the prayers of everyday Jews, much in the same way that our story in the Talmud is for everyday readers and listeners. You get the mini-string of verbs, you are told the story about the mystical experience, but there's no "there" there. Actual mystical practice is for the adepts, like Rabbi Yohanan and Rabbi Elazar.

Practice What You Preach

Yohanan further compliments his boy Elazar by telling him that he practices what he preaches. I fudged the translation a bit so it would sound more like our own idiom. It literally reads, "You expound [the Torah] well and uphold [the Torah] well." But the compliment is formulaic and is found elsewhere in the Talmud. There we are told about Rabbi Shimeon ben Azzai, himself a mystic. Ben Azzai once expounded on Genesis 1:26, which states that humanity was created in God's image and likeness. He surmised that anyone who did not father children, perforce, was guilty of diminishing God's image in the world. "They told him, Ben Azzai, there are those who preach well and practice well, and there are those who practice well but do not preach well. You, however, do not practice what you preach!" Turns out Shimeon ben Azzai was a bachelor—oops—who subsequently explained himself by saying, "What can I do? I am wedded to Torah!"

Of course, it shouldn't surprise us any longer that storytellers use well-worn formulas, any more than it would surprise us that comedians tell jokes that are remarkably similar. Stand-up performance, whether for comedy or for Torah, demands a certain regularity that comes with repeated telling of the same story. Even Homer used the same phrases (remember "rosy-fingered dawn"?) over and over again. Listeners have expectations that need to be met so they know how to interpret the genre of the tale and the point of the narration. But those expectations are toyed with by a good performer, to keep the audience's attention and interest.

We already know that if Yohanan does something with Eliezer and Elazar, his other students cannot be far behind. Let's turn to another story of a road trip, mystical exposition, heavenly display, and the mustering of angels. This time it's about Rabbi Yehoshua and Rabbi José the Priest, once more following our principle of rabbis using *Pirke Avot* as though it were a *Playbill* telling us the "Cast in Order of Appearance."

9 / ט

Anything He Can Do,
I Can Do, Too

Now we have a short interlude in which Rabbi Yehoshua and Rabbi José the Priest take their turns playing the leading roles in the "open the heavens, mystical revelation, road-trip drama." It seems as though this is a retelling of the story we've just read, with some necessary changes. But it might be that we have a number of genuine traditions about rabbinic mysticism from the early centuries. If so, we would surmise that the telling of the tales got stylized over the centuries, becoming more formulaic over time. What may have been two radically differing incidents come to appear as though they are variants on a theme. If this were the modern movie business, we'd think of one of these as the first film and the latter as its sequel or, perhaps, the remake. Well, let us hear the story and see what we can learn about both rabbinic storytelling and early Jewish mysticism.

> When these things were reported to Rabbi Yehoshua, he and Rabbi José the Priest were on a journey. They said, "Let us also investigate the works of the Chariot."
> Rabbi Yehoshua opened and expounded. Now that day was midsummer, yet the sky became knotted with clouds and something like a rainbow appeared in the clouds. The minis-

tering angels came a-mustering to hear, like folks who come to watch the entertainment of a bride and groom.

(BABYLONIAN TALMUD, HAGIGAH 14B)

Given the Talmudic segue into this story—"When these things were reported to Rabbi Yehoshua"—our text sounds a bit like the lyrics to *Annie Get Your Gun's*, "Anything you can do, I can do better." You almost expect Rabbi Elazar to pipe in with the chorus, "No you can't …" Instead we get the students' classic response, "Let us also," a somewhat more polite way of singing Annie Oakley's song. In truth Annie Oakley and Frank Butler's competition pales in comparison to the rivalry among students of Torah, so much so that the rabbis coined the phrase "the jealousy of scribes" to capture its intensity. This is a truism that finds its expression in modern academia as Sayre's Law. Wallace Sayre, the late political science professor at Columbia University, famously explained the bitterness of academic infighting: "because the stakes are so low." Yet among the rabbis, the competition was intense precisely because they perceived the stakes to be so high, quite literally to the heavens!

Mystical Speculation

We should not lightly pass over what the mystic thought he was doing. It demeans the nobility of religious yearnings to simply dismiss the practice of the mystic as no more than magic (as I did above, *mea culpa*). The rabbis took seriously the manifestations of the Divine, whether as angelic appearance or by vividly imagining God's body. In both accounts of Rabbi Yohanan's students investigating the works of the Chariot, angels appear. The advent of angels in Judaism is as old as the Torah itself. Angels appear to Abraham repeatedly, as they do to his descendants. The angels Gabriel, Michael, and Rafael are specifically named in Hebrew Scripture. A full-blown angelology (study of angels) may be found scattered through rabbinic literature, one that would give a run for its money to medieval Christian speculation about how many angels can dance on the head of a pin. Angels, being of the heavenly realm and reflecting biblical descriptions, are understood as fiery beings with sets of wings. Angel wings number as few as two and multiply seemingly exponentially, depending on the importance and power of the angel. According to both the Bible and the rabbis, there is a kind of continuum between the human and the Divine that is made up of gradations of God's messengers—from prophets (such as Malachi, which means "my angel") through heavenly angels. They are all manifestations of the Divine Being: godly, yet not God. This esoteric angelology is disturbing to many Jews, who find that it mirrors Christian theology too closely for comfort. Yet Rabbinic, Christian, and Muslim angelology all share many common features that reflect a genuine human yearning for contact with the Divine.

That yearning is also reflected in mystical speculation on topics as many and varied as God's throne room, God's chariot, God's creation of the universe, eschatology (what will come at the end of time), its corollary messianism, and finally and most radically, Jewish speculation on God's body. Around the tenth century, rabbinic mystics produced measurements of God's body. Suffice it to say that all of God's body parts are measured; God is cosmically large, and I should point out, emphatically male. One of the ironies of this explicit act of imagining God incarnate is that the numbers of the measurements are so enormously huge that the mystics had no better apprehension of the Divine once measured than at the outset. God may be measurable, yet God remains ineffable. Indeed, in the twelfth century, the austere Aristotelian thinker Rabbi Moses ben Maimon (known as Maimonides or by the Hebrew acronym of his name, Rambam) utterly rejected this kind of rabbinic mysticism as heretical.

Rambam's rationalist objections notwithstanding, all of this was the presumed backstory for those who heard the tale of Rabbis Yehoshua and José on their road trip, itching to do what their classmates had done. In truth, this background of Jewish mystical yearning for God informs the entire enterprise of sage tales. So we current listeners can calibrate our impressions of the rabbis and their legends by remembering their quest for God alongside their visitations by angels and, if we can remember all the way back at the outset of the book, the heavenly traveler, the prophet Elijah.

Openings

Let us concentrate, instead, on the details of the telling and how Yehoshua's discourse and results are the same as and different from Elazar's. To begin, Elazar did his mystical speculation in the presence of his master Yohanan ben Zakkai, while Yehoshua had a somewhat more limited audience in his pal Joey. But each investigated the "works of the Chariot," and each "opened and expounded." What did they open? They perhaps opened up a scroll to read from. They certainly opened the verses of Ezekiel to interpretation. They opened their erudite discourse. They likely opened the eyes and ears of their auditors to the wonders of their insights. And in both cases, they opened the gates of heaven so the angels could come down to witness the mystical interpretations that were offered. This broad range of meaning for the verb "opened" is found in other Jewish settings, notably Christian Scripture. In the Gospel of Luke, Jesus opens the eyes of those who see him (24:31), he opens Scriptures to them (24:32), and he opens their minds to understand those Scriptures (24:45). Luke also writes in Acts 16:14 that God opened the heart of one of Paul's followers to what he had to say.

The rabbis' respective openings of heaven are worth dwelling on further. After all, it's not every rabbi who gets the angels to come listen to him preach! The angelic advent is accompanied by various natural portents. First, although it is a midsummer day in the Land of Israel (when the weather should be entirely sunny), the sky is suddenly "knotted with clouds." We will see this very phrase again later, in another story (a Jewish equivalent of Homer's "rosy-fingered dawn"?). The Hebrew term I translated as midsummer actually reads "the summer solstice" or, even more accurately, "the season of Tammuz." Tammuz, the dying and resurrecting god of the Sumerian and Babylonian pantheons, had the month when summer began named after him. The names of the months in the Jewish calendar were actually borrowed by the rabbis from their Babylonian neighbors. Call it Tammuz, call it solstice, call it midsummer, by any other name it should be a sunny day.

Not only does the sky grow overcast (don't you think "knotted" is a much better metaphor for clouds?) but also a rainbow appears, even though no rain has fallen. Well, not actually a rainbow, but "something like a rainbow." If we look back to the beginning of chapter 8, where I quoted that doozy of a vision the prophet Ezekiel had of God's Chariot, there, too, is the rainbowlike appearance irradiating the clouds. This should be proof enough for an angel to say, as it did for Rabbi Elazar on the road with Rabbi Yohanan, "These, yes, yes, these are the works of the Chariot!" Instead, once the door of heaven, as it were, has been opened, the angels tumble out pell-mell, like the crowd at a Long Island Jewish wedding *smörgåsbord*. You can imagine the scene: the laden tables, the guests bellying up, some sharpening their appetites, others sharpening their elbows for the ruck, still others standing aside and sharpening their tongues to gossip about who is eating what.

I don't mean to sound so cynical, but I am trying to capture the inflection the rabbis intended when they chose the word I translated so blandly as "the entertainment of a bride and groom." First off, like my invocation of *smörgåsbord* in its Scandinavian spelling, they chose a foreign word, not Hebrew, to indicate "the entertainment." I suppose the word is a garbled borrowing from Greek. It only appears in one other place in all of rabbinic literature, and there it serves as a translation of the Hebrew word for "pleasantries" or "delights." When the Palestinian Talmud tells the story of our rabbis, it describes the angels mustering to see the "rejoicings of the bride and groom," using a common Hebrew term. Whatever word we may use for the size and nature of the crowd, the point is simply this: Rabbi Yehoshua brought the (heavenly) house down.

Is There a Fifth Ace in the Deck?

As the Talmud unfolds the cycle of stories of mystical discourses, four out of five of Yohanan ben Zakkai's disciples have been accounted for. Eliezer ben Hyrcanus gave his disquisition in Jerusalem. It may or may not have been mystical, I admit. But if we are being picky, the truth be told, it may or may not have ever happened. We are dwelling in a didactic form of rabbinic reminiscence, a topic we will touch on a bit more in our next chapter. For now, let's count Eliezer among the initiated. Then there is Elazar, as it were, the gold standard. He even managed to convince the master to hear his speculations, right there alongside the fiery angelic audience. And in this chapter, Rabbi Yehoshua pitched, and presumably Rabbi José the Priest served as his catcher. Our rabbinic narrators have made their way through the fabulous five, only ignoring poor Rabbi Shimeon ben Netanel, always the odd man out.

I wish I could pull a text out of my sleeve and lay it on the table, a story in which Rabbi Shimeon's mystical tour trumps that of his colleagues. Alas, there is no such tale to tell. Our obtuse friend will have to remain the fifth wheel. But what of the master himself? What did Rabbi Yohanan ben Zakkai have to say about all of his students holding forth on the mysteries of heaven? Let us turn to chapter 10 and find out.

10 / '

I Had a Dream …
I've Been to the
Mountaintop

While we are asking about what Rabbi Yohanan had to say about his students, we should also ask about what his students had to say about studying with him. Memories, especially memories of long ago, related to doing something noble or doing something with someone noble have a curious way of being remembered. In the modern world, politicians recall serving in Vietnam, even if they did not. Among academics, some remember that we studied with famous teachers or heard them lecture, even if the chronology is inconvenient to actual fact. People might recollect studying with Rabbi Abraham Joshua Heschel or hearing Martin Buber lecture about I and Thou. They reminisce about walking down Broadway with Reinhold Niebuhr or (to leap from the sublime to the ridiculous) running into Madonna in the produce section of the Fairway Market at Seventy-Fifth Street. Everybody seems to remember having been at Woodstock, no matter where they really were. Memory, reminiscence, and nostalgia are cruel mistresses. They bespeak aspirations even when not wedded to historic facts.

Many recall hearing Dr. Martin Luther King Jr. speak. Some remind us how they marched with him in Selma. Others quote the Reverend King's speeches, much as they might quote Gandhi or Shakespeare or Scripture. Such proof-texting lends authority to their claims, even when they misquote. Who among us doesn't remember when King prophetically preached, "I had a dream! I've been to the mountaintop!"? I would have sworn he gave such a speech and might even faintly summon up having heard it on television back when. Except that Dr. King did not quite say that, and what he did say came from two very different speeches. On August 28, 1963, in Washington, D.C., he famously said on the steps of the Lincoln Memorial:

> I say to you today my friends—so even though we face the difficulties of today and tomorrow, I still have a dream. It is a dream deeply rooted in the American dream.
>
> I have a dream that one day this nation will rise up and live out the true meaning of its creed: "We hold these truths to be self-evident, that all men are created equal." ... I have a dream that my four little children will one day live in a nation where they will not be judged by the color of their skin but by the content of their character. I have a dream today....

Almost five years later, in Memphis, Tennessee, on April 3, 1968, the night before he was assassinated, he proclaimed:

> Well, I don't know what will happen now. We've got some difficult days ahead. But it doesn't matter with me now. Because I've been to the mountaintop.... And He's allowed me to go up to the mountain. And I've looked over. And I've seen the promised land.... I'm not fearing any man. Mine eyes have seen the glory of the coming of the Lord.

Why do I quote Martin Luther King when I'm meant to be talking about Rabbi Yohanan ben Zakkai and his disciples? Well now, let's listen to what our rabbi, that great religious leader, had to say about his students having seen "the glory of the coming of the Lord." Right after Rabbi Yehoshua and Rabbi José the Priest brought the angels down to hear their speculation about the very vehicle in which the glory of the Lord comes and goes, the Talmud continues its tale:

> Rabbi José the Priest went and spoke of these matters to Rabbi Yohanan. To which Rabbi Yohanan said, "Happy are you and happy are they who gave birth to you! Happy are my eyes that have seen such! I had a dream. Indeed, I and you were reclining at a banquet on Mount Sinai. A voice, an echo came from heaven and said, 'Come up here! Come up here! There are great banquet tables spread with delicate foods for you. You, and your students, and your students' students are invited up to first class!'"
>
> (BABYLONIAN TALMUD, *HAGIGAH* 14B)

Our master Rabbi Yohanan had a dream! He has been to the mountaintop! I do not think for a moment that Rabbi Yohanan was quoting the Reverend Martin Luther King Jr. Nor do I even think that Dr. King was quoting our master Rabbi Yohanan. For each, the cadences of the Bible were quite natural to their discourse. Rabbi Yohanan not only invokes the now seemingly commonplace "Happy are they who gave birth to you," but he also claims that his eyes are happy to have beheld what he saw. Here, he seems to be channeling the prophet Isaiah, as did that other famous first-century rabbi, Jesus of Nazareth. In Matthew 13:16, Jesus says to his disciples, "Happy are your eyes, for they see, and your ears, for they hear." Just before he says that, he quotes from Isaiah (6:9–10), "Go, say to that people: 'Hear, indeed, but do not understand; see, indeed, but do not grasp.' ... Lest seeing with its eyes and hearing with its ears, it also grasp with its mind and repent and heal itself!" It seems that both Jesus and Rabbi Yohanan use common biblical parlance to express their delight at their students' acumen, much as did Dr. Martin Luther King.

Banquet Etiquette

The banquet on Mount Sinai that Rabbi Yohanan recalls is also curiously redolent of Jesus and his disciples. If we return to the Gospel of Luke, Jesus offers his students a parable:

> When you are invited by someone to a wedding banquet, do not recline in the top seat, in case someone of greater honor has

been invited. For then the host who invited you and him might say, "Give him your place," and you will have to take the lowest place, with shame. But when you are invited, go recline in the lowest place, so then the one who invited you will say to you, "Friend, come up higher." Then you will have glory before all who recline with you.

(LUKE 14:8–10)

Together, the stories told by Rabbi Yohanan ("I had a dream") and Jesus (in his parable) point to a brutal etiquette. Dinner parties were the daily round of Roman society. When Rabbi Yohanan invoked the banquet table in his dream sequence, he even used the Greek term *triclinium*. That low, square table accommodated guests around three (*tri-*) of the four sides, where each guest reclined (*-clinium*) for the meal. The servants used the free side of the table to bring food and clear plates. Diners leaned on pillows, propping themselves up on their left arms, which freed their right hands to reach for food and drink. Waiters mixed their wine with water, and guests ate using their fingers. In a lovely touch of antique manners, folks brought their own napkins to the banquet, saving the host the labor of laundering greasy napkins the next morning, and availing themselves a convenient wrapper with which to carry home leftovers.

Each side of the table had room for three reclining guests, for a total of nine at any given *triclinium* at a banquet. As you will notice if you lean for a moment on your left arm, you can see the person to your right but have to lean awkwardly backward to see the person to your left. This means that when guests dined at a *triclinium*, certain seats were preferable for dominating the table, while other seats put the diner essentially out of the conversation. At any given table of nine, each diner knew who was up and who was down.

To compound the potential for insult or exultation, *triclinia* were arrayed on risers around the banquet hall. Quite literally, the higher you were placed in the room, the higher your host's esteem for you. Being seated at a large banquet told you exactly where you were ranked in your host's regard. Generally, big banquets divided the guests into three classes. Those lowest in the room actually got the worst food. A Roman writer once famously complained that he was fed an eel fished from the murky waters of the Tiber and it had been cooked in oil that was used in the lamps the previous night! Is it any wonder that one might be tempted to find a seat higher up in the room? But imagine the shame of your host suggesting that you should move lower down: there were more important people in the room than you.

Who Gets a Seat at the Table?

How lovely, then, for Rabbi Yohanan to hear a heavenly voice invite him, and his disciples, and even their disciples, to move up to take their place (with God) at the great mythic banquet. Presumably, their expertise in Torah gives them a seat at the table, as it were, right up there at the top with Moses in first class on Mount Sinai. It was there, of course, that Moses received the Torah "from the mouth of God" (Numbers 9:23). In rabbinic literature, Sinai comes to be virtually synonymous with God and Torah. To the rabbis, it was not just the six hundred thousand males and their wives and children who stood at Sinai, but all Jews, even unto today. As they read Deuteronomy 29:13–14, "I make this covenant not with you alone, but with those who are standing here with us today before the Lord our God and with those who are not here with us this day," that last clause includes everybody ever: those who left Egypt, those who stood at Sinai, those who entered the Promised Land, the rabbis we've been reading about, us.

When the story of Mount Sinai is told in the book of Exodus, it has even more relevant echoes for our passage about Rabbi Yohanan's dream. We read in Exodus 24:9–11:

> Then Moses and Aaron, Nadav and Avihu, and seventy elders of Israel ascended; and they beheld the God of Israel: under God's feet was like a work of sapphire stone, like the very heavens for purity. Yet God did not lay a hand upon those leaders of Israel. They saw God, and they ate and they drank.

As with all the sightings of God we've encountered thus far, this is weird stuff. There is God in the throne room, below God's feet a sapphire stone floor. It's the final two sentences that cause consternation. Why would God wish to harm the elders who came to receive the Torah? Why do we need to be reassured that "God did not lay a hand upon" them? Well, approaching God is dangerous. A bit further on in Exodus, Moses asks to "behold God's glory" (Exodus 33:18). God replies, "You cannot see My face, for no human may behold Me and live" (Exodus 33:20).

As if this weren't fraught enough, what's with the picnic? The elders of Israel are atop Mount Sinai to receive the Torah and they stop for a snack? What could the text mean when it says, "They saw God, and they ate and they drank"? The rabbis offer an explanation that may raise more questions than answers: "They were nourished by the radiance of God's Presence" (*Leviticus Rabbah* 20:10). While we cannot even begin to imagine the divine Happy Meal God served up, we can, at least, understand the context of Rabbi Yohanan's dream. He and his disciples received a special invitation, a dispensation if you will, to ascend on high and dine with the Divine Presence, as did the elders when the Torah was first given at Sinai. The reward for their careful study of Torah is to receive more Torah, direct from the Source.

A Clear Invitation

This dream of an invitation to ascend Mount Sinai comes from the banquet's Divine Host. The voice that Yohanan heard in his dream, the echo from heaven, literally translated would be "daughter of a voice." By the rabbinic period, prophecy—direct communion from God—had given way to textual interpretation: exactly what we are doing. The sages preferred to interpret the Torah actively rather than passively awaiting new revelations. Further, I suspect that they were suspicious of new revelations, which potentially undercut their authority. They preferred an established system of commentary to charismatic religion. For the rabbis, active prophecy ended with the biblical books of the last of the Minor Prophets, Haggai, Malachi, and Zechariah. From that point onward, when it came to revelation, the rabbis engaged in midrash, the searching out of God's will through interpretation of the scriptural canon.

As one famous passage of Talmud has it, Rabbi Yehoshua quoted Deuteronomy 30:12, saying, "The Torah is not in heaven." Rabbi Yermiah explained, "Since the Torah was already given at Sinai, we do not listen to the 'daughter of a voice'" (*Bava Metzia* 59b). Indeed, when the rabbis argued in legal contexts, they followed voting procedures where majority opinion ruled. Yet in rabbinic narratives like the ones we are reading, when they wished to make God's pleasure known, either they portrayed the angels speaking in God's stead or the rabbis reluctantly made do, as it were, with heavenly echoes like the one Rabbi Yohanan ben Zakkai heard in his dream.

Rabbi Yohanan nonetheless got a pretty clear invitation to ascend to Mount Sinai with his disciples. Other rabbis had a harder time accessing God. They had to tiptoe into the throne room, as it were, in hopes of catching a glimpse of the Divine. As we will see in our next chapter, this could be a harrowing, even life-threatening procedure.

11 / כ

Paradise Ain't All It's Cracked Up to Be

R abbi Yohanan and his famous five disciples were not the only rabbis of the late first century. In fact, Yohanan's students had many contemporaries as the rabbinic movement expanded. We are focused in this book on a small cast of characters, and they help us to understand the oddities and quiddities of sage tales. But other characters will wander onto the stage now and then, as they have already. Way back in chapter 1 we met Rabbi Akiva, as he and his wife Rachel struggled with poverty. He was of the same generation as Rabbis Yehoshua, Eliezer, Elazar, Shimeon, and José. Rabbi Akiva, although he has not played a central role in our drama thus far, now steps onto center stage along with three other contemporaries in the continuation of the Talmudic tale we have been exploring.

> It was recited by our rabbis: Four entered paradise.
>
> They are Ben Azzai, and Ben Zoma, the Other, and Rabbi Akiva.
>
> Rabbi Akiva said to them, "When you arrive at the pure marble stones, do not say, 'Water, water!' for it is said, 'He who speaks falsehoods will not stand before My eyes' [Psalm 101:7]."
>
> Ben Azzai glimpsed and died. Scripture says of him, "The death of God's beloved is grievous in the eyes of the Lord" (Psalm 116:1).

> Ben Zoma glimpsed and was smitten. Scripture says of
> him, "Did you find honey? Eat only what you need, lest you
> grow too full and vomit it" (Proverbs 25:16).
>
> The Other chopped the sprouts.
>
> Rabbi Akiva went out in peace.
>
> (BABYLONIAN TALMUD, HAGIGAH 14B)

This text is utterly opaque. It is almost as though the narrator is daring us to be confused; saying, "You want mysticism? I'll mystify you!" To understand this story without getting entirely lost, we will unpack the narrative almost phrase by phrase. Each word has valence, each sentence carries its own gnomic intelligence. We'll begin explaining this difficult text with the opening of the recitation, "Four entered paradise." In this short, yet complex tale, these four rabbis seem to have done their own mystical speculation. I wrote in chapter 8 that in the early rabbinic era mysticism was not so much studied as it was *done*. Our four rabbis are reported to have *journeyed* into mysticism by having "entered paradise." But what does that practically mean? I use the word "paradise" advisedly, for it is a loan word in Hebrew (*p-r-d-s*), found also in Greek of the period. In Greek it clearly means what we mean when we say "paradise"; yet originally, in Old Persian, it could refer to a garden or an orchard. This led one modern scholar to presume that these rabbis dabbled in Epicureanism, as that school of philosophy famously met in Epicurus's garden. Most scholars, however, soundly reject this notion in favor of one of two similar approaches found among medieval interpreters of the passage.

Rabbi Solomon ben Isaac, or Rashi (as he is known by the acronym of his name), lived in eleventh-century Troyes, France. In his magisterial commentary to the Talmud (which is found in every edition of the Talmud ever printed), Rashi wrote: "*Entered paradise*: They ascended to the firmament by means of the Divine Name." For Rashi there was, indeed, a heavenly journey, accomplished by means of another mystical mantra, this one made of various permutations of the letters of the Tetragrammaton, God's four-lettered Divine Name: *Yod, Heh, Vav, Heh*. Yet a generation or two following Rashi's commentary, other Franco-German commentators offer a subtly different interpretation of what happened: *"Entered paradise*: For example, by means of the Divine Name. But they did not literally ascend to the firmament. It only appeared to them as though they had ascended." These commentators voice skepticism about our report. It was not a real journey to the heavens, but only an imaginary one. Yet for the mystic who experiences such a journey (and having survived the 1960s I am tempted to write "hallucination" in place of "journey"), the trip was real enough.

Game Over

Rabbi Akiva's seemingly off-the-wall advice about "pure marble stones" can be understood as referring to a journey into the heavenly abode of God, the divine throne room. Hai ben Sherira Gaon, a tenth- to eleventh-century predecessor to Rashi and the leader of the Babylonian Jewish community, explicated Rabbi Akiva's words in this way: Rabbi Akiva, alone among the four, had successfully negotiated the journey to heaven and back. That is what it means at the very end of our story when it says that Akiva "went out in peace." Having been within God's throne room, Akiva gives advice to his colleagues for this dangerous and arcane adventure.

We have read biblical passages that imagine the floor of God's throne room as a sapphire-like construction, made up of paving stones. This was the biblical conception of divine grandeur. Rabbi Akiva takes a contemporary Roman architectural model and represents the floor as fine marble, highly polished. The wavelike veins in the polished marble leave the floor's surface resembling water. Akiva understands this as though it were a cosmic version of a video game. If you hesitate at the threshold to the room, reluctant to step on the floor because it appears to be water, Game Over. If you so much as say, "Water, water," Game Over. Only if you stride forward do you get to enter the throne room and perhaps go on up to the next level. This was the counsel he offered to his errant colleagues. Each of them, however, failed in his quest.

As we continue in the narrative, we encounter the names of Rabbi Akiva's colleagues. Even their names leave us mystified and require some explanation. Ben Azzai, whom we have met before when he was accused of not practicing what he preached, was actually named Shimeon ben Azzai. So, too, his colleague Ben Zoma was called Shimeon ben Zoma. So why are they not called by their first names? I suspect that because they studied together and each was named Shimeon, their colleagues differentiated them by using their patronymics, rather than risk confusion like we saw in the case of Eliezer and Elazar. But when we read about Ben Azzai, we also learned that he was a bachelor. This gave pause to later commentaries, which put that fact together with the lack of mention of his personal name and concluded that it was precisely because he had no children that Jewish tradition denied him use of his first name (Ben Zoma, then, too)! According to that opinion, unless you fathered children, you weren't a real enough man to merit your own place in tradition, but were called only by your father's name. You can almost hear that macho commentator thinking, "Wuss."

To compound this nonsense, others concluded that neither Ben Azzai nor Ben Zoma was ordained as a rabbi, also because they had not married! This way of thinking makes the ancient rabbinate the very opposite, if you will, of the Catholic priesthood. If celibacy a prerequisite for the ordination of Christian leaders, goes this line of thought, then rabbis must be married and sexually active to be ordained! Of course, this presumes far too much attention to Christianity on the part of the rabbis, as well as far too much attention to the rabbis' sexual habits. There were married rabbis; there were single rabbis. There even were rabbis who performed some type of sexual renunciation. (There is a famous story about the editor of the Mishnah, Rabbi Judah the Patriarch, who was reverently called Our Holy Rabbi. When asked why he was called this, the Palestinian Talmud dryly remarks, "He never looked at his circumcision in his life" [*Megillah* 3:2 (74a)]).

Fatal Error

But enough about the secret sex lives of rabbis; let's get back to Ben Azzai's fatal error. On his journey to God's throne room, Shimeon ben

Azzai (there, we will give him the dignity of a complete name) was more successful than he was prepared for. As our text relates, "Ben Azzai glimpsed and died. Scripture says of him, 'The death of God's beloved is grievous in the eyes of the Lord' (Psalm 116:15)."

Ben Azzai apparently took a peek at the throne, saw God, and, as we learned in the last chapter, "You cannot see My face, for no human may behold Me and live" (Exodus 33:20). That was the end of Ben Azzai. Yet, despite this terrible end, God mourns the loss. Although encounters with the Divine are often fatal, the power of God's majesty overwhelming mere mortals, God finds this grievous, heavy to bear. When God's beloved die, it changes the universe. God grieves over the loss, yet is seemingly unable to change the vast, mortal disparity between Creator and creature.

Shimeon ben Zoma also failed, if not mortally. Our Talmud text reports that as a result of his journey to paradise, "Ben Zoma glimpsed and was smitten." This term can mean physically wounded, but it also can mean that he became mentally unbalanced—the ancient version of *A Beautiful Mind*. Did Shimeon ben Zoma in fact go crazy? Well, there is a famous story about him:

> Once Shimeon ben Zoma was standing bewildered. Rabbi Yehoshua passed by and asked after his health, once, then again, but he did not reply. On the third attempt, Ben Zoma replied in confusion. Yehoshua asked him, "What is this Ben Zoma? Where are your feet?"
>
> He replied, "Nothing from nothing, Rabbi."
>
> Yehoshua said, "I swear by heaven and earth, I am not moving from here until you tell me where your feet are."
>
> Ben Zoma explained, "I was speculating on the works of Creation, and it seemed to me that there is no more than two or three fingers-breadth between the upper and lower waters. Further, Genesis does not say, 'And God's wind blows,' but rather, 'God's spirit hovers' [Genesis 1:2]—which is to say it hovers like a bird hovers just over its nest as it lands, flapping its wings. And the wings do not quite touch the nest as it hovers."

Rabbi Yehoshua turned and said to his students, "Ben Zoma has gone!"

In but a few days, Ben Zoma was gone from the world.

(*GENESIS RABBAH* 2:4)

Ben Zoma may be a new character on our set, but he encounters one of our usual suspects, Rabbi Yehoshua ben Hananiah. When the elder Rabbi Yehoshua asks the spacey Ben Zoma where his head is at, or as their idiom has it, "Where are your feet?" Ben Zoma gives two peculiar answers. The first, which exercises Rabbi Yehoshua, is "Nothing from nothing." This might be the Epicurean doctrine about the self-worth of humanity: people are no more than "nothing from nothing." But, if we see it in the context of the second strange answer, it might mean that the world is nothing that came from nothing. This is a repudiation of the normative Jewish and Christian view of the Creation account, according to which God created the world *ex nihilo*, or "something from nothing." Further, it might well indicate the Gnostics' general disregard for the stuff of the world, which they considered as inherently evil. Ben Zoma is then saying that the world is nothing and it comes from nothing good. Either of these two possibilities would be sufficient to disturb Rabbi Yehoshua about the well-being of his colleague.

If we keep this in mind when we turn to Ben Zoma's speculation about the Creation, it might help us understand his bizarre conclusion. Genesis reports that God separated the upper waters in the heavens from the lower waters on the earth. Yet according to Ben Zoma, all that separates them is a couple of fingers-breadth of space, like a bird hovering over its nest. Further, the "wind" or "spirit of God," associated with the opening verses of Genesis, is now likened to the breeze that results from the bird flapping its wings. This imagery of the breath of God as a gentle breeze is also found in Gnostic writings. It is possible that Ben Zoma's mystical speculation has led him into a Gnostic heresy.

Yehoshua expresses his dismay at this heresy to his students. He tells them, "Ben Zoma has gone." Our story sadly concludes with a report of Ben Zoma's departure from the world. This could mean he died, as did his colleague Ben Azzai. But it might mean that he literally has departed the world of the rabbis for that of the Gnostic dualists with their negative worldview. To the rabbis, that was simply an insane move. And so, our Talmudic story speaks of Ben Zoma as "smitten," which is to say he was driven crazy by the nuttiness of heretical Gnostic mysticism. Or as the verse of Scripture they chose so piquantly puts it, "vomit."

The Other

I have not lost sight of the odd fact that the fourth of the colleagues who journeyed to paradise has a most unusual name—worse even than Ben Kalba Savua (that satisfied SOB) or Mr. Son of the Fringed Pillow. The fellow called the Other is referred to that way throughout rabbinic literature. His real name was Rabbi Elisha ben Avuyah. But he did something really bad, and it caused the rabbinic community to distance themselves from him. First, we'll consider his odd nickname. Then we can speculate on what it was that he might have done to cause such a negative reaction from his colleagues that they stopped even using his name. And, we won't forget those "chopped sprouts."

In biblical Hebrew, the term "other" (*aher*) has a broad range of meanings, most of which conform to our English use of the term. But sometimes, as an adjective, when someone does "the other behavior," there is a decidedly negative connotation to the term. It might even have a tinge of some kind of sexual misbehavior. This could point to the behavior that earned Elisha his nickname and the scorn of his rabbinic colleagues. In a ninth-century story (that is, a tale told seven hundred years after our paradise tale was first related), Elisha's disciple Rabbi Meir asks him about the punishment for adultery. When Elisha replies, Meir exhorts him, saying, "Rabbi, don't your ears hear what your mouth is saying! Why do you not repent?" (*Midrash Mishle* 6). This story seems to suggest that Elisha's sin was sexual and therefore his "chopping the sprouts," which the Talmud reported in the paradise tale, was that sin. I am not quite sure (okay, I am not at all sure) why adultery gets to be called "chopping the sprouts," but, hey, use your imagination!

And yet, there are other interpretations. Doesn't it seem by now there are always other interpretations? Or, in our case, "Other" interpretations. In a different passage of the Talmud (*Kiddushin* 39b), a poignant story is told about a farmer who was entertaining the rabbis. He sent his son to the birdhouse to fetch eggs for their lunch. Rabbi Elisha ben Avuyah commented that the boy, in that one act, would fulfill the only two commandments in the Torah that promise the reward of "long life." The first is "Honor your father and mother" (Exodus 20:12). The second is "When you chance upon a bird's nest ... do not take the mother with her young. Let the mother go and take only the young, in order that you fare well and have a long life" (Deuteronomy 22:6–7). According to the Talmudic story, the boy climbs up to the birdhouse and waves his arms to make the mother bird fly from her nest. At that gesture he loses his balance, falls to the ground, breaks his neck, and dies. Witnessing this tragedy, Elisha ben Avuyah loses his faith and apostatizes, becoming "the Other."

What, then, is "chopping the sprouts"? Yet another Talmudic source suggests that he was guilty of telling schoolchildren (the "sprouts") not to believe in God. In so doing, he figuratively chopped them down. I am not certain we can ever recover the offense that Elisha ben Avuyah committed to earn the enmity of his colleagues. It might have been a heresy, or it might have been objectionable sexual behavior. What we do know is this sad fact: of the four who "entered paradise," only Rabbi Akiva came out in peace.

Rumors of War

The majority of the stories we have read to this point have taken place in the mid-first century CE. The stage for most of them is set in the city of Jerusalem. In this era, while Rabbi Yohanan ben Zakkai and his students may have found some modicum of spiritual peace from their study, their prayer, and their mystical approaches to God, there was anything but peace in the Holy Land. The early to mid-first century CE was a time of ever-growing tension between the Jews of the Land of Israel and their Roman overlords. In the year 66 CE, the Jews of Roman

Palestine began a disastrous revolt against Roman hegemony. The war against Rome culminated with a blockade of Jerusalem and ultimately with the destruction of the Jerusalem Temple and the exile of the Jews from the Holy City. We turn now to read how Rabbi Yohanan and his disciples endured the vicissitudes of war against the Roman Empire and the siege of Jerusalem.

12 / ל

The
Siege

The Roman emperor Nero was not a nice person. He became emperor of Rome at age sixteen, had his mother executed when he turned twenty-one, burned Rome to the ground at twenty-six. Really not a nice person. So it came as no surprise when the Jews of the eastern province of Palestine revolted in 66 CE. Within two years of the onset of the Jewish revolt, Nero was overthrown by a military coup and, facing the high likelihood of his own assassination, committed suicide. Nero had appointed a lifelong army man, a general named Vespasian, to suppress the Jewish revolt. While Vespasian besieged Jerusalem, Rome was in turmoil. The year following Nero's death saw four different men become emperor of Rome. The first three each died in short order. None (I'm shocked, shocked) died a natural death.

As it says in one of the prophetic books, "You don't need a weatherman to know which way the wind blows." By the end of the Year of the Four Emperors, the general who commanded the armies of Rome, Vespasian, was called to be the new emperor. When Vespasian headed from Jerusalem to go to Rome, he left his elder son, Titus, to finish the job of subduing the Jews. Titus torched the Temple and so broke the back of the revolt. Vespasian ruled Rome until 79 CE, and his two sons followed him to the throne. All three of them died of natural causes while in office. When Titus died of a fever after only two years as emperor, his younger brother honored him by erecting a triumphal arch to commemorate his victory over the Jews and Jerusalem. Inside the arch there is a bas-relief of soldiers carrying off the gold and silver vessels from the Jerusalem Temple to Rome. The arch, and its depiction of the spoils of the war against Jerusalem, stands even today in the Roman forum.

In the annals of Roman history, the Jewish war was but one more provincial rebellion. For Christian theologians, it was oft trotted out as proof of divine punishment of the Jews for rejecting Christ. But for the Jews themselves, especially the rabbis, it was the paradigmatic tragedy of Jewish history. The devastation of Jerusalem and the destruction of the Temple in 70 CE eerily echoed the devastation of the First Temple by Nebuchadnezzar in 586 BCE and the ensuing exile of the Jews from the Holy Land to Babylonia. History seemed to be repeating itself so much that, by rabbinic reckoning, the desolation of both the First and the Second Temples was reported to have taken place on the same late-summer day in the Hebrew calendar, the ninth of Av. Half a millennium after the destruction by Rome, the Babylonian Talmud still struggled to find an adequate explanation, a theodicy that could account for such a grievous blow.

Some rabbis of the Talmud suggested that Jerusalem was not destroyed "until the Jewish community fractured into two dozen rival groups" (Jerusalem Talmud, *Sanhedrin* 10:6 [29c]). Yet others saw the roots of rivalry more individually and suggested that the destruction was the result of "baseless hatred" (Babylonian Talmud, *Yoma* 9b). A lengthy narrative inserted into the Talmudic tractate on divorce—for what is the destruction of Jerusalem if not God's separation from the Jewish people?—lays the cause of the destruction at the feet of two rivals who could not even bear to sit together at a celebratory meal (Babylonia Talmud, *Gittin* 56a). When one shamed the other publicly, the die was cast. Here is the Talmud's peculiar history (or better, just plain story) of the events of the Jewish war, translated from Aramaic:

> Our House [the Temple] was destroyed, our Sanctuary was burned; we were exiled from our land. He sent the caesar Nero

against them. As he came, Nero shot an arrow to the east; it landed on Jerusalem. To the west; it landed on Jerusalem. To all four points of the compass; it landed on Jerusalem.

Nero asked a child, "Tell me the verse of Scripture you are studying." The child said, "I will wreak My vengeance upon Edom, through the hand of My people Israel" (Ezekiel 25:14).

Nero reasoned, "The Blessed Holy One seeks to destroy His house and then wipe His hands on that man."

So he fled and went and converted to Judaism. His descendant was Rabbi Meir.

He sent the caesar Vespasian against them. He came and besieged them for three years. Within Jerusalem there were three rich men: Nicodemus ben Gurion, Ben Kalba Savua, and Ben Tzitzit HaKeset.

Nicodemus ben Gurion, for the sun broke through [*nakdah*] on his behalf. Ben Kalba Savua, for all who enter his house as hungry as a dog [*keleb*], leave sated [*savua*]. Ben Tzitzit HaKeset, whose ritual fringes [*tzitzit*] dragged upon throw pillows [*kesatot*]. There are those who say that his cushion for reclining at a banquet [*kisato*] was placed among those of the great men of Rome.

One of the rich men told the besieged Jerusalemites, "I will provide you all with wheat and barley." Another said, "Wine, and salt, and oil." Yet another said, "Kindling." The sages praised the one who offered kindling, for Rav Hisda used to give over all the keys of his estate to his servant except for the key to the woodshed, for Rav Hisda used to say that every storeroom of wheat required sixty storerooms of kindling. They had enough provision to feed the besieged Jerusalemites for twenty-one years!

Among them there were thugs. The rabbis said to them, "Let us go out and make peace with the Romans." But those thugs did not permit them to do so. The thugs said, "We will go out and make war upon them." The rabbis said, "The matter will not have support (from heaven)." So those thugs arose

and burned the storehouses of wheat and barley, and famine
ensued.

(BABYLONIAN TALMUD, GITTIN 56A)

The rabbis of the Talmud seem to have adopted the theology of the
biblical book of Deuteronomy: punishment is a direct result of sin.
Thus the Jews will be punished through God's scourge, Rome. The
emperor Nero, in this rabbinic version of divine history, understands
that everything is controlled by God (God is the subject of the sentence
"He sent the caesar Nero against them"). Nero reasons that although all
signs point to his victory over Jerusalem and the Jews, he will ultimately be held accountable by God for the destruction. In the story,
Nero speaks Babylonian Aramaic, marches on Jerusalem (he never set
foot there in historical reality), refers to himself superstitiously in the
third person ("that man"), and like any dutiful soldier, takes a series of
omens. In the first, no matter where he aims, his arrow falls upon
Jerusalem.

The second omen is a bit more complicated. The Romans believed
that random utterances constituted an omen—so overhearing someone
say "sell" or "buy" as you chanced to pass the grocery store might
prompt you to put in a call to your stockbroker. Or if a book were open
on a table and you happened to read a sentence, that, too, could con-
stitute a sign from the gods. Jews and Christians shared this belief.
Rabbi Elisha ben Avuyah, whom we learned about earlier under his
derisive nickname the Other, once experienced such an omen. He
overheard a teacher prompting a student to read aloud. The verse was
"Unto the evildoer [velarasha] God says, 'What have you to speak of
My laws?'" (Psalm 50:16). But when the Other heard the child read,
what he heard was "Unto Elisha God says ... " He concluded that the
door to repentance was firmly closed to him and so apostatized. We
can stipulate that Elisha ben Avuyah did not know anything at all
about Freudian slips.

Another omen delivered by hearing the voice of a child and a
verse of Scripture is related in the well-known story of St.
Augustine's conversion to Christianity. In his Confessions, Augustine

reports that he "heard the voice of a boy or a girl coming from the church" saying, "Take up and read, take up and read." Augustine took this as a personal command. He looked and there was a book nearby. He says that he snatched it up and read "the first passage on which my eyes fell." The book was the writings of Saint Paul. "No further did I desire to read, nor was there need." The passage led him to convert.

I doubt that our Talmudist knew the story of Augustine's conversion, but he surely knew the tale of the "anti-conversion" of Elisha ben Avuyah. And so, while our narrator invents omens for the soldier Nero to rely upon, he summons common motifs that his listeners know well. But all the omens in the world are not enough when our storyteller undermines his own narrative by having Nero see God's deeper plan. Nero bolts and then, in an inspired narrative flourish, converts to Judaism! This ending for Nero borders on the perverse. Surely our narrator knew that Nero did no such thing. Nero's craven suicide was infamous. So why make Nero convert? I suspect it is a sort of posthumous victory over an evil emperor. We could not defeat him in life, so we convert him, as it were, after death. Interestingly, rabbinic literature imagines the same fate for the other conqueror of Jerusalem, Nebuchadnezzar.

But wait, there's more: Nero actually gets a kind of reward for his "conversion." Once converted, he now can father a famous Jewish offspring: Rabbi Meir. We almost feel sorry for poor Rabbi Meir, being saddled with such an addled gene pool. But the rabbis meant well. Meir was one of the very few rabbis for whom we know no lineage. He is simply Rabbi Meir, never Meir ben So-and-So. Our Talmudic narrator has tidied up a loose end by giving Meir ancestry. And he has cleverly punned in doing so: *meir* means "light," and *nero* means "firelight."

Three Rich Men Again

Nero flees, Vespasian arrives, and we are besieged with puns about rich people's names. Way back in chapter 7, when Rabbi Eliezer ben Hyrcanus was studying with Rabbi Yohanan ben Zakkai in Jerusalem, we met our three rich men with the funny names. Ben Kalba Savua's name translates as "satisfied SOB." Ben Tzitzit HaKeset, you may recall, was the "son of the fringed pillow." And Nicodemus, well, he really had a Greek name but shared it with an early Christian. Now we are given more information about Nicodemus. There's a pun: "the sun broke through [nakdah] on his behalf." Nicodemus/nakdah. Get it? So what's this about the sun breaking through? Patience, we'll read that story too, but later, in chapter 16.

This time, we get the names of the three rich men within the context of the siege. Suddenly, it makes a big difference that Ben Kalba Savua's name is about satisfaction over food, when folks are starving in Jerusalem. Ben Tzitzit's name is also more understandable, especially since we've learned about Roman dining etiquette. When we heard the explanation the first time, we were told that he got to sit above all the powerful men of Jerusalem. That told us just how important he was. Here, however, we are told that his pillow merely was "among those of the great men of Rome." Either our Babylonian narrator was more modest in his ambitions for Ben Tzitzit HaKeset or he did not fully understand Roman banquet customs.

I especially like the other reason offered here for his name, that "his ritual fringes [tzitzit] dragged upon throw pillows [kesatot]." It accounts for both of the words in his name and alludes to another rich-man story. In that story (which we'll come back to later on) Ben Tzitzit is not only very rich, but he is also very fussy. He commands his servants to put down pillows, lest his delicate feet have to touch actual dirt upon bare ground. When he walks, the fringes on his garments drag on those pillows. In one telling of the story the pillows are silk, and Ben Tzitzit HaKeset leaves them behind for the poor to collect. A generous, if odd and conspicuous, way of providing charity.

It is also clear that these men use their wealth to great effect to aid the besieged in Jerusalem. Each offers staples from their vast storehouses: wheat, barley, wine, oil, salt, even kindling for fuel. That we are in the realm of rabbinic fantasy without regard for verisimilitude becomes clear when the narrator adds that they provided enough food for the Jerusalemites to hold out against Rome for twenty-one years. Here we are faced with the problem of narrative exaggeration. On the one hand, it is wonderful to know just how very rich and generous our three men were. On the other hand it strains credulity that within a besieged walled city there could be enough storage space for two decades worth of wheat, to say the least of the sixty times that volume Rav Hisda estimates as the necessary real estate to stack the wood. I suppose the narrator just flung out his exaggeration about the kindling and thought, "Let the chips fall where they may."

There's Gonna be a Rumble

This sets the stage for the scene of "thugs versus rabbis." It's choreographed to look something like *West Side Story* meets *Fiddler on the Roof*. The thugs can be the Jets or Sharks, take your pick. The rabbis are singing "Tradition" and invoking God. The rabbis want to make peace; the thugs want war. What is very clear here is the rabbinic tendency to blame the Jews themselves for the tragedy. Not Rome, but the internecine fighting is the cause of Jerusalem's destruction. There is certainly something to be said for supporting the notion of Jewish unity. It also helps to note that the rabbis here act as pacifists—which they surely were, writing centuries after the fact, following two other disastrous wars with Rome.

Given the ominous music we hear in our mind's ear, and the tragic ending of the beautifully choreographed rumble between rabbis and thugs, we can count on a Shakespearean ending. Like those Broadway plays, whether it's Tevye or Lenny Bernstein, it's Jews we're talking about—so we first worry that there won't be enough food. Or, as the guy who wrote the lyrics to Bernstein's music once wrote for another Broadway show, "Send in the clowns."

13 / מ

Comic Relief

Martha bat Boethius, the rich woman of Jerusalem, sent for her messenger and told him, "Go, bring me fine flour." By the time he went, it was sold out.

He came and told her, "There is no fine flour, but there is white flour." She told him, "Go, bring it to me." By the time he went, it was sold out.

He came and told her, "There is no white flour, but there is whole wheat flour." She told him, "Go, bring it to me." By the time he went, it was sold out.

He came and told her, "There is no whole wheat flour, but there is barley flour." She told him, "Go, bring it to me." By the time he went, it was sold out.

She removed her shoes and said, "I will go out and see if I can find anything to eat."

A piece of something stuck to her foot and she died!

Rabbi Yohanan ben Zakkai read as her eulogy, "The most tender and delicate of women, who would not allow the sole of her foot to touch the ground" (Deuteronomy 28:56).

(BABYLONIAN TALMUD, *GITTIN* 56A)

As the rabbis, even from the distance of half a millennium, confront the terrors of besieged Jerusalem and God's abandonment or punishment of the Jews, no sooner do they mention the famine than they turn to comic relief in their storytelling to mitigate the emotional turmoil. We are meant to read this episode as a bit of Keystone Kops comedy, with the benighted servant either sufficiently cowed or too stupid to act on his own authority and buy what's there in the marketplace.

It is tempting to imagine this scene set in New York City, let's say on Park Avenue, during a blackout. The elevators are not working, the lights are out, the air-conditioning is down. Martha, the rich bitch of the derisive narrative, orders her servant to go shop, utterly oblivious to the dangers (looting?) out there on the mean streets of Manhattan. And the servant, loyal to a fault, trots down the stairs, only to come home empty-handed (and empty-headed). The flour Martha requests bespeaks her socioeconomic status. First she requests fine flour—the kind that New York bakers use to make croissants and brioches. Imagine the wailing and gnashing of teeth when the servant, after climbing up the many flights of stairs (you wouldn't expect our Martha to live on a low floor, would you?), has to report to his mistress that she won't be having her fresh pastry that morning.

Off she sends him, back down the stairs, back into the growing panic in the streets, this time for white flour—which back in the first century was still very much a luxury. By now we can already anticipate that there will be none and that the servant will utterly lack the good sense to buy whatever there may be. So back he comes, climbing up the many flights of our imaginary East Side penthouse (yes, let's make it a penthouse Martha lives in!). We can imagine him arriving, huffing and puffing, only to face his mistress's wrath. Back he goes for the next round. Down the stairs, out onto the pavement. We, the listeners to this sorry tale, can join along with those who have heard it for the past fifteen hundred years, singing out in chorus: "By the time he went, it was sold out."

These days, everybody touts the benefits of whole wheat. But in the Roman world, especially in the upper classes of the Roman world, it was not done to eat whole wheat. In truth, the word that is used in our story is extremely rare, and we can only infer from its position between white flour and barley flour that this particular flour is whole wheaty. Maybe it's bran flour (also good for you, but not eaten in Martha's zip code). In fact, even though our story is being told in Babylonian Aramaic, the word for this flour, *gushkara*, is borrowed from Persian. There is a delicious irony here. A story is being told in Babylonian Aramaic about a first-century matron of Roman Palestine. But when it comes to finding low-grade flour, the narrator puts the local, sixth-century Iraqi equivalent of grits into her mouth. And even so, there is no such flour to be had. Little by little it is becoming comically but tragically clear that there really is a famine.

Finally, the poor (if really dumb) servant comes back to tell Martha that there isn't even *gushkara*, only barley flour! Barley was eaten by the poor masses, but in wealthy people's homes it was only found as animal fodder. No mushroom barley soup for Martha! Feed it to the dogs and donkeys. But even barley there was none. Ms. Martha has a problem, and the silly servant has outlived his usefulness to both her and our narrator. Exit, stage left.

Martha, My Dear

It's time for an aside on the name Martha bat Boethius. As we have seen with our other rich folks, names convey significance. Most Hebrew names have a root meaning that tells us something about the character in question. In the Bible this is true. When Abram has his name changed to Abraham, we get the explanation that AbraHAM is so named because he will be (in Hebrew: *Ab HAMon goyyim*) the "father of many nations" (Genesis 17:5). Even our famous Rabbi Yohanan ben Zakkai's name conveys meaning. His name literally means "God is gracious," son of "innocent," or of "one who is of merit." But what of our rich woman? Is her name, like those of the three rich men, descriptive of her wealth? Or is it, like Rabbi Yohanan's, indicative of sterling character? Or perhaps it is like the names Goldberg or Goldstein, which we met back in chapter 2. There, I offered them as examples of Jewish names that were, in fact, German in origin. But they also bear meaning. Goldberg means "golden mountain," while Goldstein means "golden stone." Of course, very few, if any, of the folks who have those names today think about the precious metal or mountains or stones. So *caveat lector*, be warned that while the names in these stories do bear meaning, the character they represent may be wholly unrelated to the connotation of the name.

Martha is a name found in Christian Scripture (Luke 10:38; John 11:1), as well as in our story. This tells us that Martha was a not uncommon name in the first century CE; it is an authentically Jewish name, borrowed and transliterated into the Greek of the Christian Bible. What does the name Martha mean? It is Aramaic, the feminine equivalent of *mar*. *Mar* means "sir" or "mister." So Martha means "missy" or "Ms." Given her wealth and patrician origins, I'll go with "missy." In fact, we know a good bit about our rich lady's character. According to the Babylonian Talmud she had a rather strong sense of entitlement. Indeed, after her first husband died, she wished to remarry. The trouble was that both she and her new fiancé were *kohanim*, of the priestly class. Her new beau had been nominated to become the high priest, and that priestly role expressly prohibits marriage to a widow. So, the Talmud reports, Martha paid an immense bribe and got her new husband the high priesthood anyway—never mind the rules.

Of course, other rabbinic sources point out that the Jewish king to whom Martha bat Boethius paid her golden bribe lived early in the first century BCE, a fair bit of time before the destruction of the Temple in 70 CE. If so, they sagely point out, it can hardly be the same Martha—too much time would have elapsed between her remarriage and her appearance in our narrative, during the siege of Jerusalem. True enough, except that we are dealing here with story, not history. And if our account demands a rich missy, well Martha bat Boethius she shall be. We'll see later on in chapters 21 and 22 just how fungible her name may be.

Stepping Out

Now that we know her name and character, let's walk with Martha as she goes out foraging for food. Her servant, that fool, was an utter failure. So now she, poor thing, must herself trudge down all those stairs and actually do the grocery marketing. But first, she removes her shoes. When my students discuss this gesture, it always strikes them as odd at first, and then they impute significance to it. Shoes were a sign of wealth and luxury. Perhaps she wishes to go incognito, now that she knows the streets may not be all that safe. Others have suggested that going barefoot in the park might facilitate her hunt for a meal. Here, I think we have to abandon the notion of Martha slipping off her Jimmy Choos so she won't wobble or imagining that we've seen a flash of red sole as she removes her Christian Louboutin pumps. There is another reason this rich woman may have shed being shod.

Rabbinic piety recognized that there were times such as famine and drought that the Jewish community might take extraordinary measures to implore God's mercy. In an agrarian society—in any society, really—everyone depended on rain for the crops to grow. There is an entire tractate of the Mishnah dedicated to fasting to implore God for rain. In times of scarcity, there were prescribed behaviors designed to beseech God to show compassion for the hungry. To begin with, the leaders of the community stood forth to ask God for an end to famine. Those wealthy leaders showed their sympathy with the starving, as well as their piety to God, by fasting on Monday, then Thursday, and again on Monday. These successive fasts were a way of urging God to display divine empathy. Part of rabbinic procedures of fasting (still observed on the ninth of Av and on Yom Kippur) requires eschewing outward signs of luxury. Thus the one who fasts refrains from bathing or wearing leather shoes.

I think Martha, faced with famine, has been played as comic relief. But now that even she recognizes how dire the situation has become, she shifts her role in our narrative, in an attempt to do the right thing and end the starvation. So, she removes her shoes as a sign of fasting and piety. Only then does she dare venture outside. Alas, once a character has been played for comedy, it's hard to shake that role. So although Martha as a wealthy leader fasts and goes barefoot, when she steps into the streets her delicate little foot touches "a piece of something." The unfortunate, but richly comic result: Ew! OMG!

Something sticks to her foot, and well, she just dies! The medieval commentator Rashi, writing from France, reports matter-of-factly that what she stepped in was animal dung. Later, we will learn how Rashi inferred this. For now, Ew! and OMG! again, she stepped in dog poop! No wonder she died. The death of a rich lady, played as high camp.

A Cruel Eulogy

Enter our hero, Rabbi Yohanan ben Zakkai, to deliver the eulogy. We've already seen him fund-raising among that social class, so it's not surprising that he'll do funerals, too. Nor is it surprising that our narrator brings a famous rabbi into the plot line. Like any good rabbi, Yohanan has a verse of Scripture to fit the occasion, "The most tender and delicate of women, who would not allow the sole of her foot to touch the ground" (Deuteronomy 28:56). The Talmud tells us no more about the eulogy or the funeral. But readers and listeners in the rabbinic orbit knew what it was that they weren't hearing. We, too, can fill in that gap, if we only open a Torah text to see Rabbi Yohanan's verse in its context. What we will find there, however, will wrench our narrative from comedy to stark tragedy in the briefest moment.

The verse Rabbi Yohanan has quoted is from a section of the Torah that contains the blessings and curses attached to God's covenant with the people Israel. The basic thrust of the passage is if you do God's law, you shall be blessed. And, if you disobey God's covenant, you shall be cursed. As the Torah says, "The Lord will let loose against you calamity, panic, and frustration in all that you undertake, so that you will be utterly wiped out" (Deuteronomy 28:20); you get the drift. But the section Rabbi Yohanan has quoted in his eulogy of Martha is quite particular. It begins, "The Lord will bring a nation from afar against you, from the ends of the earth, a nation whose language you cannot understand, which will swoop down like the eagle. A hard-faced nation that shows no regard to the elderly, nor mercy to the young.... It will besiege all your gates, until your high walls fall.... You shall eat the fruit of your loins, the flesh of your sons and daughters, because of the siege and desperation to which your enemy shall reduce you"

(Deuteronomy 28:49–53). This passage, the lead-up to the verse in the eulogy, sounds eerily like it predicts the very blockade that Rome (the eagle) brought against Jerusalem.

And then, there is the verse applied to Martha, "The most tender and delicate of women, who would not allow the sole of her foot to touch the ground" (Deuteronomy 28:56). That verse starkly concludes, "She shall set her evil eye against the husband of her bosom, against her son and daughter, begrudging them the afterbirth that issues from between her legs and the children she will bear; for she will eat them in secret for want of all else" (Deuteronomy 28:56–57).

The narrator of this lurid legend has expertly manipulated our emotions so that we've laughed about Martha's dilemma, even as we were sensitive to the setting of the siege. But now, having made us laugh, we are jerked harshly back to the gruesome realities of war and starvation. The laughter dies in our throats, the guilt and desperation mount, and all we can think is, "Get me out of here!" Rabbi Yohanan ben Zakkai shares that thought. Let us turn to his plan for escape from Jerusalem.

14 / ב

The Rabbi
Confronts Caesar,
or the Three Wishes

In our Talmudic story thus far, Rabbi Yohanan has arrived on the scene to conduct Martha's funeral and invoked a theodicy suggesting that God's implacable wrath is a punishment for Israel's breach of the covenant. This is very delicate territory, for it doesn't help the victims of unspeakable tragedies to find themselves blamed for their own predicament. While I am fully aware that our reaction to the Holocaust in our era may not be the same as the reaction of the Babylonian rabbis to the Temple's destruction that took place half a millennium before their time, I suggest that the rabbinic penchant for turning blame inward is not merely a propensity for Jewish guilt. There is a deep-seated philosophy among the rabbis that God's relationship to the Jews forms an unbreakable bond. Even when Israel endures disproportionate suffering, God is somehow with them. Unfortunately, the image of God here borders on that of an abusive parent. Yet for the later rabbis, explaining God's wrath was a far preferable choice than considering the possibility that God had abandoned the Jews.

With Rabbi Yohanan's dire eulogy for Martha, he returns to center stage. Yohanan and his disciples had flourished in Jerusalem up to this point. But with the city set aflame, they (and we) must shift the scene of their narrative and take the action to a different stage. Yohanan determines that it is time to escape besieged Jerusalem and develops a stratagem to do so. The question we have as we read the continuation of our tale is morally complex. How shall we understand Rabbi Yohanan's character? Are we meant to see him as the heroic savior of Judaism who risks his life to bring Judaism to its next period, from Temple sacrificial cult to People of the Book? Or is Yohanan ben Zakkai to be read as a traitor who escapes the siege, abandons his fellow Jews, and collaborates with the enemy?

> Abba Sikra, the head of a gang of thugs in Jerusalem, was the son of Rabbi Yohanan ben Zakkai's sister. Yohanan sent him the message, "Come to me in secret." When he arrived, Yohanan asked, "How long will you continue doing this, killing everyone with famine?"
>
> He replied, "What can I do? If I say anything to them they will kill *me*!"
>
> Yohanan said, "Let's see if there is a way for me to leave Jerusalem. It might be possible that I can save a small bit."
>
> He said, "Pretend that you are ill, and have everyone come and ask after you. Then put something smelly nearby and have them say your soul has gone to its rest. Let your disciples enter—and do not let anyone else do it, lest they feel that you are too light—for everyone knows that a living person feels lighter than a corpse."
>
> They did so. Rabbi Eliezer entered on one side and Rabbi Yehoshua on the other side. When they came to the gate with the "corpse," the guards sought to stab the body to be sure it was really dead. The disciples protested, "Do you want people to say that you desecrated the body of our master by stabbing him!" So they thought to just shove him. The disciples again protested, "Do you want people to say that you desecrated the

body of our master by shoving him!" They relented and opened the gate. They went out.

(BABYLONIAN TALMUD, GITTIN 56A)

To devise a plan of escape, Yohanan enlists his putative nephew, Abba Sikra. Throughout rabbinic narrative there is a tendency to imagine that all the characters are somehow related to one another. Way back in chapter 1 before we knew anything else about him, we were told that Ben Kalba Savua, one of our famous three rich men, was Rabbi Akiva's father-in-law. Could be, but it might not be so. If the plot calls for a rich man to be Akiva's father-in-law (and a nasty SOB at that), Ben Kalba Savua is the right guy for the job, whether there was a historic connection or not. And similarly, if Rabbi Yohanan needs a link to the bad guys so that he can escape the siege, well, let's make his nephew their leader. I am dubious about the historical value of these connections, even as I readily see their narrative utility. That said, I teach at a seminary where everybody really is related to everyone else. Men and women meet in rabbinical school and marry. Or their brothers marry their classmates—and rabbinic families are born. I currently teach students whose fathers and mothers I taught decades ago. So while I am suspicious of the historical value of these supposed connections reported in the ancient literature, my own experience precludes me from dismissing them out of hand.

The nephew also has a name worth noting. *Abba* means "father." It could be a title or it could be a proper name. We met an Abba Saul back in chapter 2. The name Sikra is a tough nut to crack. It might be a form of Egyptian: Saqqara, which is one of the burial grounds south of Cairo. You can find the famous step pyramid there. Maybe Abba Sikra is just a guy who came from Egypt. But the Roman Jewish historian Flavius Josephus, who wrote about the Jewish war against Rome (and who himself escaped while his colleagues were besieged, predicted Vespasian's ascent to the purple, and served the Roman emperor), told of a group of zealous assassins in Jerusalem called the Sicarii. They got their name from the stilettos (in Latin: *sicarii*) they carried to do their killing of other Jews. So Abba Sikra might mean quite literally that he was the head of the Sicarii.

I referred to his gang of thugs, who are called in Hebrew *biryoni*. Some translate it to mean "capital guards," assuming the word comes from the biblical Hebrew root for capital, *birah*. Me, I'm not so convinced. In any case, all of us who translate the term more or less are guessing from context. And it is clear from the context that these guys want to rumble, which is why I call them thugs. Abba Sikra even protests that he, poor thing, is powerless to stop them; if he suggests that they not fight, they will kill him. Abba Sikra is a craven leader who, like many modern terrorists, is content to wreak havoc without taking the responsibility of governing.

When "uncle" Yohanan pushes him, he suggests a ruse by which the rabbi might escape the besieged city. Yohanan pretends he is ill, dying. By adding some smelly item to approximate the putrefaction of a corpse, he appears to have died. Since Jerusalem is a holy city, it has long been custom not to leave ritually unfit corpses there overnight. So there is an impetus to remove the body—and no doubt the bodies of many others who died during the siege. But taking out a live person as a dead body requires a steely sense of cool. Yohanan's disciples are brought into the plot to facilitate the transfer of his "corpse." By now, you can fill in the blanks. On one side we will put Rabbi Eliezer, and on the other side Rabbi Yehoshua. Once again, the cast in order of their appearance! Our drama continues.

When they get to the gates, the guards wish to halt them. Who are these guards? Roman soldiers? Jewish zealots (our very own thugs)? We do not know. Both Romans and Jews were pious about the sanctity of corpses—one could as easily protest to a Roman as to a zealot that it is not right to desecrate a body, even to shove a corpse. I love the storyteller's keen appreciation of how a person can be pressured in such a situation. He slyly has Yohanan's pallbearers ask, "Do you want people to say ... ?" It reminds me of those who manipulate their opposition by wondering aloud what the media might think if they were asked to report it. Can't you just hear them ask, "Do you want CNN (or Fox or

MSNBC) to say you desecrated an Iraqi corpse, Sergeant?" I think it might still work.

Rabbi Yohanan has escaped Jerusalem. What next? Will he, like Josephus, also predict Vespasian's rise to emperor and also serve him? If so, is Yohanan our hero or is he a collaborator? Let's listen as our Talmudic narrator continues the tale.

Long Live the Emperor!

When Rabbi Yohanan got there, he said to Vespasian, "Peace be upon you, O King; peace be upon you, O King!"

Vespasian replied, "You have condemned yourself twice over. First, I am not emperor and yet you have committed lèse-majesté by hailing me as emperor! Further, if I were emperor, what took you so long to come?"

Rabbi Yohanan responded, "As for your saying that you are not emperor, surely you are an emperor; otherwise Jerusalem would not be given into your hands. As it is written, 'The Lebanon trees shall fall by a majesty' [Isaiah 10:34].... And as for your asking why I did not come sooner, those thugs among us would not permit it."

Vespasian said, "If you had a barrel of honey with a serpent coiled around it, would you not destroy the barrel for the sake of the serpent?"

Rabbi Yohanan was silent.

Rabbi Yosef, and some say it was Rabbi Akiva, recited the verse, "It is I, the Lord, who turns sages back and makes nonsense of their knowledge" (Isaiah 44:25). What he should have said to him was, "Take a pair of tongs, remove the serpent, and leave the honey barrel intact."

(BABYLONIAN TALMUD, *GITTIN* 56A–B)

So far, Rabbi Yohanan does not look very heroic. He comes to the Roman general Vespasian and is immediately bested by him in their exchange. Through flattery, excess of caution, or mantic reading of Scripture, Rabbi Yohanan says what everyone knows—that in a year of dire political instability in Rome, the man who controls the army will wind up on top. Seeing that probability is one thing; saying it aloud, however, is another matter entirely. As I mentioned above, Josephus had made such a prediction. When he did so, Vespasian had him imprisoned for it, actually put in chains. And the philosopher Apollonius of Tyana also predicted Vespasian's rise. In those stories (which probably were the models for the rabbinic tale we are hearing), they were rewarded by Vespasian following the news of his ascent.

Yohanan greets him by calling him "king." In a parallel version of this story in the midrash to the book of Lamentations, Yohanan's greeting is in proper Latin, carefully transliterated into Hebrew letters: *Vive domini Imperator*, "Long live the Emperor!" Vespasian parries Yohanan's dangerous greeting with a two-pronged attack. In the first place, he exposes the jeopardy Yohanan has placed them in through his treason, for Yohanan has essentially advocated overthrow of the sitting emperor of an already unstable empire. Vespasian, who likely was already plotting to take the crown, immediately distances himself from the prediction. Yohanan, however, stands by his subversive prophecy, claiming it is based in a reading of Scripture—that he understands that Jerusalem and the Temple (the cedars of Lebanon) will fall. By Yohanan's reckoning of the Bible, the one who brings them down must be royalty, hence his prediction about Vespasian.

As for Vespasian's other jibe asking why he hadn't come sooner, Rabbi Yohanan has a spineless response, on par with a callow youngster whining, "It's not my fault." This fecklessness invites Vespasian to put forward his rationale for destroying the city. He offers an analogy of the serpent coiled around a honey barrel. In using the term "serpent," rather than the common Hebrew word, our storyteller again borrows from Greek and Latin: *dracon*, or as we would say in English, dragon. It is the same word that gives us "draconian," an appropriate adjective for these circumstances. As a more recent general averred, "It became necessary to destroy the town to save it."

Yohanan is silenced by Vespasian's argument. In rabbinic narratives, it is the opponents of the rabbis who are reduced to silence in arguments, so it is an astonishing assertion our narrator offers. Indeed, Yohanan's helpless silence brings condemnation from other sages. The first to jump in is Rabbi Yosef, a prominent Babylonian who lived in the third to fourth centuries, some 250 years and 550 miles distant from the siege. But others attribute the critique to Rabbi Yohanan's contemporary, Rabbi Akiva. To place the criticism of Yohanan into the mouth of such a famous rabbi underscores the Talmudic discomfort with Rabbi Yohanan's role here. The quotation from Isaiah, "It is I, the Lord, who turns sages back and makes nonsense of their knowledge" is a barely polite way of calling Rabbi Yohanan's response to Vespasian idiotic.

With the benefit of hindsight we are told what Yohanan should have said. In general, that phrase "he should have said" evokes sadness or pathos. Here, Yohanan's failure to reply properly brings down a once great city. So has our storyteller condemned our once great teacher's reputation to disgrace and infamy? Let's return to the Talmud's tale and watch whether Rabbi Yohanan might redeem himself.

The Three Wishes

Just then a military attaché arrived from Rome and said, "Arise, for Caesar has died, and the nobles of Rome wish to seat you as their head."

Vespasian had just put on one boot; but when he tried to put on the second, it would not go on. So he tried to remove the first boot but could not. He asked, "What's this?"

Rabbi Yohanan explained, "Don't worry, it's just the good news you've received, as it is said, 'Good tidings fatten the bone' [Proverbs 15:30]. What is the remedy? Bring someone with whom you are unhappy and have him pass before you, as it is said, 'Despondency dries up the bones' (Proverbs 17:22)."

He did so and his boot went on!... Vespasian said, "I must leave now and will send someone in my stead. But ask of me some boon that I may grant it."

He said, "Give me Yavneh and its sages, and the Gamalielite line, and a physician to heal Rabbi Tzadok."

Rabbi Yosef, and some say it was Rabbi Akiva, recited the verse, "It is I, the Lord, who turns sages back and makes nonsense of their knowledge" (Isaiah 44:25). What he should have said to him was, "Let Jerusalem go this time." But Yohanan worried that he would not do that much, and then he would not have saved even a small bit.

As for the physician to heal Rabbi Tzadok (for Rabbi Tzadok had fasted for forty years trying to prevent the destruction of Jerusalem; he became so thin that when he ate something, you could watch it go down his gullet from outside!), the physician fed him fruit juice on the first day, on the next day broth, and then gruel, until little by little his innards healed.

(Babylonian Talmud, *Gittin* 56b)

Our story shifts when Rabbi Yohanan's prediction bears fruit. When the attaché arrives from Rome with the news of Vespasian's election to emperor, we might expect that Vespasian will appear even more powerful compared to our rabbi. Instead, Vespasian, the new emperor of Rome, is played for a fool, hopping on one foot with a stuck boot—recalling the nursery rhyme of "Diddle Diddle Dumpling." Still speaking with Yohanan in Babylonian Aramaic (a curious fact, that), he asks, "What's this?" In Aramaic this is almost slang: *Mai hai?* But for the niceties of diction, it could read, "Wassup?" And now Rabbi Yohanan has the snappy answers, each from Scripture. You gotta love the rabbis and their storytellers—they have a verse for every occasion: stuck boots, loose boots, idiotic answers, and all else. As it is written, "How good is a verse at the right time" (Proverbs 15:23).

The theater here should not be ignored. We move Vespasian, hopping, from center stage, while Yohanan enters the spotlight to recite his verses. When our rabbi suggests that Vespasian bring someone whom he dislikes into the tent, there he is waiting in the wings. The staging and timing of the entrances and exits are the stuff of comic farce. The audience smirks at Vespasian during what should be his finest hour. He, a common soldier, will now be elevated to the purple, to replace the dynasty of the Julio-Claudians. Yet even as he establishes his own Flavian dynasty, he needs a rabbi to give him advice on footwear. So much for all the folk adages about generals with their boots on. Indeed, the comedy smacks of folktale as Vespasian now announces that although he will not lift the siege of Jerusalem, Yohanan can have three wishes.

Well, Vespasian says he's going to send someone else in his stead, but Yohanan can ask a favor. It is really our rabbi who enters the realm of folktale by invoking the "rule of three." And what a strange list of three wishes Rabbi Yohanan asks for. The first is Yavneh and its sages. In the late first and early second century CE, the town of Yavneh was famous for the rabbis and sages who gathered there to study Torah and so reconstitute Judaism as a rabbinic religion. We heard about Yavneh back in chapter 4. It's where Yohanan's disciples chose to go when Elazar ben Arakh decided to go to the beach instead. But when Yohanan and Vespasian had their tête-à-tête, Yavneh was not even called Yavneh; it was still Jamnia, a Roman garrison town! Yes, it appears that Yohanan was asking the general to be housed among the Roman soldiers—perhaps for protection from the Jewish rebels who might have seen him as a collaborator?

As it turned out, Rabbi Yohanan was prescient (or our narrator anachronistic). Yavneh did turn out to be one of the great centers of rabbinic learning. But how did its name change from Jamnia to Yavneh? The soldiers who served in the eastern provinces of the Roman Empire, like those besieging Jerusalem, were native Greek speakers. So the Jews referred to Jamnia as Greek-town, which in Hebrew is Yevani. It was a great pun to change the nickname from Yevani to Yavneh, because the latter either derives from the Hebrew root for "building" (as in: we will rebuild Judaism) or for "understanding" (as in: we are rabbis and sages who understand Torah correctly). Jews and their rabbis flourished at Yavneh until, well, until the next Jewish revolt against Rome in the years 132–135 CE.

The next wish is even more mystifying. Yohanan ben Zakkai asks for the preservation of the line of Gamalielites. In Christian Scripture, Saint Paul says he studied with Gamaliel. According to rabbinic literature, Gamaliel and his family held hereditary office for hundreds of years, serving the community as patriarch of the Jews. But the office of patriarch was the job Rabbi Yohanan claimed at Yavneh. It would have been an apt moment for Yohanan to usurp the role, since the Gamalielite dynasty bore some responsibility for the revolt against Rome. If he really was the patriarch, Yohanan was the one and only non-Gamalielite to ever hold that title. But the history of the office and its holders is murky, exacerbated by the fact that rabbinic literature by and large idolizes Rabbi Yohanan ben Zakkai. So he may get credit for a leadership role that he never actually held. No matter what the real history, throughout rabbinic literature Yohanan ben Zakkai and the family of Gamaliel are depicted as political enemies of one another. So why is Rabbi Yohanan asking Vespasian to spare his own political opposition? Why wish that Rome give comfort to the antagonist it might otherwise see fit to discomfit?

Almost every historian of this period writes about this story as the "foundation myth" of Yavneh and rabbinic Judaism. If we take that point of view, I suppose it is important that such a myth benefit not only Rabbi Yohanan and his disciples, but the other leadership of the Jewish community, as well. So it's nice that Rabbi Yohanan saves the Gamalielites and at Yavneh the rabbis all learn to get along with one another. As legend, it is a powerful antidote to the rabbinic notion that Jerusalem was destroyed because the Jewish community was riven by factionalism. But a cynical part of me imagines that this particular story cycle might be pro-Gamaliel and actually anti–Rabbi Yohanan. I take this jaundiced view based on the possibility of reading the first part of the story as an indictment of Yohanan's collaboration with Rome. When he comes to Vespasian, we are told by the pro-Gamalielite narrator, even Yohanan is forced to admit that the Gamalielites are the rightful rulers and so he supplicates Vespasian to save them. We can look at this as a story of "let's all get along," or we can see it as a piece of

political theater tarring the opposition and forcing them to acknowledge the legitimacy of their adversary.

Woulda, Shoulda, Coulda

This leaves us to account for Rabbi Yohanan's third wish, a physician to
heal the cartoonishly skinny Rabbi Tzadok. I confess that I tinkered
with the text and used parentheses to bring the account of his emacia-
tion into our narrative from an earlier part of the Talmudic story that I
had skipped over. Originally, it was in the story of Martha bat Boethius.
We read in chapter 13 that she died when a piece of something stuck
to her foot. I glossed over an alternative explanation, which was that
she had stepped on a piece of the already-been-chewed fruit that
Tzadok sucked on to regain his strength after his forty years of fasting.
Once more, all together now, "Ew!"

Rabbi Tzadok had hoped his piety and fasting could preclude
the destruction of Jerusalem. What intrigues me about our tale are
two tacit admissions that the text seems to acknowledge. First, that
since the 30s of the first century CE, there were Jews who could readily see that the Temple would be destroyed. The conflict with Rome
had been long simmering. Other Jews—like the ones who removed
themselves from Jerusalem and sought refuge in Qumran, near the
shores of the Dead Sea—had utterly rejected Temple leadership as
corrupt and destructive. Still others, like Jesus as depicted in the
Gospel of John, predicted the Temple's destruction at the same time
that Tzadok began his pietistic regimen.

The last acknowledgment comes when Yohanan asks for a
physician to heal Rabbi Tzadok. That is Yohanan's recognition that
Rome will win, Jerusalem will fall, and Tzadok's decades of fasting
will have been to no avail. When Vespasian tells him that he will send
someone else in his stead to continue the siege, Rabbi Yohanan
accepts the inevitable and prepares for it. Although his later colleagues again sing their chorus of "he should have …," we know only
too well, "woulda, shoulda, coulda," it's all for naught. The only
solace here is that Rabbi Tzadok eventually recovered. Perhaps we

can see his return to health as a metaphor that even as Jerusalem is razed and the Temple torched, Judaism too will recover, like Tzadok, little by little.

With Rabbi Yohanan, we bow to the inevitable. Vespasian sent his son to destroy the Holy City. We turn to read the Talmud's account of the tragedy and its aftermath.

15 / ס

The Gnat's Revenge

We learned in chapter 12, back when we began to unfold the story of the fall of Jerusalem, that when Vespasian went to Rome to become emperor he left his son Titus behind to finish off the Jewish revolt. Titus not only breached the walls of Jerusalem, ending the siege, but he also put the city and its Temple to the torch. Titus carried the precious spoils of the Temple back to a spectacular triumph in Rome, described at length by Josephus, and commemorated to this very day on the arch his brother erected to honor him there. The extended Talmudic narrative we have been studying about the siege now turns its gaze to Titus. Predictably, given his responsibility for the destruction of God's House, the Talmud treats him as a blasphemer and archenemy of God. Typically in this kind of storytelling, the bad guy will get his comeuppance.

Vespasian went and sent Titus. "And he said, 'Where is their God, the Rock in whom they sought refuge' (Deuteronomy 32:37)?" This verse refers to Titus, that evil one, who blasphemed against Heaven. What did he do? He took a prostitute by the hand, entered into the Holy of Holies, spread forth a Torah scroll, and committed a transgression upon it. Then he took his sword, penetrated the veil of the Temple, and a miracle occurred and blood spurted forth. Titus thought he had killed

Himself, as it is said, "Your foes roar in the midst of Your meeting place, they place their standards as ensigns" (Psalm 74:4).

Abba Hanan said, "'Who is mighty like You, O Lord?'
[Psalm 89:9]. Who is as mighty hard as You, that You witness
the curses and blasphemy of that evil one and yet are silent?"
Among the school of Rabbi Ishmael they taught, "'Who is like
You among the mighty [ba'elim], O Lord?' [Exodus 15:11].
Who is like You among the mute [ba'elmim]?"

What did Titus do? He took the veil of the Temple and
used it like a basket in which he put all of the vessels of the
Sanctuary. He loaded them on a ship and went to celebrate a
triumph in his city of Rome....

(BABYLONIAN TALMUD, *GITTIN* 56B)

Once again, our tale-spinner invokes just the right verse of Scripture to
capture the essence of the story he tells. Or, equally likely, his thorough-
going knowledge of the Bible shapes the tale even as he tells it. His
verse from Deuteronomy, with which this section of the narrative
begins, is actually more slippery than it seems on the surface. In its
biblical context, it is God speaking, "And He said, 'Where are their
gods, the rock in whom they sought refuge' (Deuteronomy 32:37)?"
God is disdainful of the Israelites for having put their trust in false
gods. But even as our narrator subverts its meaning, the context offers
hope to the listeners and a clue to the end of our tale. The immediately
preceding verse reads, "For the Lord will vindicate God's people and
take revenge for God's servants" (Deuteronomy 32:36). Even as Titus
blasphemes and crows his triumph, we who are familiar with Scripture
know that he will get his just deserts. Revenge, yes! But not just yet.

Unforgivable Sins

First we need to appreciate the delicious description of Titus's sacrilege. The scene is set in the Jerusalem Temple's *sanctum sanctorum*. No
Jew, save the high priest on Yom Kippur, would ever venture to step
foot into that holy space. So how does our narrator know what took

place? Well, he just knows that Titus had to be doing the very worst things a person could possibly do. So our talebearer indicts him by fantasizing just how bad that bad boy could be.

In rabbinic thinking there are three sins so evil that one should prefer to die rather than commit them: idolatry, sexual transgression (as spelled out in Leviticus 18), and spilling blood. Our narrator ingeniously imagines a scene in which Titus can transgress all three in one fell swoop. There on God's altar, hooker in hand, he commits sacral prostitution. That's a twofer, since it counts as both a sexual transgression and an act of idolatry. Then with his sword, he slashes the curtain separating the Holy of Holies from the rest of the Sanctuary and so spills blood. Now he's three for three! And yes, Dr. Freud, we did notice the juxtaposition of the naked whore and Titus's penetrating "sword"!

Titus, that evil fool, thinks he has killed God. Our text euphemizes. In typically Aramaic fashion, it does not utter the sacrilege directly, but rather says, "Titus thought he had killed Himself." I capitalized that final pronoun so that we understand that Titus did not think he had committed suicide. Ironically, that is exactly what he accomplished through his sacrilege, as we will soon see.

There is a set of asides here that are breathtaking. Overwhelmingly, rabbinic literature justifies God's actions—that is literally what theodicy is all about. Yet Abba Hanan, and some even attribute the sentiments to the school of the great early rabbinic leader Rabbi Ishmael, raises a voice of protest. In these interpretations of two similar verses, God is made to play the role of *Deus absconditus*—the absent or hidden God. This sounds remarkably like modern theologians who wonder where God was during the Holocaust. In our text, these two still, small voices cry out their protest and indict God's silence during the siege and destruction. God is either hard-hearted or rendered mute. This type of complaint against God, once regular in biblical prophetic literature and Psalms, is so rare in rabbinic literature that medieval commentators on this passage seek to explain it away as a compliment for God's restraint. I think not. Here, in a mere two lines out of thousands, the rabbis mark the damage that the Temple and Jerusalem's destruction has inflicted upon their relationship with God.

Sinus Trouble

At first, it appears that Titus will get away with the devastation he has wrought, as well as with his blasphemy. Having destroyed and despoiled God's House, he returns in triumph to Rome. Historically, this is precisely what happened. But in rabbinic fantasy, the rabbis can remember the event with a much more satisfying conclusion—one in which God wreaks vengeance upon Titus in the cruelest fashion.

A storm arose on the sea and threatened to capsize him. Titus reasoned, "It seems to me that their god only has power upon water. When Pharaoh came, he drowned him in water. When Sisera came, he drowned him in water. Now he wants to drown me in water! If the god of the Jews really has power, let him make war with me upon dry land!"

A voice came forth and said to him, "Evil one, son of an evil one, offspring of the evil Esau! I have a simple creature in My world named a gnat." *Why is it called "a simple creature"? For it has a mouth but has no rectum.* "Get up on dry land and make war with it!"

When Titus arrived at dry land, a gnat flew up his nose and drilled into his brain for seven years.

One day when he was passing the gate of a blacksmith's shop, he heard the sound of the hammer hitting the anvil and the gnat was silenced. Titus thought, "There's a solution!"

Each day he brought a smith who hammered in his presence. He paid a gentile four *zuz* to hammer, but to a Jewish smith he said, "It's enough that you have seen your enemy so." This worked for thirty days, but then the sound of the hammering no longer availed to silence the gnat.

It is taught: Rabbi Pinchas ben Aroba said, "I was among the great men of Rome; and when Titus died they split open his head and found that the gnat had grown to the size of a free-range bird weighing two kilos."

As it is taught in the Mishnah: Like a one-year-old pigeon weighing two kilos.

(BABYLONIAN TALMUD, GITTIN 56B)

Titus compounds his blasphemy with hubris. Surely our storyteller understands that hubris was the great engine of Greek tragedy and theater. In the rabbinic telling, however, he weds hubris to farce, so that the narrative (from a safe distance of miles and centuries) can drip disdain upon the Jews' tormentor. No sooner does he set sail to Rome than God begins to exact retribution. While Titus is depicted as having an idiosyncratic awareness of biblical history, he fails theology.

It is fairly common knowledge that Pharaoh met his end when the Reed Sea closed upon him and his Egyptian chariots. But knowing about Sisera's demise counts as useful for Trivial Pursuit or *Jeopardy!* Titus is recalling the peculiar account of a general who rose up against biblical Israel, whose story is recounted in the book of Judges. There we are taught that Sisera struck fear into the hearts of the Israelites when he raised an infantry that included "nine hundred iron chariots" (Judges 4:13). Sisera led his troops into the dry riverbed of Kishon. Then, according to the poetic recounting, "The heavens dripped, yea, the clouds dripped water.... The river-torrent of Kishon swept them away" (Judges 5:4, 5:21). With his chariots mired in the suddenly rushing wadi, Sisera ignominiously fled. The heroine Yael lured him to her tent and, once he was asleep, pounded a tent peg into his brain. Nice foreshadowing of Titus's own demise.

The Anvil Chorus

Titus committed the fatal error of thinking that the Creator of heaven and earth had no more power than Neptune, Roman god of the seas. He compounded his error with his blasphemous challenge to God, who blithely met it. Enter the gnat. God scorns Titus by refusing to fight with him at all. Instead, God dispatched the smallest and simplest of all creatures to put an end to Titus and his blaspheming ways. How small and simple is the gnat? Why, the gnat is so simple that ... the punch line is reported as an aside in Aramaic in an otherwise Hebrew section of our narrative. It is the voice of our storyteller, interrupting God's echoed voice—a "daughter of a voice" like the one we encountered back in chapter 10 coming down from Mount Sinai. Here, too, we're meant to chuckle at the thought of the half-assed gnat (actually, the non-assed gnat) flitting up Titus's nose and driving him to distraction. In another telling of this tale, the gnat flies up Titus's nose at the very moment he is quaffing wine from the victory cup presented to him at his triumph.

What a glorious and destructive distraction the gnat provides. Titus is so bothered by the buzzing and drilling that he finds relief in the sound of a blacksmith hammering away at his anvil. How stupid do you have to be, or how disabling must the sound of the gnat's drilling be, that you might prefer the hocking on an anvil to the buzz in your brain? Titus is not even an equal opportunity employer—he has differing pay scales for gentiles and Jews. Here again, we can enjoy the laugh the Jews have at his expense as they imagine forgoing payment for the joy of watching their enemy suffer. And, truly a sign of the fantasy of the rabbis, in the story even Titus realizes they are taking pleasure from his suffering!

Still, all good things must come to an end, and the gnat grows used to the sound of the anvil. Once the gnat has acclimated to the hammering, it resumes its insidious buzzing in Titus's brain. But let us not forget that Titus destroyed the Jerusalem Temple, God's Holy House. No buzzing gnat is sufficient punishment for such an atrocity. With a cruel twist, our narrator allows the gnat to grow, eating away at Titus's brain like a malignant tumor. The tumor kills him, and at his autopsy, it is found to have grown to enormous size. The measure of its final weight is twofold. First, in a display of narrative genius, the storyteller places an eyewitness at the scene. That the rabbi who testifies is all but unknown in rabbinic literature (he's mentioned only once more in the entire Talmud) undermines the verisimilitude even as it enhances the fantasy.

But why have a second testimony about the size of the tumor, likening it to what appears to be a ruling of the Mishnah about the size of a sacrificial bird? Here, we enter truly subtle territory. The text that is quoted as explicating the birdlike weight of the gnat that grew in Titus's brain actually is not found in the Mishnah. To what end, then, might our narrator have made up a faux text? I think that the rabbinic principle of measure for measure is being cunningly invoked. Titus destroyed the very altar where birds were daily sacrificed to God's honor. So our pseudo-Mishnah invents a fantasy bird-offering from the now destroyed altar. Message: There's more than one place to honor God. Sometimes the altar of dreamed vengeance is the only place left for offerings to God.

16 / ע

Rainmaker

The rabbis told stories in which they redressed their grievances against God and against the vicissitudes of Jewish history. In their narratives, as opposed to historical reality, tyrants were punished. We have seen how the rabbinic retelling of history might set right histori-cal wrongs or explain them so that God continued to be a faithful part-ner to the Jewish people, no matter what their suffering. Much of the rabbinic narrative focused on Temple times, back in the first century CE. They recalled it as a halcyon period, when the detailed command-ments of the Pentateuch could be carried out with exacting piety. Sacrifices could be offered as prescribed. Rain fell in its season. Crops flourished. Jews prospered. The virus of nostalgia deeply infected these rabbinic narratives.

Yet even in our brief survey of these rabbinic fantasies, we have noted the intrusion of stark reality onto the stage. All was not well. The Temple stood no more. Famine abounded. Jews fell hard from their former glory. One can hear the lament sounded offstage, "Lo! How the mighty have fallen!" (2 Samuel 1:19). Or as played from the orchestra pit, "Zion's roads mourn, empty of pilgrims; her gates are devastated" (Lamentations 1:4). There is a cognitive dissonance between story and history. One of the functions of our sage tales is to mediate that dissonance and in so doing to assuage the sorrows of reality. Let's listen as our rabbis spin such a story from back when the

Temple still stood. Not coincidently, the hero of this telling is one of our three rich men.

> The rabbis recited: Once upon a time all of Israel had gone up on pilgrimage to Jerusalem to celebrate the festival, but they had no water to drink. Nicodemus ben Gurion approached a local grandee and asked, "Loan me twelve wells worth of water for the pilgrims and I shall repay you those twelve wells. But if I cannot repay you on time, I pledge to give you twelve talents of silver."
>
> He agreed and set a time for repayment. When the time came and it had still not rained, he sent this message in the morning, "Remit to me the water or the money that you owe me."
>
> Nicodemus replied, "I still have time. The entire day is mine."
>
> At noontime he sent this message, "Remit to me either the water or my money that is in your hands."
>
> He replied, "I still have waiting time in the day."
>
> In the afternoon he sent, "Remit to me either the water or my money that is in your hands."
>
> He replied, "I still have waiting time in the day."
>
> That grandee sneered at Nicodemus, "All year long it has not rained. Do you think it will rain now?" He entered the bathhouse in joy.
>
> (BABYLONIAN TALMUD, *TAANIT* 19B–20A)

We are in pre-war Jerusalem. Our setting is one of the three biblically prescribed pilgrimage festivals. Shall we say Sukkot? I want to set the scene during that holiday for three reasons. First, for the rabbis, the fall harvest festival of Sukkot was "festival" par excellence. It not only marked the end of the summer harvest, but for the rabbinic community it also brought to a grand finale the seemingly endless month of Tishri, with its New Year's festival of Rosh HaShanah, the Day of Atonement or Yom Kippur, and then (still within the same two-week period) the eight-day-long holiday of Sukkot. The end of the holiday and harvest season was truly a cause for celebration.

Then there are the pilgrims themselves. They came to Jerusalem in great numbers for Sukkot, not only because it was time to take a few days off once the harvest had been gathered, but also because they brought their accommodations with them. How did they bring their own accommodations? The Torah commands that Sukkot be celebrated by dwelling in temporary booths commemorating both the harvest and the years the Israelites wandered in the Sinai wilderness without permanent structures. So, the pilgrims brought along their own booths (in Hebrew, *sukkot*) with them for the holiday in the capital. The mishnah that teaches that "no one ever said, I have no room to lodge in Jerusalem" (*Pirke Avot* 5) must have been thinking of Sukkot (and clearly not the story of the birth of Jesus in the Gospels). Free lodging!

Third, I like Sukkot as the festival because by then summer had passed and it was quite common that there would be no water left in the cisterns. The rabbis remark that one should, in fact, begin praying for the rainy season to begin at the outset of Sukkot. But, they deferred those prayers until the festival's end, lest they be drenched in a downpour while staying in their flimsy booths. Clearly, the rabbis believed in the efficacy of praying for rain—despite what that Roman grandee may sneer.

Neither a Borrower nor a Lender Be

Which brings us to Nicodemus's borrowing of water. We might remark that at a time of drought, a person who speculates by loaning water should be regarded as despicable. Even so, the pilgrims were thirsty, so Nicodemus did what was necessary and struck a deal with a "local grandee," however slimy that speculator may be. Curiously, manuscripts differ in how they refer to this fellow. Some texts use the Hebrew term for "lord" or "master," *adon*. But older manuscripts have the term in Greek, *hegemon*, as in the English term "hegemony." It leaves a distinct impression that this water speculator was a pagan gentile. In any case, I would imagine that had the water man been a Jew, Nicodemus would have leaned on him to make the water a charitable contribution for the welfare of the Jewish community.

Instead, they agree to the terms of a loan. Yet the very loan bespeaks an agreement between two Jews, as it is carefully constructed to avoid interest payments. The Torah prohibits interest between members of the covenantal community, so the rabbis determined ways to enact non-interest-bearing loans for the sake of ongoing commerce and agriculture. With interest, the repayment fee would grow by a specified percentage as each day passed. Without interest, the loan of water would fall due on a given date. If the rain falls by that day (or before), no extra money changes hand, and the water lender has not made any profit on the loan. But if repayment of the water takes place after that date, a penalty clause is invoked and extra cash payment is due. In our case, let's say that Nicodemus borrows his twelve wells worth of water on, for example, September 15. And let's say that he agrees to return the water by October 15. If he is late, he still owes the water, but also a penalty of twelve talents of silver. If Nicodemus has been so careful as to make this non-interest agreement with a pagan, it is a remarkable display of his Jewish piety.

In the first century, twelve talents (a set weight, like a kilogram) of silver was an astronomical sum of money. The entire tax burden of the eastern Mediterranean province of the Roman Empire was thirty-six talents. So Nicodemus is more than betting the farm on this loan—he is betting the entire capital of the worldwide Jewish community. This is a foolish benefaction. No one should be betting on rain to fall, no matter how pious or generous, and he certainly should not be betting with those stakes.

Is it any wonder that our local grandee sneers? The give-and-take between Nicodemus and "Mr. Waterman" is exemplary. On one side we see unbridled greed. Once the cash is in hand, the speculator will be fabulously, unimaginably wealthy. Nicodemus, for his part, shows true sangfroid. With remarkable aplomb he pushes back each demand for cash in hand. Nicodemus's equanimity is tested when his nasty counterpart sneers at him—not so much from the sneer itself as from the accuracy of the observation. In that moment, if not before, Nicodemus must realize what a foolish deal he has struck.

Rain Man

Nicodemus went from "The entire day is mine" to the limp "I still have waiting time" in the space of a few hours. We imagine the pressure ratcheting up for Nicodemus while the water speculator grows ever more confident of his imminent fortune. Our tale continues according to the rules of Greek theater. Indeed, our protagonist and antagonist are virtually depicted as those famous paired masks that adorned the Hellenistic stage. Not only is one smiling and one frowning, but also in the waning moments of their contest, each retreats to the classic edifice of his cultural affiliation: our pagan water speculator goes to the Greco-Roman gymnasium, or bathhouse, while Nicodemus heads to the Jerusalem Temple.

> While the grandee was going to the bathhouse in his delight, Nicodemus entered the Jerusalem Temple in his sorrow. Nicodemus wrapped himself in his cloak and stood in prayer. He said to God, "Master of the Universe, it is revealed and known before You that I did this not for my own glory, nor for the glory of my father's house. I did this for Your glory, that there might be water for the pilgrims to drink!"
>
> Immediately the sky became knotted with clouds and rain fell until the twelve wells were filled with water and there was even more in addition.
>
> As the grandee left the bathhouse, Nicodemus left the Jerusalem Temple. When they confronted one another Nicodemus said, "Give me the value of my extra water that is in your hands!"
>
> He replied, "I realize that the Blessed Holy One disturbed the world on your behalf, yet I still have an opening to extract my money from you. The sun has already set, so the rains actually fell in my dominion!"
>
> (BABYLONIAN TALMUD, TAANIT 20A)

Wow, that almost worked! Nicodemus's piety and sincerity were sufficient to convince God to send rain during a time of drought. Not on
Nicodemus's behalf, per se, but for the glory of God. The U.S. Army
chaplains' Latin motto is *Pro Deo et Patria*, "For God and Fatherland."
Nicodemus, as it were, demurs and lets God know that it was not for
the glory of his father's house, but for God alone. That is efficacious
prayer, but only to a point. The rains did fall, but, oops, not quite soon
enough.

Given the goading that the grandee gave to Nicodemus, when the
rains fell our man in Jerusalem could not resist tweaking his adversary.
But his asking payment for the extra water stirred the pagan poseur to
summon his lawyerly skills and insist that both the rains and the silver
belong to him. What bitter irony that the very miracle that darkened
the skies with rain clouds brought an end to that same day with the fall
of darkness. In a world of no clocks, only sunlight was a reliable measure of time. Dark equals evening. And as Genesis tells it, "It was
evening, it was morning, day one/two/three...." Jewish days begin at
sundown, so the sky knotting with clouds spelled Nicodemus's doom.

But I Just Dried My Hair!

Of course, when Nicodemus and the grandee confront one another,
Nicodemus has not quite realized that the seeds of his defeat are
hydroponically planted among the raindrops. We imagine the entire
scene like a Greek theater performance, but if I may import a moment
of modernity into our discussion, let's see it as though it were playing
out on a split-screen movie. Delight in our storyteller's insouciance as
he has the pagan enter the baths while Nicodemus stands in the
Temple. We are told that Nicodemus "wrapped himself in his cloak
and stood in prayer." We need not hear our narrator instruct us to
imagine the opposite on the other half of our screen. Propriety precludes him from saying aloud what we can now imagine. As
Nicodemus wraps up, the water speculator unwraps. As Nicodemus
elevates himself in prayer, the grandee lowers himself into the baths.
And while we are gazing at the unmentioned portion of the divided

screen, imagine that pagan luxuriating in water while the Jews suffer drought. The pilgrims thirst while our grandee immerses first in the tepid pool, then the hot pool, and finally swims a few laps in the cool waters of the Roman bathhouse.

This imaginary scene sets a sharp contrast to their respective exits from bathhouse and Temple—if you will, the temple of the body versus the Temple of the spirit. See our nasty speculator, freshly garbed, anticipating immense wealth, just having blow-dried his hair. Laugh as we watch his face fall as he walks out into the pouring rain! And laugh more with the glee Nicodemus must feel at having had his prayer answered, his possibility of crushing debt relieved, and, not least, having produced water for the parched pilgrims. One more note on the storyteller's art: When the rains do come, "immediately the sky became knotted with clouds." This lovely phrase tips us to the divine intervention. We've actually heard exactly these words once before, in chapter 9, when we read about Rabbi Yehoshua and Rabbi José the Priest investigating the works of God's Chariot while on their own road trip.

But as we've noted, "the sky knotted with clouds" actually spells Nicodemus's doom. We can see the Greek masks change once more, so that the pagan is again smiling and Nicodemus is frowning. And then, we can imagine Nicodemus shout, "Wait! Stay right there! I'll just duck into the Temple for a sec and be right back! Really! I promise!"

Nicodemus went back into the Jerusalem Temple, wrapped himself in his cloak, and stood once more in prayer. He said to God, "Master of the Universe! Make it known that You have beloved ones in Your world."

Immediately, the clouds dispersed and the sun shone. At that moment, the grandee said, "Had the sun not broken through [*nikdarah*], I would have had an opening to extract my money from you."

It was taught that his name was not Nicodemus, but rather Buni. So why was he called Nicodemus? For the sun broke through [*nikdarah*] on his behalf.

(BABYLONIAN TALMUD, *TAANIT* 20A)

Here Comes the Sun

Here's a happy ending to our story. Nicodemus, once more into the breach, prays again to God to set things right. It seems our rainmaker needs to tweak things just a tad to get them right. But right they are, as right as rain! All Nicodemus needs to do is give God the slightest hint: "Make it known that You have beloved ones in Your world." Nicodemus's prayer serves as a midrashic hint to God; there is a subtle biblical allusion here. The story of Titus and the gnat gives us our clue. We will recall that Titus had worried that he might suffer the same fate as the general Sisera.

In the same passage of the book of Judges where we read of Sisera and how his chariots got stuck in the mud, the prophet Deborah sang her song of thanksgiving to God for the victory. Her lyric: "May God's *beloved* be like the sun going forth in its might" (Judges 5:31). I imagine God hearing Nicodemus's prayer and thinking, "Make it known that I have beloved in the world? Whatever does he mean? How shall I make it known that I have beloved? Ah, yes! 'Like the sun going forth in its might.' That's what Nicodemus wants from Me. Sun, sun, sun, here it comes."

With the twelve wells filled and then some, the sun can now pierce the clouds and give us a glorious ending to the story. Better still, our hero can ride off, as it were, into a proper sunset. Even that pernicious pagan has to admit that while he woulda, and maybe shoulda, in the end he couldn't get his lucre. The pilgrims have water, Nicodemus his cash, and the water hoarder has only his drenched toga and soggy coif.

We're almost done, but for the odd coda to our tale. We learn that the name Nicodemus comes from the miracle he performed. The sun broke through (*nikdarah*), which sounds like Nicodemus. But, what do you mean his name wasn't really Nicodemus? Who, in heaven's name, is Buni? Where'd he come from? When we first met Nicodemus back in chapter 7 along with the other rich men, I hinted that perhaps the rabbis were disturbed that we might confuse him with the Nicodemus mentioned in the Gospel of John. In the Gospel, Nicodemus is described as a great man of the Pharisees who begins opposed to, but ends the Gospel supporting, Jesus of Nazareth. Could the rabbis have been concerned that their listeners might confuse the two? Would they be concerned that this rich man who could apparently work miracles, or at least bring rain, might be thought to be a Christian? Just how much were the rabbis exposed to or concerned with Christianity anyway?

17 / פ

Nicodemus and Buni— Uncensored!

The early rabbis ignored Christianity. Perhaps they thought of it as just another minor Jewish sect. Perhaps they thought of it as an ineffectual, non-law-observant breakaway group. Perhaps the early Christian community was simply too small to be of much notice. The rabbis had so many other things to worry about, both within the Jewish community and outside it. There were many other forms of Judaism. There was Gnostic dualist thought (remember poor Ben Zoma?). And, always, there was the looming threat of Rome. Christianity did not exercise the rabbis all that much until it firmly became the Roman Empire in the late fourth century.

I have spent more than three decades studying the relationships between Judaism and Christianity in the first five centuries of the Common Era, precisely the time in which both rabbinic Judaism and Christianity took shape as what ultimately became separate religions. In my estimation, by and large, Christianity was formed with an eye to differentiating itself from Judaism. But Judaism, on the whole, dealt with Christianity in only a miniscule portion of its literature. So, it is worth noting when Christianity does intrude into rabbinic stories, as long as we have a sense of proportion. Our study of sage tales thus far has had very little to do with Christianity, and rightly so. Now and again, we made allusion to parallels in Christian literature, in recognition of the prominence Christianity holds in modern American culture.

But the stories of our three rich men and how they got their names now have bumped us up against one of the most famous, or infamous, texts about Christianity found in the rabbinic repertoire.

Dead Man Walking

We begin with a difficult matter of Jewish law. In the tractate of the Mishnah dealing with the theoretical powers of a Jewish court, the rabbis discuss the strictures on capital punishment. I say theoretical, because Rome did not allow the Jewish community to execute those sentenced to death. Roman "justice" reserved for itself the exclusive right to execute. But because the Torah advocated capital punishment for a number of sins, the rabbis debated the issue. After determining the various ways to administer the death sentence and the qualifications of a court to do so, and after discussing rules of evidence that intentionally made it exceptionally difficult to actually convict, the rabbis also discussed an appeals process that followed sentencing. We will begin with the Mishnah on the subject and then the commentary of the Talmud. Soon after that discussion begins, we will take an unexpected turn toward Christianity and find another text of rabbinic literature that mentions Buni, which we just learned was the "real name" of Nicodemus.

> MISHNAH: If he is found innocent [following sentencing], they release him. If not, he goes forth to execution. The herald goes before him saying: "So-and-so is going to be stoned for such-and-such a sin. So-and-so and so-and-so are the witnesses. Anyone who has testimony to his innocence, come and testify."
>
> TALMUD: Abbaye said, "And the herald must say, 'On such-and-such a day, at such-and-such an hour, at such-and-such a place,' in case there are those who have information; so that they can come to impugn the false witnesses." *The herald goes before him*: "before him" physically, but not "before him" temporally.
>
> (BABYLONIAN TALMUD, *SANHEDRIN* 43A)

Thus far, our Mishnah and the Talmud's commentary. Let's begin by noting that it seems as though the Mishnah intends to give every opportunity to the one convicted of a capital crime to prove his innocence. So, even after sentencing the Mishnah provides an appeals process. It demands that a herald or town crier go forth announcing the upcoming execution (the generic term used is "stoning"). The Mishnah goes so far as to invite any overlooked witnesses to come forward. And Abbaye, in the Talmud commentary, seeks to extend this tendency of the Mishnah by demanding that the herald mention other details about the sin. The purpose is explicitly stated: the more details there are available, the better possibility that someone might come forward to undermine the testimony of false witnesses. Since the offense carries the death penalty, there should be every opportunity to test the witnesses to make sure that they have not conspired to abuse the court and so murder someone.

It is significant that the rabbi who is proposing this expansion of convicts' rights is Abbaye. He lived in late-third- to early-fourth-century Babylonia and was head of the famous rabbinic academy at Pumbedita. His argumentation (engaging with his dialogue partner Rava bar Yosef) marks the pinnacle of Talmudic dialectic. His commentary, more than a century after the redaction of the Mishnah, shows a keen appreciation of the liberalizing tendency of both the Mishnah in Roman Palestine and subsequent Babylonian rabbis.

But then, the Talmud turns everything on its head. The anonymous editor of the Talmud, working in the early sixth century (two hundred years after Abbaye and more than three hundred years after the Mishnah), undermines the intention of both our Mishnah and Abbaye's commentary through one restrictive interpretation. The Mishnah mandates that the herald "goes before him." Now within the context it seems as though the words "before him" should refer to time—for there must need to be enough time between the herald's announcement and the potential coming forward of new witnesses to impugn those who falsely spoke on behalf of conviction. At least, that seems to be the intention of the Mishnah and Abbaye. But the anonymous Talmudic voice informs us that the phrase really means "'before him' physically, but not 'before him' temporally."

Yeow! That interpretation seems to make a travesty of justice. Talk about your strict construction. Now all the town crier needs to do is walk a few steps ahead of the convict on his way to execution. We might as well have the herald just say, "Dead man walking." Obviously the editor of the Talmud has a profoundly different attitude about the death penalty than earlier rabbis. And, with the mere rereading of two words (in Hebrew, a one-word preposition), he changes the entire meaning of our text.

Censorship

Is there no other evidence to support the more lenient understanding of convict's rights? As a matter of fact, yes, there is. The Talmud's editor knows of an early rabbinic source that testifies that the herald should go crying out the details *forty days* in advance of an execution. We have just read: "*The herald goes before him*: 'before him' physically, but not 'before him' temporally." Here is the continuation of our Talmudic text. Enter Jesus!

> But it is taught: They hung up Jesus of Nazareth on the eve of Passover. And the herald went before him by forty days, saying: "Jesus of Nazareth is going out to be executed for practicing sorcery, and he enticed and misled the Jews. Anyone who has exculpatory evidence, come forth and testify." Yet they found no evidence of innocence and they hung him up on the eve of Passover.
>
> (BABYLONIAN TALMUD, SANHEDRIN 43A)

Before I say anything at all about this text, let me point out this: it was deleted in editions of the Talmud printed in Europe from the advent of printing (in the sixteenth century) until the mid-twentieth century. Christian censors had banned this passage from Talmud texts. They were offended at the accusations about Jesus and so, quite literally, removed the lead plates from which the text was printed. In fact, in my own set of Talmud, which was photo-offset from those European editions, the bottom third of the page is blank. Its layout looks something like this (see Fig. A):

[Fig. A]

The missing text was restored on the basis of manuscripts and Talmud texts printed in non-Christian countries. There was also one Christian source that helped scholars restore the censored text. In the late thirteenth century, the Dominican friar Raymundo Martini wrote a work instructing Catholics on how to use rabbinic literature to accuse Jews from their own texts during the disputations of the Inquisition. In that work, called *Pugio Fidei* (the Dagger of Faith), Martini quoted many rabbinic texts in order to provide the inquisitors with a broad array of "evidence" with which they might entrap the Jews. Today, only historians of the Inquisition and Talmud scholars make use of Raymundo's book. I can only hope he is rolling over in his grave as you read about his unwitting contribution to Talmud scholarship. I recommend toasting him—perhaps with a martini.

Crucifixion

Now, let us return to the outrageous content of the early rabbinic teaching quoted by the Talmud. Jesus of Nazareth is quoted here (and some of the texts that do have the passage nonetheless censor or alter the name). Well, it may not actually say "of Nazareth." The ancestral village of Jesus is not mentioned as a place in the Hebrew Bible, so we are hard-pressed to guess at its Hebrew etymology. Our text has *notzri*, which well might be the town of Nazareth. But it may mean something like "he of the sprout"—perhaps this means he is the scion of the messianic line, but maybe not. It might come from the Hebrew root *nazar*, as in a Nazarite vow, and indicate Christian asceticism. So, there are three possible meanings here: it's a place-name, a messianic name, or a name indicating some form of religious renunciation.

In any case, our text says that Jesus was "hung up" on the eve of Passover. "Hung up" could mean he was executed and then his body was displayed for all to see, as in Deuteronomy 21:22, "When someone is guilty of a capital offense and executed, hang him up upon a tree." Saint Paul, by the way, actually applies the very next verse of Deuteronomy, "for anyone hung upon a tree is cursed by God," to Jesus (see Galatians 3:13). But translating our text is complicated by the fact that the Hebrew used for "hung up" equally well may be translated as "crucified."

Here is where modern bias looms large. Many, many scholars (and non-scholars) have written about this material. In fact, my "rabbi" in all things regarding Christian Scripture, Father Raymond Brown, of blessed memory, wrote a two-volume work called *The Death of the Messiah*, in which he devotes just over sixteen hundred pages to discussing the crucifixion of Jesus. As Ray and I regularly noted when he was alive, bias cuts both ways. So, Jews tend to see materials about Jesus's death in one way, while Christians see it another way. I acknowledge that I may be biased in my presentation of this rabbinic passage. I am vulnerable to accusations that I am engaging in apologetic on behalf of my rabbinic forbears. But, my presentation also is informed by years of study with Father Brown and careful reading of his works.

As I pointed out above, the Romans did not permit Jews to execute. So, although our text might appear at first blush to mean that Jews killed Jesus, if we know that fact about Roman restrictions, the "they" of "they hung up" or "they crucified" should refer to Roman soldiers executing Jesus, not Jews doing so. Exactly as it says in the Gospels. But wait, do the Gospels also say that Jesus was hung up on the eve of Passover? Don't they say that Jesus was crucified on Passover itself, the day following the "Last Supper" (which most folks take to be a Passover Seder)? And what about the slur that "they found no evidence of innocence"? How about Jesus's twelve disciples? Didn't they come forward in his defense?

These questions beg a more basic query: are we actually looking at early rabbinic evidence of a Jewish role in the death of Jesus? Here, my answer is an unequivocal no—this is not early evidence. Quite the contrary, this "early" passage dates from the late second century, at least 150 years after the crucifixion. Further, the Gospel of John does report that Jesus was executed on "the eve of Passover." And, all of the passion narratives report how the disciples abandoned Jesus following his arrest. In other words, there is no fresh evidence here at all of Jewish complicity, just secondhand reports of what's already in the Christian Testament, reported in rabbinic literature a century after the Gospels were edited. Finally, only the Babylonian Talmud reports this tradition, which means that it circulated far away in both time and space from the actual events.

Forty Days

One curious note is the accusation that Jesus committed sorcery. Interestingly, the Jews were not the only ones who accused Jesus of being a magician; pagans did, too. Calling someone a magician or sorcerer simply meant that you disagreed with him. Were you to agree with him, the very same acts he performed would be deemed "miracles." But here, too, the book of Deuteronomy is being referenced. In Deuteronomy 18:10 we read, "Let no one be found among you ... who practices sorcery." And while we are in the book of Deuteronomy, we can see how it has midrashically influenced the remainder of our story about Jesus: "If your brother ... entices you … stone him to death, for he misled you away from the Lord your God" (Deuteronomy 13:7, 13:11).

That one remaining loose end, the forty days of advance notice, is what caused this astonishing passage to be schlepped into the Talmud text in the first place. How will our pro-death-penalty editor of the

Talmud account for this case that seems to so thoroughly undermine his argument? Just a few more lines of Talmud text will answer that question and offer us so much more to chew on:

> Ulla said, "Does this make sense? Jesus of Nazareth was a man of overturned merit! He was an enticer! The Merciful One said, 'Show him no pity or compassion' [Deuteronomy 13:9]. But the case of Jesus is an exception as he was close to the government."
>
> The rabbis taught: Jesus of Nazareth had five disciples: Mattai, Niccai, Netzer, Buni, and Thoda.
>
> (BABYLONIAN TALMUD, SANHEDRIN 43A)

Ulla was an older contemporary of Abbaye. Ulla was born in Roman Palestine but later moved to Jewish Babylonia. He is reported to have traveled back and forth regularly, so he is a transmitter of the traditions of the Land of Israel among the Babylonians. He asks about the death of Jesus and seemingly assures later readers that the sentence was carried out according to biblical justice. He hearkens once more to that same passage of Deuteronomy 13, when he reports that God, ironically here called "The Merciful One," demands that no mercy ("pity or compassion") be shown to the enticer. Jesus had his own merit overturned by leading Israel astray, according to this report, or it could mean that he overturned the merit of others by misleading them.

Ulla also wonders why Jesus got forty days of advance notice, since he deserved death. His answer: Jesus was an exception to the rule (no matter what your theology, Jesus apparently will always be an exception to the rule). So, we cannot learn any precedent from the case of Jesus at all. He "was close to the government." This could mean that his case was of special concern to Rome, and so the herald went far in advance of the legal requirement. Or it can be understood that Ulla, who knew the west, saw that the government of Palestine was Christian, so he presumed that the treatment of Jesus would not follow normal procedure.

Let us also give credit to the Talmud's editor. He clearly believes that the death penalty should be applied and works hard to interpret the Mishnah to reduce the potential for endless appeals. To his credit, given his own strict construction of the law, he quotes a text that provides evidence against his interpretation. This is excellent rhetoric, for like a good lawyer, he must anticipate the objections to his case and account for them. So, our anonymous editor trots out the infamous case of the death of Jesus, which has the ostensibly probative detail that the herald went forth forty days in advance of the execution. Forty days is a damn sight longer than having the herald walk the convict to the place of his stoning. But the editor can also rely on Ulla's conclusion that the exceptional case of Jesus does not teach us about proper legal procedure for post-verdict appeals.

Five Disciples

And as is so often the case in the Talmud, there's one more thing—in this case, another early teaching about Jesus and his disciples. "Jesus of Nazareth had five disciples: Mattai, Niccai, Netzer, Buni, and Thoda." The text of the Talmud actually continues to discuss each of their fates. But we have what we came looking for, the name Buni. Before we discuss our dear rich friend Buni, a.k.a. Nicodemus, let's wonder in astonishment at our Talmud editor's assertion that Jesus had five disciples. Yes, he was all the way over in Babylonia, there between the rivers Tigris and Euphrates, but really, he'd have to be living under a rock not to know that Jesus had *twelve* disciples. Hello? How is it possible that our rabbi thought Jesus had only five disciples? Need we worry about the missing seven or is something else afoot?

Any, indeed *every* rabbinic storyteller knew absolutely and totally the text of the Mishnah that has been driving this entire book: "Rabban Yohanan ben Zakkai had five disciples." By now, we can recite their names in order: "Rabbi Eliezer ben Hyrcanus, Rabbi Yehoshua ben Hananiah, Rabbi José the Priest, Rabbi Shimeon ben Netanel, and Rabbi Elazar ben Arakh." Here, I think that we are dealing with a counter-text about Jesus. The rabbis somehow see him as a photo negative, if you will, of our sainted Rabbi Yohanan ben Zakkai. His father's name, Zakkai, you might recall, means "innocent" or "one who is of merit." And Jesus has just been described as "a man of overturned merit." The corollary to this is simple: if Yohanan had five disciples, our rabbinic narrator was certainly not giving Jesus any more! Five is the limit. *Basta!*

So, five disciples it shall be. Mattai is most likely Matthew. This is somewhat ironic, as Matthew is a Greek rendering of the Hebrew name Matityahu (like the Maccabee hero Mattathias). Here, the Greek has been re-Hebraized into Mattai. Next comes Niccai, most likely our Nicodemus. So far, we are in the realm of persons associated with Jesus in the Gospels. But next comes Netzer. As we saw earlier, that can translate as "Sprout." Since I very much doubt that the reference is to the Jolly Green Giant's little friend, I'll go with "sprout, offspring, scion of the messianic line of David." This would be an appropriate nickname for Jesus, but not, alas, for one of his disciples. The fourth disciple, Thoda, is a good Hebrew word; it means "thanksgiving." The best testimony we have for it as a proper name is as it is transliterated into Greek, Thaddeus. He is listed as one of Jesus's twelve disciples in the Gospels.

Which leaves Buni. Here he is on the list of disciples of Jesus. But didn't I end the last chapter by suggesting that the rabbis renamed Nicodemus and called him Buni precisely because they did not want him confused with the disciples of Jesus? And yet here he is, perhaps even alongside Nicodemus, as a student of Jesus. So what's the deal with Buni?

It is not a very common Hebrew name, but it is found in the biblical book of Nehemiah (11:15) on a list of Levites who returned to Jerusalem from the Babylonian captivity. It appears as a name of a rabbi now and again, too. So maybe our rich man's Hebrew name was Buni, while his Greek name was Nicodemus. Some Jews actually had both a Hebrew name and then a Greek one for official government documents. Or, we could speculate that his name was only Nicodemus, but the rabbis saw him as one of their own. When we talked about the name of the town Yavneh (where Yohanan fled from the siege), we saw that the same Hebrew root (*b-n-h*) could mean "builder" or "understander." Buni and Yavneh share the same *b-n-h* root; so the name Buni can presage the advent of Rabbi Yohanan and his disciples at Yavneh. It is possible, then, that the rabbis have given Nicodemus the suggestive nickname Buni. Or not. One thing is fairly sure, though—I was wrong when I suggested that the rabbis called him Buni to avoid confusion about Nicodemus and Christianity. We are more confused than ever.

18 / צ

Rainmaker—
The Sequel

Sometimes it's hard not to be confused. We are trying to unravel stories from a distant past. They were told in a language famous for its ambiguities—witness the multiple interpretations I have had to offer for proper names and other multivalent terms. We do not always know the historical background that might help inform our interpretation. And, as we have been trying to demonstrate, these stories were performed. That means that they can change from performance to performance. Even when the words stay the same, the audience might differ, or the conditions of the telling (a room too hot, too crowded, too cold). We have hinted at still another problem, which we turn now to confront head-on. Often there are multiple versions of a story—not unlike the Gospels in Christian Scripture—in which the words really do change from telling to telling. This can be a function of differing performers, different audiences requiring changes in local details, or different centuries and countries of telling (e.g., pagan Palestine, Zoroastrian Babylonia, Christian Byzantium, or the Muslim Mediterranean). Sometimes the rabbis recycle folktales that come in different flavors, as it were, from different cultures.

Folklorists study the cross-cultural phenomenon of the folktale with utmost seriousness. This gives rise to erudite articles on the "Three Little Pigs," true, but it equally gave us the majestic collection of folktales in various Germanic dialects by the brothers Grimm. A good example of a folktale is our story of how Nicodemus got the rain to fall and then the sun to shine again. As a folk motif, this would qualify as a "rainmaker" narrative. If we think for a moment about the "rainmaker," we will realize that we can find such a story in any society that depends upon rain for the crops to grow. That means *every* society. So it should not surprise us to find more than one version of the rainmaker folktale among our rabbinic sage tales. Of course, the very fact that we can recognize these stories as folktales means that they share common elements with one another, as well as with "rainmaker" tales from other cultures. As we read our next story, think back on Nicodemus making it rain and how these tales are alike or different.

> The rabbis taught: Once most of the month of Adar had passed but it had not rained. They sent a message to Honi the Me`Aggel: "Pray that the rain may fall!" He prayed but the rains did not fall.
>
> He made a circle and stood within, the way that the prophet Habakkuk did, as it is said, "I will stand upon my watch, take my place along the tower" (Habakkuk 2:1).
>
> Honi said to God, "Master of the Universe, your children look to me, for I am like a member of Your household. I vow by Your great name that I shall not stir from here until You have mercy upon Your children."
>
> It began to drizzle.
>
> His disciples said to him, "Rabbi, we look to you that we may not die! It seems to us that these rains are only falling to release you from your vow!"
>
> Honi said, "I did not ask for thus, but for rains to fill cisterns, irrigation ditches, and wells!" So the rain came down in force, so that each drop could fill the mouth of a barrel. The sages measured that no drop was smaller than a liter.
>
> His disciples said, "Rabbi, we look to you that we may not die! It seems to us that these rains are only falling to destroy the world!"

Honi said to God, "I did not ask for thus, but for rains of bounty, blessing, and beneficence." Then the rain fell normally, continuing until everyone had to go to the Temple Mount because of the rain.

They said, "Rabbi, just as you prayed that the rains would fall, now pray that they may go away."

He replied, "I have received a tradition that one does not pray about too much of a good thing! Nevertheless, bring me a bullock for a thanksgiving offering."

Honi laid his two hands upon the bullock and said to God, "Master of the Universe, Your people Israel whom You have brought forth from Egypt cannot endure too much good or too much punishment. When You were angry at them, they could not endure. When You suffused them with good, they could not endure. May it be Your will that the rains may cease and there be relief for the world." Immediately, the wind blew, the clouds dispersed, and the sun shone. And everyone went out to the fields to gather mushrooms and truffles.

(BABYLONIAN TALMUD, *TAANIT* 23A)

Let the Rain Come

This is a very sweet second telling of our rainmaker motif. It's found in the same tractate of Talmud just four pages away from the Nicodemus rainmaking tale (see chapter 16). This proximity is not entirely surprising given that the tractate of the Talmud is dedicated to the role of fasting in the time of drought. In order to appreciate the story of Honi, I want to read it through twice. The first reading will be with an eye to explaining some of the obscure or the more colorful details. In our second read-through—wait, I hear myself sounding like a theater director. Next thing you know, I'll be asking you to think about your character's motivation and backstory. Where was I? Oh, yes, our second read-through will focus on how Honi's rainmaker tale compares with the Nicodemus rainmaker story. When we've read it through twice over, we will turn to the Talmud's surprise ending to this episode.

We begin with the setting. We are told that "most of the month of Adar had passed," which teaches us a number of useful things. If most of Adar has passed, the next month, Nisan, is about to begin. Passover falls in the middle of Nisan; it is the spring festival. But if it's almost spring and it has yet to rain, uh-oh! That means the almost entire rainy season has passed without any rain. A couple of more rainless weeks and it will be too late to plant. Drought will ensue! Right from the get-go, our storyteller spells the trouble that's brewing.

Enter Honi the *Me'Aggel*. As I've pointed out, some of these Hebrew names are ambiguous. Honi the *Me'Aggel* is certainly a tough nut to crack. His first name, Honi, comes from the Hebrew root *h-n-n*, which means "grace." An appropriate name for the one who embodies God's grace as a religious adept who can bring rain. I should note that Greek sources transliterate the name as Onias, and the historian Josephus seems to know that in the first or second century BCE, there was a certain Onias who was a rainmaker and miracle worker—which is to say that either the rabbis are writing about a real guy or the folktale of Onias the rainmaker is very old among Jewish legends.

His last name or title is a bit of a conundrum. I punted and did not translate *HaMe'Aggel*, except to take the first syllable and render it as "the." What about the *Me'Aggel*? Well, it is most often translated as "Circle Drawer," and Honi certainly did draw a circle. The Hebrew root *a-g-l* can, indeed, mean "circle." So why am I reluctant to adopt that translation? Because when our story talks about Honi actually drawing his circle, it uses a different Hebrew verb and noun entirely, that's why. This brings me back to pondering the apparent title *Me'Aggel*. It might refer to a wheel, which, I hasten to remind you, is most often circular. So his name might be Honi the Wainwright. Or, even Honi the Wagon Driver. But I like another possibility for the meaning of the term, using the Aramaic root of *Me'Aggel*. In Aramaic *a-g-l* means "speedy." So, I am tempted to translate his name as Honi the Impatient—the guy who needs stuff done speedily, right now! Since he's the guy who wants the rain now, or he'll hold his breath until he turns blue, let's call him Honi the Precipitant.

The Circle Game

Yet he does draw a circle and stand in it. We must ask ourselves, why? Some have said it is a magic circle, and he stands within to gain power to adjure God, like one who draws a pentagram. Others have pointed to a Roman parallel that leads us to assume it is an act of impatience. In the Roman story, a general demands an answer to his ultimatum. With his sword he draws a circle, stands within, and tells his victim to take all the time he needs to answer the ultimatum— just as long as the answer is given while he is still in that circle, that is. It is a way of forcing the hand of the other. And so, Honi is trying to force God's hand here. This makes the analogy to the prophet Habakkuk a very good one. He was a prophet who demanded, "How long, God, shall I cry out and You not listen?" (Habakkuk 1:1). In fact, the verse that our story quotes, "I will stand upon my watch, take my place along the tower," continues, "and wait to see what God will say to me" (Habakkuk 2:1). I especially like the way Habakkuk has paraphrased Bob Dylan and Jimi Hendrix's "All Along the Watchtower." As the prophet said, "The hour is getting late."

Honi is not a modest fellow. In fact, he is particularly arrogant about his special status. He scolds God, as if saying, "Look here, God, You had better deliver. They came to me because I have access to You!" It's almost as though Honi has flourished his West Wing pass and demanded to see the president in his East Wing bedroom. To make matters worse, Honi actually takes a vow in God's name. From the rabbis' perspective, this is never a good thing to do. Vows schlep God into your business whether God wants to be there or not. Forcing God to be a partner in your doings, especially if it is against God's desire, can be most dangerous. The rabbis suggest that whether you are innocent or guilty, you should always flee from a vow. But this does not stop Honi.

First, he prays for rain and no rain comes. This makes it fairly clear that God does not intend there to be rain. But then Honi makes his vow, and God, reluctantly, allows it to drizzle. Honi's disciples call him on this. It is curious that this charismatic, the one with special access to God, is depicted as a rabbi with disciples. Honi lived well before the era of the rabbis. Honi was not a legalist or an interpreter of Scripture. He was, rather, God's own naughty boy. So the rabbis proceed to tame him, to rabbanize him, as it were. We will see this phenomenon come to full fruition for Honi in the next chapter. But for now, we note that even as his disciples call him "rabbi," he forces God's hand.

It does not rain at first, then it drizzles, then there is what we may call chubby rain. How big was the rain? Why it was so big that every drop was a gallon and could fill a barrel! I suspect this is exaggeration, but it is completely in keeping with the tall tales transmitted as folklore. Finally, after a number of goes, God gets it right and the rains fall normally. But even then, they fall in such unremitting abundance that folks have to flee to high ground and take shelter under the marble porticoes of the Temple Mount. Rain in its season is good. Too much rain can wash away the soil and bring dangerous flooding.

Once more into the breach, they turn to Honi and ask him now to stop what his intervention has unleashed. Honi says he has a received tradition that one should not pray about "too much of a good thing." And then, with the arrogant insouciance of a true charismatic, he says, "Nevertheless." Again, even as the rabbis seek to tame Honi by rabbanizing him, even in the legend of their own making, he is resistant. Received tradition is what rabbis are all about. They pass down the received oral tradition that they trace back to the time of the revelation at Sinai. For his part, Honi says, "Nevertheless," and blithely proceeds to ignore received tradition. He asks for a bullock to be offered and lays hands upon it. This is correct procedure for offering a bullock for slaughter, but also when ordaining a rabbi. Hmmm. Is the message here about Honi's refusal to be tamed, or is the Talmud wryly contemplating how congregants really treat their clergy?

Pasta al Tartufo

The prayer that our storyteller imagines for Honi is also instructive. He actually sounds like a rabbi preaching. First, we note that he is seasonal. In the waning weeks of Adar and early Nisan, everyone in the

Jewish community is anticipating Passover and planning their Seders. So it is apposite that Honi is imagined to invoke the Exodus when speaking to God, "Your people Israel whom You have brought forth from Egypt." And then Honi rehearses the well-known narrative of Scripture: the Jews do not endure God's wrath well, nor can they endure too much good. God's wrath against Israel can be found repeatedly in the biblical narratives about their wilderness wanderings. But the episode of "too much good" most likely refers to the incident of the quail. Daily, the Israelites were graced with bread from heaven, a portion of manna. Even so, they complained. So God gave them the very meat they asked for, and they ate of the quail until they were sick—or as Numbers 11:20 piquantly puts it, "until it comes out of your noses and becomes repugnant to you." They truly could not endure the good with which God suffused them.

No matter what our rabbinic storytellers are intending to signal by Honi's imagery, his prayer works. The rains cease, and in a beautiful flourish we are informed, "Immediately, the wind blew, the clouds dispersed, and the sun shone." That actually sounds familiar, doesn't it? When Nicodemus ducked into the Temple to ask God to show that God has "beloved ones," that story also reported, "Immediately, the clouds dispersed and the sun shone" (Babylonian Talmud, *Taanit* 20a). Here again, we see the art of the oral performer. Like Homer's "rosy-fingered dawn," our rabbi uses stock phrases to fill in the details of his tale. If it is a story in which a little rain must fall, then we can end it with the stock phrase leading to our happy ending. We already have seen a stock phrase for the onset of the rains, "The sky became knotted with clouds." Now we have another stock phrase, "Immediately, the clouds dispersed and the sun shone," for the departure of those rains.

There is a final note of local color. Every folktale shares universal aspects, but when it is told in a given place, details are added to make it familiar to the listeners. It gives them a sense of ownership—that the tale really is about them. In the case of the Honi story, it is a wonderfully bucolic image. After the rains, mushrooms spring up. And so, our storyteller gleefully imagines the bounty of the rains. Everyone is out gathering mushrooms, even truffles. Next we'll be drinking Chianti and eating *pasta al tartufo*! Sweet.

Enter Kate Hepburn

Now, our second read-through, this time with an eye to structural similarities. When I say "structural," I am thinking of a school of literary criticism that has been profitably applied to folklore studies: structuralism. It assumes that folktales share a common skeleton, if you will. This deep-boned structure is what allows us to call disparate tellings of a tale the same basic story. For instance, for a "rainmaker" story to work, there needs to be a minimum of two things: a drought and a rainmaker. But when these stories are studied cross-culturally, many other commonalities become apparent. By comparing Honi and Nicodemus, we can uncover some of the deep structure.

In both stories, there is not only a drought, but it also takes place as a festival is approaching. This means that the drought has special significance, because those who need water are on their way to pray to God. Of course, this is exactly what the rainmaker will do as well. In Nicodemus's case, he is explicit that he is not praying for his own aggrandizement. Honi, on the other hand, is less humble. He considers himself one of God's own retinue. In both cases, however, the rainmaker does hold special status that allows his prayer to be answered. In both cases, the Temple, God's House par excellence, is the scene of the rainmaker's entreaty. In both cases, something goes wrong and the rainmaker is forced to pray more than once. And in both cases, someone sneers, as it were, at the rainmaker. In Nicodemus's case, the sneer is quite literal. In Honi's story, it is in the form of his disciples' rebuke of their master about his vow.

More surprising is that in both cases the rain turns out to be potentially ruinous—for Nicodemus of his wealth, for Honi due to flooding. And so, in each case, the rainmaker is left praying for the rain to stop! Once we know from Honi that he has a tradition not to pray about too much good, we can better understand why Nicodemus only hints to God with his coy, "Make it known that you have beloved ones," rather than ask outright for the rain to stop. And in both of our rainmaker tales, the scene ends with the sun shining. If it were a movie, we would cue the rainbow—or at least the credits, as our hero rides into the sunset.

In fact, that is exactly how the 1956 movie *The Rainmaker*, starring Burt Lancaster and Katherine Hepburn, ends. In that film the rainmaker (Lancaster) is certainly sneered at. It takes the whole movie for the rain to finally fall. When Burt rides off on his buckboard (almost getting Kate to come with him), the rain is pouring down, saving the farmers from a drought. But by the end of the credits, "the clouds dispersed and the sun shone."

It might be unfair to do our comparative work with a Kate Hepburn movie. After all, no Temple, no pilgrimage festival, and most of all neither Nicodemus nor Honi had to reckon with Ms. Hepburn. So let us go far afield from modern American culture, back to the ninth century. There, we turn to Hadith, oral traditions about the prophet Muhammad and his circle. These are sacred texts in the Muslim community, and we will rely on two of the most authentic, those of the ninth-century Hadith collection of Sahih al-Bukhari and Muslim ibn al-Hajjaj, for the following tale:

It is related from Anas ibn Malik that a man entered the Mosque while the Messenger of God, may Allah bless him and grant him peace, was giving the Friday sermon. He stood in front of the Messenger of God and said, "O Messenger of God, our livestock are dying and the roads are blocked, so pray to Allah to give us rain." He said, "The Messenger of God raised his hands and said, 'O Allah, give us rain! O Allah, give us rain! O Allah, give us rain!'"

Anas said, "By Allah, we could not see a cloud or even a speck of cloud or anything else in the sky. Then a cloud looking like a shield rose up behind him, and when it reached the middle of the sky it spread out and then it rained." He said, "By Allah, we did not see the sun for a week."

Then a man entered the Mosque while the Messenger of God, may Allah bless him and grant him peace, was giving the sermon on the next Friday. He stood in front of him and said, "Messenger of God, our property is being destroyed and the roads are blocked, so make supplication to Allah to stop it." He said, "The Messenger of God, may Allah bless him and grant him peace, raised his hands and then said, 'O Allah, around us and not on us! O Allah, on the hilltops and mountains, and the places where trees grow.'" He said, "It stopped and we left walking in the sunshine."

(2:17:126–132)

In this Muslim tradition, which I have adapted from al-Bukhari's Arabic, we can see many elements in common with our two Talmudic tales. Muhammad, of course, is the charismatic Messenger of God, beloved and blessed by Allah. The festival is the Friday, or *Jumaah,* service, where the Prophet, preaching in the Mosque (Temple), is confronted by a man who asks him to pray for rain, as there is a drought. On the following Friday, the rain has become so plentiful that the Prophet is asked to make it stop, lest disaster befall the countryside. Muhammad specifies where the rain should fall, not unlike Honi's request for "rains to fill cisterns, irrigation ditches, and wells." The Hadith tradition also ends with the sun coming out.

Now it is not impossible that the narrators of this Hadith might have known the Talmudic tales. But the stories of Muhammad are told in multiple versions and recorded in the soundest Islamic traditions. I think the tale that Anas ibn Malik related shows us the deep structural similarities among various folk traditions. I should point out, of course, that what pious Muslims will testify about this story of the Prophet Muhammad, peace be upon him, is that the story is told this way because it happened this way.

The Spoiled Brat

I promised at the outset of this chapter that our story of Honi would have a surprising ending. Actually, it has two surprising endings. One is the finale of the rainmaking affair. The second ending is really about Honi's own end. That we will reserve for the next chapter of this book. But for now, let's go back to our rainmaking scene. It has now rained. There will be water for the Passover holidays. The pilgrims will bring their offerings to God. Honi has saved the day! He is our charismatic hero, right? Well, not so much. Let's see how the rabbis end this episode:

> Shimeon ben Shetah sent Honi the following message: "Were you not Honi, I would have decreed a ban upon you! For if these years had been like those of the prophet Elijah—who had the keys to rain in his hand—would you not have profaned God's name? Yet what shall I do? You offend God and God still does what you ask for! You are like a spoiled child who offends his father and that father does what the child asks anyway. He says, 'Daddy, take me to the hot baths, rinse me in the cold pool, gimme peanuts, almonds, peaches, pomegranates'—and the father gives it to him! It is about you that Scripture says, 'May your father rejoice, and the mother who bore you delight' (Proverbs 23:25)."
>
> (BABYLONIAN TALMUD, TAANIT 23A)

Shimeon ben Shetah is remembered by the rabbis as their pre-rabbinic forebear back in the days of the Maccabees. As they retell the history of that period, he was the proto-rabbinic head of the community. As such, Shimeon stands in for rabbinic leadership back in Honi's days, the second century BCE. And Shimeon is not happy. If he could, he would have banned Honi. That rain man is out of control—especially out of rabbinic control. They just don't like charismatics, who are a threat to organized rabbinic Judaism. Like the Grand Inquisitor in Dostoevsky's classic novel *The Brothers Karamazov*, he's too threatening to be left unchallenged.

Shimeon makes explicit what bothers him—it is related to a rabbinic hero who, truth be told, was also a charismatic—Elijah the prophet (whom we met in chapter 1 and will meet again in our next chapter). In the Bible (1 Kings 17:1), Elijah goes up against King Ahab, his evil queen, Jezebel, and the false prophets of Baal. Elijah declares

"As God lives ... there will be no dew or rain these years except at my word." Shimeon equates Honi with Elijah. Both take vows involving God. Both use the phrase (at least as Shimeon tells it) "these years." Both arrogantly seek to control the rain. But here's the rub. Elijah wanted the rain to cease, while Honi wanted it to fall. Shimeon says that had those two charismatics lived at the same time, one would have vowed to stop the rain and the other to make it fall. The end result? One way or the other God's name would be profaned, because one would succeed while the other would fail. Either way, God looks bad. It's a zero sum game with God the loser.

And then, almost as though we were still in Nicodemus's story, we are suddenly back in the bathhouse in the midst of the drought. Shimeon likens Honi to a spoiled child at the baths. You know the type—the one who is so annoying you are thinking about saying something to the kid's parent or, worse, are silently rooting for the kid to get a spanking (this despite the fact that you actually disapprove of spanking). And just when you are about to speak up and censure the obnoxious behavior, daddy pats the little brat on the head and gives him what he wants. Damn!

Shimeon expresses his dismay with what I can only assume is bitter sarcasm. Dripping with irony, he offers to Honi the compliment Rabbi Yohanan ben Zakkai trotted out back in chapter 2, when he applied the verse of Proverbs to Rabbi Yehoshua. Next time I'm on the Broadway bus and find myself beleaguered by some spoiled brat, I'll just sweetly say, "May your father rejoice, and the mother who bore you delight." But I confess I might be thinking, "And the horse you rode in on!"

19 / ק

The Rabbis'
Rip Van Winkle

Honi the *Me`Aggel* remained an object of fascination for the rabbis, despite his charismatic, outlier status and Shimeon ben Shetah's censure. Perhaps this is because he came to the rabbis more or less fully formed as a Jewish folk hero. Josephus knew he was a rainmaker from a century earlier, and the rabbis place him in the era of Shimeon. This means that there has been a hundred years and more for his legendary status to ripen. Honi, like our three rich men, became a magnet for folktales. Indeed, in the tractate of Talmud from which we have been drawing our stories, there is an entire cycle of rainmaker tales—not only about Honi, but about his grandsons, as well. Apparently, rainmaking ran in the family.

These were tales told in days of yore. We will not take too much more time following Honi or comparing other rainmakers to him. But I did promise that we would learn how that arrogant charismatic met his end. I remind you, the story you are about to hear is didactic fiction. It is not told to teach us the history of the Second Temple period or even Honi's biography. Rather, it is told to teach the moral and religious truths that the rabbis wish us to learn, even now. Again, we note the difference between what actually happened historically and what sage tales may tell us to convey eternal verities.

In fact, this next folktale has its own life, independent of Honi. It is told many places in rabbinic literature and could be characterized as the folk motif of "man planting the tree." It has been schlepped into the Honi legend by our Talmudic storyteller—one folktale illustrating yet another. That other folktale, with apologies to Woody Allen, could be called "Sleeper."

> That righteous man was troubled all his days by this verse: "A Song of Ascents. We were like dreamers when God returned the captivity of Zion" (Psalm 126:1). He asked, "Who can nap for seventy years?"
>
> One day he was traveling on the road and saw a man planting a carob tree. He asked him, "How long will it take for that tree to bear fruit?"
>
> The man answered, "Up to seventy years."
>
> Honi asked, "Are you sure you will live for seventy years?"
>
> He replied, "This man found the world with carob trees. Just as my forefathers planted for me, I too plant for those who come after me."
>
> Honi sat and ate a sandwich. Then sleep overcame him. He napped. While he was sleeping, a stony outcropping surrounded him, hiding him from view. He napped for seventy years. When he awoke, he saw that man collecting carobs from the tree. He asked, "Are you the one who planted it?"
>
> He said, "I am his son's son."
>
> Honi reasoned, "I infer from this that I had a seventy-year nap!"
>
> And he saw that his donkey had given birth to many offspring.
>
> (BABYLONIAN TALMUD, TAANIT 23A)

This is the first part to the dénouement of the Honi story cycle. It is a complicated tale that opens with a play on a very well-known verse from Psalms. The verse is chanted as part of the introduction to the Blessing after Meals recited by obervant Jews. You may recall that Rabbi Yohanan asked young (okay, young-ish) Eliezer ben Hyrcanus whether he had ever learned that prayer and was astonished that he had not. Our verse is from a psalm of praise to God. The end of the Babylonian exile, the return to Jerusalem from the captivity of Zion, is depicted as a dream. The psalm later includes the memorable line "Those who sow in tears, will reap in joy" (Psalm 126:6). Presumably, this is what will happen to those who return from the exile. It is equally apposite to our story of the man planting a tree.

Yet Honi seems to willfully misunderstand this verse of Scripture. He takes the verse to refer not to the actual return, but to the length of the exile, alluded to in the biblical book of Daniel (9:2) as seventy years. This requires his reading of the verse's "dream" to be a "nightmare." For Honi, the exile was a seventy-year-long nightmare. No wonder he was troubled by that verse all his life. And note, please, that Honi is referred to in this story as "that righteous man." I am not sure whether to read this as more rabbinic irony or an admission by the narrator that if Honi can bring rain, he must be righteous. Once Honi has assumed the exile was a seventy-year nightmare, he questions the veracity of the metaphor, for "who can nap for seventy years?" I translated the verb "nap" because that's the term Honi uses—and not the usual verb for "sleep." (I can hear my sainted grandfather grousing in Yiddish, "Can't a man take a damn nap without interruption!")

Sleeper

With Honi's question, the scene is set and the plot is off and running. Enter the "man planting a tree." Honi sees the guy, asks how long it takes for a carob to bear fruit, and we have our requisite seventy years. Then Honi sits down for lunch (it literally says, "he wraps his loaf," like at those fast-food wrap joints) and, following his meal, predictably nods off. As can only happen in folktales, he is magically surrounded by a rocky formation and is hidden from view and interruption. Finally, no one to bother him while he naps. And what a glorious nap he takes. When Washington Irving told the tale of "Rip Van Winkle," he only let him nap for twenty years. Honi had threescore and ten years to dream. It makes me sleepy just thinking about it. But as we will shortly see, it foreshadows his own exile.

Before we get to Honi's rude awakening, let's return for a few moments to the roadside where our other fellow is planting his carob tree. An earlier rabbinic version of this folktale imagines the Roman emperor Hadrian passing by an elderly tree planter. Hadrian rebukes him, saying, "Had you planted early in your youth, you wouldn't need to be working so hard late in your old age." That tree planter says, "Early or late, I do what pleases my Master in heaven." Hadrian is tickled by this answer and commands that if the fellow should ever reap what he sows, he should come see him and be rewarded. The old tree planter eventually makes his way to the emperor, who trades his basket of fruit for a basket of gold! (*Leviticus Rabbah* 25:5).

There are at least eight other versions of this folktale recounted in rabbinic literature. And two modern folklorists have trotted out another dozen cross-cultural examples. Like rainmakers, tree planters are rather ubiquitous (think Johnny Appleseed). My all-time favorite invocation of the "man planting the tree" motif was its use some years ago on fund-raising posters by the United Jewish Appeal: "Just as my forefathers planted for me, I too plant for those who come after me." The tree was no longer literal, but the desired basket of gold surely was.

In our story, Honi wakes to find the carob tree bearing fruit. He coyly asks the man collecting the carobs, "Are you the guy who planted it?" The answer, "I am his son's son," serves as evidence of the extraordinary length of the nap. If that weren't enough, Honi notices that the donkey, which he had no doubt firmly tethered to a nearby tree when he sat down to eat his sandwich, has given birth to generation upon generation of donkeys. This is an odd touch of local color. Its very strangeness as a detail lends the story a certain "truthiness" (as Stephen Colbert might say).

Either/Or

Our two folktales have been trotted out in the service of our Honi stories. Now our "rainmaker" has encountered the "man planting tree" and then turned into a "sleeper." The ubiquity of these motifs clues the listeners in to the lack of historical fact contained in the tales. Instead, they are cued to listen to how the narrator has artfully manipulated these old saws in the service of his new moral. We will see that in this very rabbinic telling of the tale, Honi, like the charismatic Elijah the prophet before him, is tamed and rabbanized. By the time this tale has reached its sad conclusion, Honi will be just another rabbi (but maybe with a sadder ending).

> Honi went to his home. He asked them, "Is the son of Honi the Me`Aggel still alive?"
>
> They said, "His son is not; his grandson is."
>
> He told them, "I am Honi the Me`Aggel!" But they did not believe him.
>
> So he went to the study house. He overheard the rabbis saying, "The law is as clear as in the days of Honi the Me`Aggel. For when he entered the study house, he would resolve any difficulties that the rabbis had."
>
> He announced to them, "I am he!" Not only did they not believe him, but they did not pay him the respect he deserved.
>
> His spirit became weak. He prayed for God's mercy and died.
>
> Rava said, "It's what folks say: 'Either companionship or death.'"
>
> (BABYLONIAN TALMUD, TAANIT 23A)

Note how carefully our storyteller has constructed this poignant ending to the Honi saga. The question and answer to the tree harvester above and then to the person at his own home echo one another. Having learned from the first instance about the depredations of passing time, Honi inquires cautiously. Obviously, he cannot ask whether he himself is there. He asks instead for his son and, stunningly, learns that he is dead. His only consolation is that his grandson yet lives. But when Honi declares himself (with his grand title: the Me`Aggel), he is not believed. How clever of the storyteller to go mum here and not fill in the rejection that we and other readers/listeners can all too painfully imagine.

Sent away from his own home, Honi turns to his second home, as it were. In this moment, the arrogant charismatic is humbled—reduced to mere rabbinic status. When he gets to the rabbinic academy (apparently the brick-and-mortar type of building common in later Jewish Babylonia), Honi overhears the rabbis arguing. One voice declares the law, the received tradition, as clear as in the good old days when Honi used to resolve rabbinic disputes. We might be surprised to learn that Honi resolved rabbinic disputes. Who would have thought that the rainmaker was a rabbi? In fact, he was not. But in the convenient retelling of rabbinic proto-history, Honi can be made to play that role. Even so, despite his stellar reputation, when he declares himself as Honi, he is once again not believed. This time the Talmud is more expansive, if still somewhat delicate. We are told, "They did not pay him the respect he deserved." This is a polite way of telling listeners that the rabbis threw him out on his ear.

Notably, throughout the telling of this tale Honi is supplied with the vocabulary of a Babylonian rabbi. When he asks the tree planter, "Are you sure?" it is in the common parlance of Babylonian rabbinic dialectic. When he wakes up and sees the donkey and its many offspring, he proclaims, "I infer from this," much as would a rabbi at the conclusion of legal dialectic. It is of a piece with pretending that he resolved rabbinic disputes, what I have called the rabbanizing of Honi. The best way to tame the charismatic is to depict him as though he was just one more among the many rabbis of the academy.

Yet Honi also is depicted in the same ways that the prophet Elijah is described in the Babylonian Talmud—as a kind of über-rabbi. This, too, is a way of rabbanizing the charismatic (both Honi and Elijah). The rabbis say of Elijah that when he comes as forerunner to the Messiah, he will resolve all the legal difficulties of the rabbis. But there is a further analogy being made between Honi and Elijah the prophet. In the Bible, when Elijah had his dispute with King Ahab over the rains and won his spectacular victory over the false prophets of the god Baal, he became depressed. He actually begged for mercy from God to let him die. But God had other plans for Elijah.

Not so poor Honi. He has gone from being a charismatic, arrogant rainmaker to a depressed wretch begging for God to let him die. What I translated as "his spirit became weak," could equally translate as "his mind weakened" or even "his will grew weak." Unlike Elijah, Honi's prayer for mercy is answered. He is given a death marked by bathos. The rabbis, centuries after his historic death, got even with Honi for rocking the boat. The great rabbinic dialectician Rava in essence writes Honi's epitaph when he quotes the folksaying as a fitting end to our folktale: "Either companionship or death." It has a rhythm and rhyme in Aramaic. But it has a moral, too. The rabbis thrive on companionship. Their hallmark dialectic depends upon companionship. And we saw what happened to Rabbi Elazar ben Arakh when he wandered away from his fellow students.

Honi chose the path of a loner. He thought it was just him and God. He could disdain everyone else as he stood in his circle, because he presumed that he had special status. He proclaimed himself like a member of God's household. The rabbis, ever wary of such hubris, fashion a crude warning in telling the tale of Honi's end. He dies like every other mortal. But Honi dies alone, unremembered, and disrespected. "Lo, how the mighty have fallen!" (2 Samuel 1:19).

Honi lived two centuries before the destruction of Jerusalem. But the sage tales recounted in this book have by and large studied the rainmakers, scholars, and saints who lived immediately before, during, and just after the destruction of Jerusalem. In our next chapter, we return to the aftermath of the siege to learn what became of our rich men, their families, and their seemingly unlimited prosperity.

20 / ר

Pretty Woman
1 and 2

We have traveled a long road together encountering many interesting characters along the way. As though we were pilgrims in Chaucer's *Canterbury Tales*, we pause to refresh and hear a good yarn. And like those famous stories, the narratives we read have been either overtly or implicitly teaching their own morality and worldview. Sometimes the morals to the story are right out there; other times we have to dig a bit beneath the surface to see what it is the rabbis are getting at. Having spent this much time together, we're getting fairly adept at learning the mechanics of the tales—how they are spun and how the narrators ply their arts. We know our cast of characters, the plots are fairly simple (if sometimes disheartening), the performances enjoyable. But always, our sage tales are thought provoking. We have delved into theology, Jewish history, and the relationship between them. Together, we have pondered death, mysticism, the study of Torah and how certain rabbis came to it. Indeed, we have been reading the tales of the founding of rabbinic Judaism and how it survived the incredible trauma of the destruction of Jerusalem in the first century. We've also heard tales of miracle workers, including the rabbis' take on that most famous of them, Jesus of Nazareth. And let us not forget the folktales of rainmakers, tree planters, and even sleepers. As I said, we have traveled a long road together.

Just as our plots have not been overly complex, neither have our characters. They are almost caricatures. At best, the thumbnail sketches the rabbinic storytellers performed allowed us to distinguish one rabbi from another or one of their rich supporters from his wealthy colleague. But often, minor characters have been more or less interchangeable, fungible fellows that they are. They function more as symbols than as real people. This, of course, is a by-product of reading didactic narratives, lives of the saints. This is not biography. We need not fully realize these characters. But we do need to know what they represent: the rich man, the sage, the evil other. Now and then, as we will soon see, certain characters stand for corporate Israel—one person represents the Jewish people as a whole. It reminds me of those Roman coins that depict a solitary woman seated abjectly beneath a palm tree. The caption on the coin reads: *Iudea Capta* (Judea captured). They were issued by the emperor Vespasian to commemorate the destruction of Jerusalem. Here's the coin, with Vespasian on one side and our fallen woman on the other side, seated on the ground under the watchful gaze of a Roman soldier.

Vespasian and his sons liked the image so much that they issued *Iudea Capta* coins for twenty-five years following the destruction of Jerusalem. As a result, coins with the image of the captured woman were found everywhere in the eastern part of the Roman Empire. In fact, the imagery of the lonely woman was found much earlier than Rome. It is already in the Bible. For example, in Lamentations 1:1 we read, "Like a widow, the city once great among the nations sits desolate."

It was only natural then that this imaginary woman, bereft of family and children, became a symbol for the rabbis, too, when they spoke about the aftermath of Jerusalem's destruction.

> "If you know not, O fairest of women" (Song of Songs 1:8).
>
> "Because you would not serve the Lord your God ... you shall have to serve your enemies" (Deuteronomy 28:47–48).
>
> Once, when Rabbi Yohanan ben Zakkai was going up to Maon Yehuda, he saw a young woman collecting barleycorns from horse dung. Rabbi Yohanan ben Zakkai asked them [his disciples], "Did you see that young woman? What is she?"
>
> His disciples replied, "Jewish."
>
> He asked, "Who owns the horse?"
>
> They replied, "An Arabian traveler."
>
> Rabbi Yohanan ben Zakkai said to his disciples, "All my life I was troubled by this verse. I would read it and not understand it: 'If you know not, O fairest of women' [Song of Songs 1:8]."
>
> Because you did not want to serve Heaven, behold you now serve the lowest of the Arabian gentiles. Because you did not want to pay a *beka* as the head tax to Heaven, behold you now pay fifteen *shekel*s to the government of your enemy.
>
> (Mekhilta DeRabbi Ishmael, Yitro 1)

There is a remarkable dynamic at work in this story. It is clearly a tale told to make a point, almost sermonic in driving home the moral to the story. In fact, it has other earmarks that make it look homiletic, as though it had been delivered in a synagogue to exhort the congregants to shape up or else. This sermonette has a double heading of two scriptural passages. We have seen again and again in our rabbis' stories how their narratives engage Scripture. The Hebrew Bible is quoted, embraced, played with—always lovingly and joyfully. Here, too, even when the message is severe, there is clever quotation of biblical text. The unlikely juxtaposition of a bucolic verse from the Song of Songs with the terrifyingly stern imprecation of Deuteronomy's covenantal curses alerts us that something is afoot.

Let us turn to that beautiful idyllic passage in Song of Songs to see the context. The famous female lover of the Bible asks, "Tell me, my soul's beloved; where do you graze your flock? Where do you rest at noontide?" (Song of Songs 1:7). Her beloved's reply, "If you know not, O fairest of women, follow the tracks of the sheep and graze your kids among the shepherds' tents" (Song of Songs 1:8). It is astonishing to think that such a pastoral image could be used to paint a portrait of subjugation—unless, perhaps, the second-century rabbinic author of this text had read Philip Roth's *American Pastoral* and its bleak portrait of a much later empire.

The verses from Deuteronomy that follow are ferocious. Let's quote them more fully here:

"Because you would not serve the Lord your God in joy and with good heart when you had abundance of everything, you shall have to serve your enemies hungry and thirsty, naked and lacking everything … and God will bring an enemy against you from afar" (Deuteronomy 28:47–49).

This scathing excoriation overwhelms the subsequent rabbinic narrative. Our story is all about unpacking these two verses of Bible. They are not only the headers for the tale, but they also drive the plot. The Song of Song verse gives us our girl who follows in the tracks of animals to graze, while the Deuteronomy verse is paraphrased as the moral to the Jews. You did not serve God, so now you serve Rome. You didn't pay the Temple tax, so now you pay taxes to the imperial *fisc*.

A Teaching Moment

To give our story and its embodiment of Scripture some narrative legs, enter Rabbi Yohanan and his disciples, once more on a road trip. This time they are given a specific locale for their travel: Maon Yehuda. This is a nice touch; the place lends credence to the events. Except that we know of no place called Maon Yehuda, either now or back then. It seems to be a fictional town, made up by our narrator. The medieval scribes who copied the tale were stymied by this place-name. They changed the name (some wrote Emmaus) or miscopied it. It's not even on Google. It matters not, for this is not a tale about what happened, when, and where. It is an illustration of Scripture, plain and simple. How do I know this? Because I want to believe that were there really a starving young Jewish girl, Rabbi Yohanan would have just gone over and fed her. Of course, we have encountered his bad manners in another tale, when Rabbi Yohanan left Eliezer ben Hyrcanus hungry until his breath fairly reeked. I prefer to think of it as a literary tic, a motif, rather than inexcusable behavior on the part of our good rabbi.

Rabbi Yohanan quizzes his students: Do you see that girl sifting in the dung for any undigested barley kernels she might find to eat? Do you realize who she is? And what about that man who owns the horse? Here we need to stop and explain Rabbi Yohanan's comment about the Arabian horseman. He is described as an "Arabian traveler." This character played the functional equivalent of the traveling salesman in jokes from the 1950s. Calling him this does not implicate Arabs, per se. Nor do I believe there is racism here (says this rabbi, apologetically). Rather, the caravan man, the sojourner-salesman was of ill repute as a man of loose morals. He would seduce your daughter and rob you blind given half a chance. Okay, maybe there was rabbinic racism in this characterization. But the point was not so much to slur those from the pre-Islamic Arabian Peninsula as it was to cast aspersions on the morals of the horse's owner, the "enemy from afar." The reason for this characterization will only be apparent to us later in this chapter, once we've heard a second performance of the tale.

Now, Rabbi Yohanan can tell his disciples why he has deigned to take note of the foraging female in the first place. He's been troubled by the meaning of a verse of Scripture, in the same way that our rainmaker Honi had been troubled by not understanding the meaning of his verse. Again, we see the storyteller's technique at work. Having a character be "troubled by a verse" is just a rabbinic way of introducing a novel understanding to a passage of the Bible—not a recounting of historic events, but interpretation of Scripture. What this verse means is that the girl is following in the tracks of the grazing horse to feed herself. In this narrative, she is an all too literal embodiment of a peculiar reading of the verse in which she stands in for the grazing flocks of baby goats. Here, too, the next telling of the tale will flesh out this replacement of the goat by the girl.

Before we turn to that telling, a final note on how some things never change. The curses of the book of Deuteronomy determine the fallen state of the young woman in our story. The moral to the tale echoes the verse of Deuteronomy invoked at the outset of the telling. But the biblical curses nowhere mention the curse of having to pay taxes. The rabbi refers to the biblical measures *beka* and *shekel*, but the taxes were most certainly exacted by Rome, "the government of your enemy." It is, at least from the distance of eighteen hundred years, humorous to note that the storyteller invokes the payment of taxes as yet another curse laid upon the Jews. *Plus ça change, plus c'est la même chose.*

From Riches to Rags

The "historian" Josephus anticipated the rabbis by a century when he told his own version of the pretty woman foraging during the siege of Jerusalem. In his description in his book *The Jewish War*, he wrote about a certain Miriam or Mary from the town of Beth Ezuba who was driven by hunger to unspeakable acts of desperation. In fact, Josephus's lurid account mirrors a much earlier narrative from the Bible that tells of a famine in Samaria when a small portion of dove's dung sold for five *shekel*s of silver (2 Kings 6:25). This biblical account not only inspired Josephus's descriptions of the siege of Jerusalem, but also helps us account for the dung and *shekel*s in our rabbinic story of the foraging woman. These antecedents to our tale duly noted, we are ready for Pretty Woman 2.

> A story is told about Rabbi Yohanan ben Zakkai, who was riding a donkey and his disciples were following behind him. He saw a young woman collecting barley from beneath the hooves of the cattle of Arabians. When she saw Rabbi Yohanan ben

Zakkai, she wrapped herself in her hair and stood before him. She said, "Rabbi, sustain me."

He asked, "Whose daughter are you?"

She replied, "I am the daughter of Nicodemus ben Gurion. Rabbi, do you remember when you signed my marriage agreement?"

Rabbi Yohanan ben Zakkai said to his disciples, "I signed her marriage agreement and read therein a million gold dinars promised by her in-laws as a bride price. As for this young woman's family, they would not go to worship in the Temple Mount until woolen carpets were laid beneath their feet. Then they would enter, worship, and return to their homes in joy. All my life I have searched for the meaning of this verse, and now I have found it, 'If you know not, O fairest of women, follow the tracks of the sheep and graze your kids among the shepherds' tents' [Song of Songs 1:8]."

Do not read the verse as saying "your kids" [*gediyotayikh*], but as though it says "your corpses" [*geviyotayikh*].

For so long as the Jews do the will of the Omnipresent, no nation or government can rule them. But when the Jews do not do the will of the Omnipresent, they are given into the hands of a lowly nation. And not just into the hands of a lowly nation, but beneath the feet of the cattle of a lowly nation.

(*Sifre Deuteronomy* 305)

This sage tale comes from the early third century, contemporary with the earlier telling we read above. This version is found in the earliest rabbinic commentary on Deuteronomy, which is ironic because this telling of our "girl foraging" tale never mentions a verse of Deuteronomy, only the verse we've seen from Song of Songs. But don't fret, we can see that missing verse lurking below the surface, embedded in the moral to the story about the Jews doing God's will or being handed over to a lowly nation.

There is so much else familiar to us in this second telling of the tale. I hope you were calling out or nodding at the recognizable tropes, names, and character tics. In fact, there are so many common motifs and fill-ins that our storytelling is beginning to resemble the old party game of Mad Libs. The scene opens with Rabbi Yohanan on his road trip, riding on a donkey with his disciples following behind. The report is almost the same as the one we saw in chapter 8, when Yohanan and Elazar ben Arakh were on their magical mystical tour. The one difference between the formulations is this: when Elazar was accompanying Rabbi Yohanan, Elazar did the driving (of the donkey). Here, we have unnamed disciples who are walking behind—we do not know who is behind the wheel, as it were.

When our young miss goes foraging, it is described in somewhat more delicate language. Now she gathers barley from beneath the hooves of the cattle. We still understand that she is sorting through the manure to find undigested barleycorn, but it isn't quite as graphically expressed as before. And the horse has been traded for cattle, in the plural. This adjustment better accounts for the animals in the grazing flock mentioned in the verse of Song of Songs. The storyteller here allows Scripture to dictate the details of his narrative.

But then we have a new fact introduced into the story. The girl wraps herself in her hair. The same verb was used in the Yohanan-Elazar narrative, when Yohanan wrapped himself in his cloak. Either there is something about a road trip that requires wrapping or I am making too much of mere coincidence on this one. And, before you also make too much of it, when Honi "wrapped" his sandwich, the Hebrew word was different from the one used here.

Of course, we just have to ask why "she wrapped herself in her hair." It is possible, and judging from the work of Roman historians of the period, even likely that the girl was nearly or entirely naked. It was all too common for the abject poor to wander naked through the urban streets, begging for their bread. And so, Godiva-like, our young woman modestly covers herself before approaching the great rabbi. That possibility opens the door to yet another staging of this scene, in which the young woman is clothed but covers her face with her hair, again from modesty. But this explanation presumes that Jewish women in the first or second century would veil themselves. I am not at all sure this was so, despite the evidence from Roman statuary that shows pagan Roman matrons with a head covering demurely clasped in one hand, as if ready to veil their faces at any moment.

Yet the Mishnah attributes the custom of veiling to Arabian women, making it seem as though Jewish women do not veil. Perhaps she just wants to hide her identity from Rabbi Yohanan, whom she recognizes. She might be ashamed. She might think hiding this way is a better strategy for getting him to pony up some *shekels*. What marks this narrative account from our previous "girl foraging" tale is much more profound: she speaks! No longer is she a mere object lesson for the elucidation of Scripture; here our young woman has a personality, a voice, a family.

Just How Rich Was She?

Indeed, Rabbi Yohanan is depicted reacting in his usual fashion, asking after lineage. Do you remember when he asked Eliezer ben Hyrcanus, "My son, whose son are you?" (see chapter 6). One of the very early manuscripts of this version of the girl foraging story has Yohanan ask her, "My daughter, whose daughter are you?" In both cases, the irony of his address to them as "my child," followed by the inquiry about parentage, underscores the absurdity and inappropriateness of the question given the circumstances. Yet in both instances Yohanan gets eye-popping answers. Each of his hungry waifs has a very rich father. For Eliezer, it was Hyrcanus. And for our young lady, quick: name a rich man! Nicodemus ben Gurion—that is correct! You win a fabulous vacation in besieged Jerusalem!

Just how rich was this dirty, naked beggar sifting shit to find her morning meal? Why, she was so rich that Yohanan ben Zakkai himself performed her wedding. We've already learned that he would do the funerals of the very rich, so why not weddings? And oh, what a wedding it was! Why the very angels came down from heaven to the *smörgåsbord*—no, never mind, they came down for a mystical sermon. I really have to try to keep my stories straight. But you really can't blame me—these stories all borrow so much from one another.

Her in-laws ponied up a million dinars as her bride price. As for her own parents, well, they were as rich as, as Ben Tzitzit HaKeset. Remember how his garment's ritual fringes (*tzitzit*) used to drag upon pillows (*keset*)? Here is another case of fungability, where the motif of "wealth demonstrated by not putting your delicate foot on the ground" has been translated from one rich man to another. And speaking of "not putting your delicate foot on the ground" might just call to mind yet another rich character, also from Yohanan's circle of supporters, our very own Martha bat Boethius. What goes around comes around.

I am rapidly running out of clichés for the recurrence of motifs in these rabbinic narratives, so I'll bring this chapter to a close with but a few brief remarks (you should always be on your guard when a rabbi says this). Yohanan has a new formulation for his scriptural offering. Instead of being troubled by it all his life, he has been "searching for meaning." Who among us hasn't? But when he trots out that verse of Song of Songs (we're still mulling the absence of Deuteronomy here), we notice that maybe the verse isn't as perfect as it seemed when we first used it as our proof-text. Like the chiropractor says, it needs some adjustment.

No longer should we read the verse as though we are grazing our baby goats. We should read it, which is to say make a pun on it, as though it says "our corpses" (Hebrew: *geviyotayikh*) in lieu of "our kids"

(Hebrew: *gediyotayikh*). All we need to do is change but one letter. So far so good. But as often happens once you are on the chiropractor's table, one adjustment begs for another small adjustment. And so, we get a do-over for the moral to the story. No longer will the Jews be put into the hand of a lowly nation. Taking the metaphor exceedingly literally, our storyteller insists that we say instead that the Jews will be remanded beneath the hooves of the cattle of the lowly nation. And to be sure we understand what we're talking about, we even name the "lowly nation." Well, alrighty then. But really, is that necessary? Must we be quite so literal?

As we will see in our next chapter, this oft-told tale introduces different quirks with each telling. What intrigues me is to wonder if, like in some vast game of telephone, we can watch the story travel around the room, or through time and space, and record its permutations from one teller's mouth to the next performer's ear. Can we recover the *original* story of the girl foraging if we lay out all the versions of the tale next to one another? Was there, in fact, ever an original story? Did it actually happen? Does the moral ever change? What might it teach us about the rabbis, Jewish history, and storytelling?

21 / שׁ

Pretty Woman
3, 4, 5

The story of the girl foraging was quite popular in rabbinic circles. It was told and performed in many venues, like a rabbinic version of *Annie*. It is found in a variety of presentations: some long, some short. As I mentioned earlier, each storyteller tweaked the details, embellishing or editing depending on the audience. The narrative motif could even be invoked as a kind of shorthand, much the same way as we might refer to news stories or television shows with a quick title or brief allusion. Once the story was in wide circulation, it underwent even further transformations. Having gone viral, it takes modern readers some keen parsing to recognize that there beneath the surface of a seemingly random reference to something else we can still see our poor little rich girl. She might have been mercifully stripped of the ponderous moral to the story about obeying God, but she's still sifting her way to a meal. Let's watch as the story and its often bizarre details transform in two versions of it from the Palestinian Talmud. The two narratives in chapter 20 came from early-third-century rabbinic commentaries on the Bible; these stories come from a commentary on the Mishnah, edited around 425 CE.

The context is an extended discussion of women's rights in certain aspects of Jewish law. The Jewish marriage document (referred to in the previous chapter when the girl foraging reminded Rabbi Yohanan that he had signed her richly endowed contract) serves as a form of prenuptial agreement. Like virtually every other contract, a marriage contract can be subject to litigation. When that occurred, a rabbinic court was convened to determine what a given widow or divorcée might receive from an estate as her fair share of post-matrimonial maintenance. It is not uncommon in discussions of the details of these laws to cite previous cases as legal precedent. Whether these cases actually happened or not is subject to debate among Jewish historians. But we are not here to debate Jewish law or history. Let's focus on the *story* contained in the so-called precedent. And keep an eye on the plaintiff while you're at it.

> A case is cited regarding Martha bat Boethius. The sages ruled that she could receive two barrels of wine as a daily maintenance allowance. This proves that the sages have the right to rule on wine allowances....
>
> Rabbi Hezekiah quoted Rabbi Abbahu in the name of Rabbi Yohanan, "They also ruled about a daily cooked-food allowance."
>
> Despite this, she cursed the court, saying, "You should only give this to your own daughters!"
>
> Rabbi Akhah said, "We all replied to her, 'Amen!'"
>
> Rabbi Elazar ben Tzadok said, "May I never see consolation if what I say is not true. I saw her collecting barleycorns from between the hooves of horses in Acre. I recited the following verse about her: 'The most tender and delicate of women, who would not allow the sole of her foot to touch the ground' [Deuteronomy 28:56]. 'If you know not, O fairest of women, follow the tracks of the sheep' [Song of Songs 1:8]."

As Alice famously said in *Wonderland*, "Curiouser and curiouser." Martha bat Boethius is involved with this story? We will recall that she was a divorcée with a strong sense of entitlement. And we certainly recall that our poor girl foraging claimed to Rabbi Yohanan that she came from an extraordinarily wealthy family. But, that girl said she was

Nicodemus's daughter, while Martha ... well, it doesn't really matter, does it? Josephus said *his* starving young woman was Miriam or Mary. Mary, Martha, they all sound the same (and in fact, Miriam/Mary and Martha regularly were confused in Christian tradition, as Jesus had female followers by both names).

Whatever her name is in a given story, we still want to know: "How rich was she?" Why, Martha bat Boethius was so rich that the sages allowed her to fund wine and cooked food from her alimony settlement. Many rabbinic names are trotted out here to lend authority to this generous ruling. The rabbis had a principle that people should be kept in the style they were accustomed to, which sounds like something a cliché 1950s' dad might ask of a prospective groom, but was a reasonable principle of equity when the rabbis settled estates or gave from charitable funds. Martha, true to form, thinks this is too little and far beneath her needs. She curses the court, telling the sages disdainfully that they should give such a mere pittance to their own daughters. To quote another famous fictional protagonist, "The rich are different from you and me." Although Martha cannot conceive that anyone could get along on so little, the rabbis of the court could not conceive that anyone could ever have so much. In a brilliant piece of rabbinic humor, Rabbi Akhah tells us his colleagues all answered hopefully, "Amen!" If only they could provide that for their daughters!

Stepping In

As though it weren't strange enough that Martha has traipsed (barefoot?) back into our story, she does so in the guise of the girl foraging. Ah! Now we understand why Rashi, the famous Talmud commentator, thought that it was dung she had stepped in back when we were reading about the siege of Jerusalem. He knew this story and understood that rich Martha was interchangeable for rich girl foraging. Actually, if we think about it, Martha *was* a rich woman foraging. It is totally the same story! To remind you of how *that* tale ended, here are the final few lines of that performance:

She removed her shoes and said, "I will go out and see if I can find anything to eat."

A piece of something stuck to her foot and she died!

Rabbi Yohanan ben Zakkai read as her eulogy, "The most tender and delicate of women, who would not allow the sole of her foot to touch the ground" (Deuteronomy 28:56).

(Babylonian Talmud, *Gittin* 56a)

So, now we understand that Martha steps in it and a famous rabbi eulogizes her with an appropriate verse from Deuteronomy. If we know the story of the rich girl foraging, we get that Martha is there following the herd to find her lunch. As we have so often said when we read about my dear Martha, "Ew!"

Now, let's take another look at the verse from Deuteronomy 28:56 that Rabbi Yohanan ben Zakkai quoted about her. It's only a very few short verses away from the verse that was quoted as the header in our "first" telling of the girl foraging tale, at the outset of the last chapter, "Because you would not serve the Lord your God ... you shall have to serve your enemies" (Deuteronomy 28:47–48). We really are in Wonderland here. I do not think this juxtaposition of verses is mere coincidence. As we see from the verse(s) Rabbi Elazar ben Tzadok quoted at the outset of this chapter, the Martha verse from Deuteronomy and the girl foraging verse from Song of Songs are also interchangeable.

In fact, the Deuteronomy verse fits the girl foraging story pretty well, without all of the chiropractic adjustments. What a sermon it would be to have *two* verses of Deuteronomy, only nine verses apart, serving as the introduction to a homily in which one of those verses illustrates our girl foraging, while the other verse illustrates the moral to the story about Israel. Let me summarize this hypothetical sermon for you in outline form, like this:

a. "The most tender and delicate of women, who would not allow the sole of her foot to touch the ground" (Deuteronomy 28:56).

  b. "Because you would not serve the Lord your God in joy and
   with good heart when you had abundance of everything;
   you shall have to serve your enemies hungry and thirsty,
   naked and lacking everything" (Deuteronomy 28:47–48).
  c. Once there was a poor little rich girl out foraging among
   the animals to find her next meal ...
  d. And the moral to the story is, when the Jews obey God ...
   and when they disobey God ...

Or we could mix it up a bit, with a journalistic lede on a particular victim, followed by the broader story:

  a. Once there was a poor little rich girl out foraging among
   the animals to find her next meal ...
  b. "The most tender and delicate of women, who would not
   allow the sole of her foot to touch the ground"
   (Deuteronomy 28:56).
  c. And the moral to the story is, when the Jews obey God ...
   and when they disobey God ...
  d. "Because you would not serve the Lord your God in joy and
   with good heart when you had abundance of everything,
   you shall have to serve your enemies hungry and thirsty,
   naked and lacking everything" (Deuteronomy 28:47).

Not coincidently, these two topic verses that drive the plot and the
moral to the story come from the part of Deuteronomy that lays out the
curses God will bring for abandonment of the covenant. Traditionally,
they are read together, quickly, and in a low voice, so as not to extend or
spread too wide the horror of this section of the Torah. The sermon outlined above, then, would be for a very narrow slice of the Torah reading.
It would be a sermon that held Israel accountable for her sins and laid
out the consequences most graphically with a poignant example.

  Once we see how readily interchangeable are the various parts of
this sermon, we appreciate all the more the art of rabbinic storytelling.
We have observed how thoroughly interchangeable the characters'
names are. Using what we learned from the rainmaker folktales, we see

that Martha and the woman foraging share a common narrative skeleton. As the names of the characters shift, so do locales and other such details. In the Martha story, it was Rabbi Yohanan ben Zakkai who recited the verse from Deuteronomy as his eulogy. In the story from the Palestinian Talmud about Martha's marriage settlement, it is Rabbi Elazar ben Tzadok who quotes both the Deuteronomy verse *and* the Song of Songs verse. We can actually watch one verse in the process of replacing the other during the history of the various tellings of this tale.

And I want to focus on the name of the second rabbi for a moment, the one who is not Yohanan ben Zakkai. He is the son of Rabbi Tzadok, the same fellow who fasted for forty years to try to forestall the destruction of Jerusalem. You may recall that Rabbi Yohanan asked Vespasian for a physician to heal him. Tzadok had sucked the juice out of fruit and spit out the fiber. And some say that "piece of something" was what Martha stepped on with her bare foot. This is fun! It's like playing Six Degrees of Kevin Bacon.

Just the Facts

If you are confused at this point, that's okay. There are so many interchangeable details, like so many Lego parts to snap in and out of our stories. If you are not confused at this point, you might be qualified to be a rabbinic storyteller. But before you go off to perform your very own sage tales, here's one final version from the Palestinian Talmud. If we count the story of Martha as one more version, she brings us up to Pretty Woman 4.

The remaining tale of the woman foraging is from the section of the Talmud that is offering precedents about the court's power to determine an appropriate allowance from the estate. In this case, they do so for a widow. But there is a twist to the legal fact pattern, because this is not just any widow. She lost her husband before they had children. According to biblical law in Deuteronomy 25:5–6, "Her husband's brother shall cohabit with her.... The son she bears will be raised in the name of the dead brother." This archaic law was rarely put into practice, as there was a ceremony by which she could repudiate her brother-in-law. But this could only happen if the surviving brother did not want to take her as a levirate wife.

Stay with me now, because it gets a bit more complicated here. As if this were not odd enough a circumstance to introduce our woman foraging story, there's an even stranger twist. What if the husband dies and leaves behind an indecisive or a very young brother? If the boy is too young, he has neither the legal standing to participate in the ceremony nor, well, the *cojones* to do the deed. What, then, is the status of the poor widow? Must she wait until the little brother grows up enough to perform his brotherly duty? And if the brother is indecisive, she is in a legal limbo until he decides what to do. How long can a widow wait on events like that? And does she get an allowance from her late husband's estate to survive while she is waiting for Junior? If so, does the rabbinic court get to decide her alimony? This is the bizarre fact pattern leading to our next telling of the tale, what I've dubbed PW5.

> A story is told about Miriam, daughter of Shimeon ben Gurion. The sages ruled that she should have a five hundred dinar per diem perfume allowance, although she was only waiting for her brother-in-law to do his levirate duty.
>
> Despite this, she cursed the court, saying, "You should only give this to your own daughters!"
>
> Rabbi Akhah said, "We all replied to her, 'Amen!'"
>
> Rabbi Elazar ben Tzadok said, "May I never see consolation if what I say is not true. I saw her tied by her hair to the tail of a horse in Acre. I recited the following verse about her, 'The most tender and delicate of women, who would not allow the sole of her foot to touch the ground' [Deuteronomy 28:56]."
>
> (Palestinian Talmud, Ketubot 5:7)

Go ahead and giggle if you like. I know, it's really bordering on the absurd. It looks as though "the names have been changed to protect the innocent." Martha or Mary is now emphatically Miriam. And her dad is Shimeon ben Gurion, who I suppose was the long-lost brother of both Nicodemus and David ben Gurion! Forgive my cynicism about the historicity of this name, but this is the one and only time it is mentioned in all of rabbinic literature, so I suspect it's here in error or from whimsy. And did we mention that her family was rich? Why Ms. Miriam was so rich that she had a daily perfume allowance. And it, too, was a tidy sum of *Gelt*.

But, what truly makes me laugh is that twentieth-century Jewish historians (best left unnamed), writing about the siege of Jerusalem, note with apparently straight faces how the women of Jerusalem were taken captive and marched away with their hair tied to the tails of their Roman conqueror's horses. Where they see "just the facts, ma'am," I see a game of storytelling telephone gone awry. Let's add the image of the "girl foraging behind the horses" to the image of the "young woman covering herself with her hair." We have here a case of 2 + 2 = 5. The different details of the story lead this Talmudic tale to a bizarre conclusion about what the girl and her hair were doing behind that horse. Of course, given that the alternative is sifting through the dung for a meal, maybe it's not so bad that she's now fit to be tied.

Tall Tales

We have now meandered through a series of stories about Rabbi Yohanan (or someone like him) and a woman foraging for food in the aftermath of the siege of Jerusalem. These narratives illustrate the biblical theme of "how the mighty have fallen," or if you prefer it in American parlance, "from riches to rags." During the past twenty chapters we have stayed reasonably focused on Yohanan and company. I chose them because there are stories, folktales, legends, and lore associated with them at that seminal moment of Jewish history. But like the tales told about Founding Fathers of American history, not all the tales are necessarily factual (e.g., "I cannot tell a lie. I chopped down the cherry tree"). Nevertheless, they do teach us the common morality and ethos of the emerging rabbinic sensibility (like Washington's father's supposed reply, "My son, that you should not be afraid to tell the truth is more to me than a thousand trees, though they were blossomed with silver and had leaves of the purest gold!").

The rabbis were great masters of Jewish law. They debated and prescribed behaviors to replace the destroyed Jerusalem Temple and its moribund cult. But they found, as do all great teachers, that stories draw the heart more readily than do the dictates of the law. And so, with a combination of storytelling and interpretation of God's commandments, they set about to find a middle path for Jews to walk, a balance by which to survive the end of the sacrificial cult and the traumatic razing of God's capital. Finding that middle road took constant negotiation and adjustment, as we will see in our final chapter.

22 / ת

The End:
We Hope

The sage tales we have been reading were edited into the forms we have them over a long period of time. The earliest rabbinic texts were compiled in the early third century, and the latest texts we have quoted in this book date from the ninth century. During that period of more than half a millennium, Jews in the Land of Israel experienced pagan Roman rule, Christian rule, and Muslim rule. Jews in Babylonia went from Sasanian Zoroastrian rulers to Parthian overlords and, finally, also lived under Muslim rule (albeit not the same Islamic authority). Throughout this lengthy period, rabbis in these two centers of Jewish life reacted differently, generation by generation, and sometimes rabbi by rabbi, to relations with their overlords. Attitudes toward the imperial other varied widely.

Much of Jewish life was focused inward. Yet here, too, Jews differed on what constituted Jewish identity, on norms of behavior both ethical and ritual, and on spiritual matters. There were some constants within the rabbinic world. Adherence to God's commandments was one of those constants, even as differing rabbis in varying locales debated the details of observance of those divine laws. And, as we have seen now in abundance in this book, the other constant in Jewish life was the power of stories to teach moral lessons and Jewish self-definition. Attitudes about leadership, charity, study, wealth, miracles, and tragedies were among the themes reflected in the narratives the rabbis performed for their students and rapt audiences.

On occasion, the rabbis told stories about the particular observance of a commandment. These tales limned the parameters of behavior in the Jewish community: what was right and what went too far; what might express identity and what became impossible as a standard of behavior. In this, the discussion resembles the ongoing debate and dialogue among various factions of the Jewish community even today. When we turn to the telling of these tales at the very outset of the rabbinic enterprise following the fall of Jerusalem in 70 CE, we understand that the stakes were much higher. Where to draw the line in piety, and how we represent that process of even finding that line, served as a rhetoric of identity formation for rabbinic Jews. The stories we tell teach us who we are and to what we aspire.

> Rabbi Ishmael said, "From the day the Temple was destroyed, by rights we Jews should no longer eat meat nor drink wine, as an expression of mourning for our lost Sanctuary. Yet it is our principle that the rabbinic court should not enact decrees upon the Jews that they will not observe."
>
> He also said, "Since the Romans have uprooted Torah from amongst us through their decrees, we no longer have a raison d'être. So we should decree an end to Judaism! Let no man marry a wife or bear children. Let there no longer be circumcision ceremonies, until the seed of Abraham run its course and is no more."
>
> They said to him, "It is better that the Jews continue in error than that you make such decrees and they continue their behavior in defiance of rabbinic law."
>
> (TOSEFTA SOTA 15:10–15)

This story tells us about a thwarted rabbi, a would-be lawmaker who understands that there are genuine constraints on his rabbinic power. He theorizes that it would be appropriate to decree perpetual mourning on the Jewish people over the loss of Jerusalem and the Temple cult. Much of the Torah comes to naught with the loss of that central shrine. Virtually the entire biblical book of Leviticus is in abeyance, absent a sacrificial altar in Jerusalem. And so, Rabbi Akiva's contemporary Rabbi Ishmael wistfully wishes he could command and all would obey his severe demand for asceticism as a response to Rome's destruction of Jerusalem. But, he is all too realistic. No one would obey such a rabbinic enactment. Folks like to eat a burger now and then. And red wine is good for you, Rabbi. So Rabbi Ishmael admits defeat. He and his colleagues are wise enough not to undermine their own power by demanding things that their Jewish followers will never do.

It's almost as though his bowing to reality makes him even more romantic about giving it all up. Rabbi Ishmael lived in the mid-second century CE, well after the destruction of the Temple, but contemporary with the next failed war against Rome. The utter disaster of what is called the Bar Kokhba rebellion, from 132 to 135 CE, resulted in the deaths of tens of thousands of Jews and their exile from Judea to the Galilee. Jerusalem was now lost, it seemed, forever. And Rome legislated against religious practices that defined Judaism for the rabbis, such as circumcision. Rabbi Ishmael woefully seeks to throw in the towel. No more marriage, no more babies, no more circumcision, no more Jews! His rhetoric is a tad over the top, wouldn't you say? Thankfully, the anonymous "they" remind him not to decree any really stupid enactments. It is better that Jews sin in ignorance than to have rabbis making decrees they willfully ignore. In rabbinic thinking, ignorance of the law *is* an excuse. Sometimes it's better for a rabbi to keep his mouth shut than it is to drive away his congregants.

This extreme rhetoric puts into the mouth of a prominent rabbi the dilemma Jews faced after the two failed wars against Rome. The old system was over, and it would not ever be the same again. Further, rabbinic Judaism was just in the process of establishing itself. These stories were told to remind everyone what the stakes were and how much compromise was necessary. That there would be no more Temple was terrible to contemplate. That Jerusalem was razed to its foundations and rebuilt as a pagan capital was awful to behold. That Jews were exiled within their own land so that they could no longer step foot in the Holy City left them inconsolable. But these stories and their cautious reinvention of a different form of Judaism were their hope against the possibility of Judaism disappearing forever.

Foolish Piety

This was the battle they fought: hope against despair. This was why they told their sage tales, to buttress faith in the future, even as they were inventing the very architecture of the refurbished sanctuary that was rabbinic Judaism. Story and law, narrative and *nomos*, served as the builders' stones that would hold the edifice firm. When the Holy City and the Jerusalem Temple lay in smoldering rubble, the rabbis imitated God, who created the world through speech. Rabbinic Judaism would be a religion of words, legal pronouncements, and capacious narrative.

> When the last Temple was destroyed, separatists multiplied among the Jews, who would not eat meat or drink wine. Rabbi Yehoshua dealt with them.
>
> He said, "My children, why do you not eat meat?"
>
> They replied, "Shall we eat meat, which was offered daily as a perpetual sacrifice upon the altar, but it is no more!"
>
> He said, "Fine, we shall not eat meat. But why do you not drink wine?"
>
> They replied, "Shall we drink wine, which was daily poured as a libation upon the altar, but it is no more!"
>
> He said to them, "Fine, we shall not drink it. But if so, perhaps we should not eat bread, for they brought two ceremonial loaves and the showbread in the Temple. And perhaps we should not drink water, which was also poured as a libation upon the altar. And then we should not eat figs or grapes, which were brought as first fruit offerings at Pentecost."
>
> They were silenced.
>
> (*TOSEFTA SOTA* 15:10–15)

In our story, we have leapt backward in time, some fifty years earlier. The scene is set directly after the destruction of Jerusalem, at a time when mourning the Temple loomed large and despair was a constant companion to both physical and spiritual hunger. With the loss of the cult, there were many pietists who, lacking an altar, found new ascetic rigors to feel holier than thou. This inclination to religious extremism rears its ugly head in every generation. In the aftermath of the destruction, Rabbi Yohanan ben Zakkai's great disciple Rabbi Yehoshua ben Hananiah takes in hand those who would engage in the downward spiral of perpetual mourning.

Note the resignation of the narrator. He opens by saying, "When the *last* Temple was destroyed." Already by the early third century when this story was being told, the rabbis had reconciled to the loss of cult and Temple. Elsewhere, the rabbis speak of the destruction of the First Temple (in 586 BCE) and the destruction of the Second Temple (in 70 CE). But here there is no apparent wish for any immediate rebuilding. No more desire for a destructive war leading to a messianic restoration of a Davidic king. Rabbinic Judaism became a religion of reconciliation. No longer a sacrificial cult, Judaism was now a religion of the Book, of Torah study, of rabbinic interpretation of the law, and of repeated performances of the stories that reified the rabbinic enterprise. The "last Temple" was destroyed; long live rabbinic Judaism!

To appreciate this sea change, it helps to do some historical calculation. This story is told about Rabbi Yehoshua coming on stage right after the destruction of Jerusalem in 70 CE, true. But it is found in a collection that was edited about 220 CE. One hundred fifty years is a long time in passing. If I were to tell you such a tale today, it would have to be a story with all the immediacy of the Civil War. Now it is true that there are those, especially Southerners, for whom the Civil War is still being fought. And it is true that there are those like me, from Illinois, for whom President Lincoln still speaks. But by and large the Civil War is the domain of reenactors, tourists, and schoolchildren. Nevertheless, we make reference to "the better angels of our nature" precisely to recapture Lincoln's ethos and greatness.

So, too, our tale of Rabbi Yehoshua and his teetotalers. He surely appreciates their need to mourn. Yet he is mindful of behaviors that lead to a fragmented Jewish community at a time of mortal danger to the body politic. The rabbis are accordingly cautious about going too far. And so, Rabbi Yehoshua engages those ultra-pious Jews in a bit of *reductio ad absurdum*. One imagines the staging of this scene à la Tom Stoppard's *Rosencrantz and Guildenstern Are Dead*. Witty repartee leaving the antagonist in tatters and the audience in titters. Okay to no wine or meat, but what about bread? Fruit? Water? If you really want piety, you ought to starve! Fade to black.

A Golden Mean

The extremists are, of course, silenced in this theatrical argument. After all, the story is told by the rabbis, who not only back their hero but also back moderation. You may recall that when Yehoshua's teacher Rabbi Yohanan ben Zakkai argued with Vespasian, he, too, was silenced. For rabbinic Jews, silence is defeat; it spells the end of dialogue. Having caused the separatists loss of face, Rabbi Yehoshua seeks to engage them once more, but with a nod to the *via media*. Here is his suggestion of how to get on with daily life in the face of such a soul-shattering loss.

> He said to them, "My children, it is not permissible to mourn excessively. Yet neither is it permissible to not mourn at all. Rather, this is what our sages suggest: 'You should paint your house with lime, but leave a small patch unpainted, as a remembrance of Jerusalem. You should prepare all the dishes for a banquet, yet refrain from serving one, as a remembrance of Jerusalem. And a woman should put on her jewelry, yet remove a piece, as a remembrance of Jerusalem.' As it is said, 'If I forget you, Jerusalem, may my right hand wither; may my tongue stick to my palate if I do not remember you, if I do not place Jerusalem above my highest joy' [Psalm 137:5–6]. For all who mourn Jerusalem will merit seeing her joy, as it is said, 'Rejoice with Jerusalem and be glad for her, all who love her; all who mourned her will rejoice with her!' [Isaiah 66:10]."
>
> (TOSEFTA SOTA 15:10–15)

Rabbi Yehoshua counsels reason. It is a dangerous thing to give yourself over to excessive mourning and piety. Such extremism yields bitterness and breeds hatred for those with whom you must learn to coexist. He suggests that to foster cooperation, we need to find ways to commemorate Jerusalem in the quotidian, that the memory of her may never leave you. Rabbi Yehoshua almost literally tells them (and so, us) to find a middle way. Don't leave it behind, but don't let it consume you.

Even today in certain Jewish households it is possible to find an unpainted patch of wall commemorating Jerusalem's destruction almost two thousand years ago. You might have to peek behind a picture frame, but there is that unadorned bit of wall, commemorating Jerusalem. My mother, may she rest in peace, was famous for throwing a fabulous dinner party and, when all the guests had gone home, finding the green beans or some other vegetable she forgot to serve. A senior moment? Perhaps, but I prefer to think it was in commemoration of Jerusalem. And wasn't it Jackie Kennedy who counseled women to put on their jewelry for the evening and then remove one piece? They said it was elegant fashion advice, but I prefer to think it was in commemoration of Jerusalem.

O Jerusalem

The first time I stepped foot in Jerusalem was in early July 1967, one month after Israel's stunning victory in the Six-Day War. I was on a Jewish teen tour, which at the end of six weeks of wide-eyed wonder had its culmination by bringing us to visit the Wailing Wall on the ninth of Av. This date commemorates the destruction of both the First and Second Temples, as we learned when we read the stories of Vespasian and Titus. It has always been a somber day of semi-mourning, fasting, and lamentation. But 9 Av in the year 1967 CE was, in the newly reunited Jerusalem, a day of carnival-like celebration. Even I, at the tender age of fifteen, saw long-lost friends there standing before the Wall. It seemed like everyone I knew was there, and everyone had the same rabbinic adage on his or her lips: "All who mourn Jerusalem will merit seeing her joy."

For Muslim Arabs, Jerusalem is also a holy city, al-Quds. And Jerusalem holds sacred status for Christians, too. This is an instance where physical real estate does not conform to the mental map of the three Abrahamic religions, each with its own overlay of sacrosanct cartography. We pray for the possibility that all peoples can celebrate Jerusalem as their holy city, their sacred shrine, as one. In the meanwhile, modern Jerusalem builds, ever more divided. And the Jerusalem that we might all share seems to recede ever upwards into the firmament, as Heavenly Jerusalem. That Jerusalem is one on which all can pin their hopes and prayers. For the Heavenly Jerusalem, unlike the one here on earth, is truly eternal, and truly a city for all God's creatures.

As for earthly Jerusalem, I fear we may need Elijah to visit us once more, this time in his role as forerunner to the Messiah. As the prophet says, "Behold, I will send Elijah the prophet to you in advance of the coming great and awesome Day of the Lord" (Malachi 3:23). Until that great and awesome day, we console ourselves with stories. We mourn our losses and we remember our joys through our telling of tales. Whatever your Jerusalem may be—a place, an idea, a sense of self, a spiritual journey—tell your sage tales and rejoice. All of us who love Jerusalem: rejoice and hope.

Appendix 1

The Complete Texts

1 / א Elijah the Prophet

Rav Kahana was reduced by poverty to selling wicker baskets in the women's marketplace. There, a matron importuned him for sexual favors. He said, "Wait, while I go make myself pretty for you." He went up to the roof and flung himself to the ground, rather than succumb to his libidinous urges. Elijah came and caught him. Elijah said to Rav Kahana, "You've troubled me to travel four hundred miles to catch you." Kahana replied, "And what caused me to be sitting here in the marketplace open to temptation? Was it not my poverty?" So Elijah gave him a jar of gold coins.

(BABYLONIAN TALMUD, *KIDDUSHIN* 40A)

Once upon a time the Jews wished to send a bribe to the court of Caesar. They wondered who to send and settled on Nahum of Gimzo, who was experienced in miracles. They sent him with a sack of precious gems and pearls in hand. On the way he stayed at an inn. During the night the innkeepers took what was in his bag and filled it with dust. When Nahum got to the court of the Caesar and they opened the sack and saw it was full of dust, they wanted to kill everyone, for Caesar said, "The Jews are mocking me!"

Elijah appeared to them in the guise of one of their royal courtiers and suggested, "Perhaps that dust is the dust of their ancestor Abraham, who when he threw dust, it turned into swords, and when he threw straw, it turned into arrows, as it is written in Scripture, 'His sword is like the dust, his bow like the wind-driven straw' [Isaiah 41:2]."

There was a city that Caesar had been unable to conquer. He tried the dust and captured the city! So he took Nahum into his treasury, filled the sack with precious gems and pearls, and sent him home with great honors.

When Nahum returned to the inn, the innkeepers asked, "What did you bring him that you are given such honor?" Nahum replied, "What I took from here, I brought there." They demolished the inn and brought it to the court of Caesar. They said, "That dust that he brought you, it was ours!" They tried the dust, but of course it didn't work. So they executed those innkeepers.

(BABYLONIAN TALMUD, *TAANIT* 21A)

Rabbi Akiva, a poor shepherd, betrothed the daughter of Ben Kalba Savua, a very rich man. When he heard about their impending marriage, her father vowed to disinherit her. It was winter when they married, and they had nothing but straw for their bedding. Rabbi Akiva said to his bride, "If I could, I would adorn you with a tiara of gold, shaped like the skyline of Jerusalem."

Elijah came to them in the guise of a poor man. He begged them for a bit of straw, "My wife is about to give birth and she has nothing to rest upon."

Akiva said to his wife, "See, here is a man who doesn't even have straw …"

(BABYLONIAN TALMUD, *NEDARIM* 50A)

2/ב The Cast of Characters

Moses received the Torah at Sinai and transmitted it to Joshua. From Joshua to the Elders; from the Elders to the Prophets; and the Prophets transmitted it to the Men of the Great Assembly.... Shimeon the Righteous was among the remnant of the Great Assembly.... Antigonus of Sokho received the tradition from Shimeon.... Yosé ben Yoezer of Tzeraidah and Yosé ben Yohanan of Jerusalem received the tradition from them.... Hillel and Shammai received the tradition from them....

Rabbi Yohanan ben Zakkai received the tradition from Hillel and Shammai. He used to say, "If you have studied much Torah, don't claim merit for yourself, for you were created to do so." Rabbi Yohanan ben Zakkai had five disciples. These are they: Rabbi Eliezer ben Hyrcanus, Rabbi Yehoshua ben Hananiah, Rabbi José the Priest, Rabbi Shimeon ben Netanel, and Rabbi Elazar ben Arakh.

He recounted their virtues: "Eliezer ben Hyrcanus is a lime-plastered cistern that doesn't lose a drop; Yehoshua ben Hananiah: happy is she who bore him! José the Priest is pious; and Shimeon ben Netanel fears sin; while Elazar ben Arakh is an overflowing wellspring."

He used to say, "If all of the sages of Israel were on one scale of the balance and Eliezer ben Hyrcanus were on the other scale, he would outweigh them all."

But Abba Saul quoted in his name, "If all of the sages of Israel were on one scale of the balance, and even if Eliezer ben Hyrcanus were among them, Elazar ben Arakh would outweigh them all."

He asked his disciples, "Go forth and see: what is the good way that a man should adhere to?"

Rabbi Eliezer said, "A good eye."

Rabbi Yehoshua said, "A good colleague."

Rabbi José said, "A good neighbor."

Rabbi Shimeon said, "The one who sees that which is born."

Rabbi Elazar said, "A good heart."

He said to them, "I prefer the words of Elazar ben Arakh, for his words include your words."

He asked his disciples, "Go forth and see: what is the bad way from which a man should distance himself?"

Rabbi Eliezer said, "A bad eye."

Rabbi Yehoshua said, "A bad colleague."

Rabbi José said, "A bad neighbor."

Rabbi Shimeon said, "The one who borrows and does not repay." One who borrows from a human is like one who borrows from the Omnipresent, as it is said, "The wicked borrows and does not repay, while the righteous gives generously" (Psalm 37:21).

Rabbi Elazar said, "A bad heart."

He said to them, "I prefer the words of Elazar ben Arakh, for his words include your words."

They each said three things.

Rabbi Eliezer said, "Let your friend's honor be as dear to you as your own. Do not easily anger. Repent one day before your death. Warm yourself at the hearth of the sages, but be wary not to get scorched by their coals; for their bite is the bite of a fox, their sting is the sting of a scorpion, and their hiss is the hiss of an asp. All of their words are like fiery coals!"

Rabbi Yehoshua said, "A bad eye, a bad libido, and misanthropy remove a person from the world."

Rabbi José said, "Let your friend's money be as dear to you as your own. Prepare yourself to study Torah, for it is not automatically bequeathed to you. Let all your doings be in God's name."

Rabbi Shimeon said, "Be punctilious in the recitation of the *Shema* and in the Prayer. When you pray, do not pray by rote, but address God in supplication and desire for mercy; as it is said, 'For God is gracious and compassionate, slow to anger, abounding in kindness, and renouncing punishment' [Joel 2:13]. Do not consider yourself evil."

Rabbi Elazar said, "Be diligent to study Torah. Know what to reply to Epicurus. Know before whom you labor, who is the Master of your labors who will reward you for your deeds."

Rabbi Tarphon said, "It is not yours to complete the task, but neither are you free to abandon it."

(*PIRKE AVOT* 1–2)

3/ב A Story Well Told Is Worth Retelling

A story is told about a gentile who came to Shammai and said to him, "Convert me, but on the condition that you can teach me the entire Torah while I stand on one foot."

Shammai repelled him with the builder's cubit in his hand.

He came to Hillel, who converted him. Hillel said to him, "Don't do anything to a friend that you hate yourself. This is the entire Torah. The rest is commentary. Go study." (Babylonian Talmud, *Shabbat* 31a)

Rabbi Yohanan ben Zakkai had five disciples. He gave them each nicknames. He called Eliezer ben Hyrcanus a limed cistern that does not lose a drop, a pitch-coated amphora that preserves its wine. He called Yehoshua ben Hananiah "a three-fold cord not easily broken" (Ecclesiastes 4:12). José the Priest he called a pious one of his generation. Shimeon ben Netanel he called a succulent plant in the wilderness that holds fast to its water. Blessed is the disciple whose master compliments him and testifies about him. He called Elazar ben Arakh a flowing stream and an overflowing wellspring whose waters overflow outside, to fulfill that which is written, "Your wellsprings will gush forth in streams in the public squares" (Proverbs 5:16).

(Avot DeRabbi Nathan A, chap. 14)

4 / ד On Loan

When Rabbi Yohanan ben Zakkai's son died, his students came to comfort him. Rabbi Eliezer entered and sat before him, saying, "Rabbi, may I say something to you?" Rabbi Yohanan replied, "Speak."

He told him, "Adam had a son who died and he accepted comfort. Where does Scripture speak of his accepting comfort? As it is said, 'Adam again knew his wife' [Genesis 4:25]. So too, you should find comfort."

He replied, "Is it not enough that I have my own troubles that you remind me of the sorrows of Adam?"

Rabbi Yehoshua entered and said to him, "May I say something to you?" He said, "Speak."

He told him, "Job's sons and daughters all perished on the same day, and yet he was comforted for his loss of them. You, too, should find comfort. Where does Scripture speak of his accepting comfort? As it is said, 'The Lord gives and the Lord takes away, blessed be the name of the Lord' [Job 1:21]."

He replied, "Is it not enough that I have my own troubles that you remind me of the sorrows of Job?"

Rabbi José entered and sat before him, saying, "Rabbi, may I say something to you?" Rabbi Yohanan replied, "Speak."

He told him, "Aaron had two adult sons who both died on the same day. Yet he was comforted, as it is said, 'Aaron was silent'

[Leviticus 10:3]. Silence here means comfort, so you, too, should be comforted."

He replied, "Is it not enough that I have my own troubles that you remind me of the sorrows of Aaron?"

Rabbi Shimeon entered and said to him, "May I say something to you?" He said, "Speak."

He said, "King David had a son who died and he was comforted, so you, too, should be comforted. Where does Scripture speak of David receiving comfort? As it is said, 'David comforted his wife Bat Sheva, he came unto her and lay with her. She gave birth and called the child Solomon' [2 Samuel 12:24]. So you, Rabbi, should accept comfort."

He replied, "Is it not enough that I have my own troubles that you remind me of the sorrows of King David?"

Rabbi Elazar ben Arakh entered. When Yohanan saw him he told his servant, "Gather my clothing and prepare to follow me to the bathhouse; for Rabbi Elazar is a great man and I shall not withstand him."

Elazar entered and sat down before Yohanan. He said to him, "I will give you an analogy. This is like a man with whom the king has entrusted a deposit of some value. Each and every day that man would wail and moan, 'Oy for the time that I will return this deposit in peace and fullness!' So you, Rabbi, had a son. He studied Torah: Pentateuch, Prophets, Writings, Mishnah, Laws, and Narrative. And he departed this world without sin. You should take comfort that you have returned your deposit in peace and fullness."

Rabbi Yohanan said to him, "Elazar, my son, you have comforted me like a Mensch."

When they left Yohanan, Elazar said, "I will go to Damasit, a place of beauty with pleasant and beautiful waters."

The other four disciples said, "We will go to Yavneh, a place where so many disciples of the sages love the Torah."

He who went to Damasit, the place of beauty with pleasant and beautiful waters, his name diminished in Torah. They who went to Yavneh, the place where so many disciples of the sages love the Torah, their names were exalted in Torah.

(AVOT DERABBI NATHAN A, CHAP. 14)

5 / ה The Woman of Valor

"A woman of valor, who can find?" (Proverbs 31:10) They told a tale of Rabbi Meir who was sitting and expounding in the study house one Shabbat afternoon when his two sons died. What did their mother do? She rested the two of them upon the bed and spread a sheet over them. When Shabbat had ended Rabbi Meir returned home from the study house. He asked, "Where are my two boys?"

She told him, "They went to the study house."

He replied, "I looked for them at the study house, but I didn't see them."

She gave him a cup of wine to pronounce the blessings for ending Shabbat, and he recited them. He asked again, "Where are my two sons?"

She said, "Sometimes they go to some Place; they're on their way now." She put dinner before him and he ate. After he had recited the blessings following the meal, she said to him, "Rabbi, I have a question to ask."

He said to her, "Ask your question."

She asked, "Rabbi, earlier a man came and left me something on deposit. Now he has come to collect that deposit. Shall we return it or not?"

He said, "My daughter, is it not clear that one who is entrusted with a deposit must return it to its master!"

She said, "I wouldn't have returned it without your consent." What did she do? She took him by his hand, led him up to that room, brought him close to the bed, and removed the sheet from them. He saw the two of them lying dead upon the bed and began to weep.

He said, "My sons, my sons, my rabbis, my rabbis! My sons by nature, but my rabbis in that they enlightened me with their Torah."

At that time she said to Rabbi Meir, "Rabbi, did you not tell me that we must return the deposit to its Master? Thus it says, 'The Lord gives and the Lord takes away. Blessed be the name of the Lord' [Job 1:21]."

Rabbi Hannina said, "With these words she comforted him and settled his mind. That is why it says, 'A woman of valor, who can find?' [Proverbs 31:10]."

(*Midrash Mishle* 31)

6/ז How a Boy Became a Rabbi

A tale is told of Rabbi Eliezer ben Hyrcanus, whose father had plow-men who would plow the furrow, while Eliezer plowed the stony hillocks. He sat and wept. His father asked him, "Why do you cry? Perhaps you are upset that you are plowing the stony hillocks? Now, go plow the furrow."

Eliezer sat upon the furrow and wept. His father asked him, "Now why do you cry? Are you upset at having to plow the furrow?" He replied, "No."

He asked, "So why do you cry?"

Eliezer said, "Because I want to learn Torah."

His father replied, "Look, you are twenty-eight years old! *Now* you want to study Torah? Get yourself a wife, have kids, take *them* to school!"

Eliezer went for two weeks without eating a thing, until Elijah— may he be remembered for good—appeared to him. He said, "Son of Hyrcanus, why do you cry?"

Eliezer said, "Because I want to learn Torah."

Elijah said, "If you wish to study Torah, go up to Jerusalem to Rabbi Yohanan ben Zakkai."

Eliezer arose and went up to Jerusalem to Rabbi Yohanan ben Zakkai. He sat and wept.

Yohanan asked him, "Why do you cry?"

He replied, "Because I want to learn Torah!"

Yohanan asked him, "Whose son are you?" But he did not tell him. Yohanan then asked, "In all your days have you not learned to recite the *Shema*, or the Prayer, or the Blessing after Meals?"

He replied, "No."

Yohanan said, "Arise and I will teach you all three."

He sat and wept.

He asked him, "My son, why do you cry?"

He answered, "Because I want to learn Torah!"

So Yohanan recited two laws of Mishnah each day of the week, and Eliezer would review them until they stuck. Eliezer went eight days without eating a thing, until the smell from his mouth came to Rabbi Yohanan ben Zakkai's attention. Then he stood away from him. Eliezer sat and wept.

Yohanan asked him, "Why do you cry?"

He replied, "Because you stood away from me as though I were covered in boils!"

Yohanan said, "My son, just as the scent of your breath has come to my notice, so may the savor of the laws of the Torah ascend from your mouth to heaven."

He asked, "My son, whose son are you?"

He confessed, "I am the son of Hyrcanus."

Yohanan exclaimed, "Are you not the son of one of the great men of the world! By your life, today you will dine with me!"

Eliezer replied, "I already ate at my hostel."

Yohanan asked, "And who, then, are your hosts?"

He said, "Rabbi Yehoshua ben Hananiah and Rabbi José the Priest."

Rabbi Yohanan sent a messenger and asked the hosts, "Did Eliezer eat with you today?"

They replied, "No. It's been eight days since he tasted anything."

After that Rabbi Yehoshua ben Hananiah and Rabbi José the Priest went themselves to tell Rabbi Yohanan ben Zakkai, "It's been eight days since he tasted anything."

(*PIRKE RABBI ELIEZER* 1)

7/ז Meanwhile Back at the Ranch

Hyrcanus's sons said to their father, "Go up to Jerusalem and disown your son Eliezer from your properties."

When he went up to Jerusalem to disown him, he found a festive banquet taking place honoring Rabbi Yohanan ben Zakkai. All the powerful men of the city were banqueting there: Ben Tzitzit HaKeset, Nicodemus ben Gurion, and Ben Kalba Savua.

Why was he called Ben Tzitzit HaKeset? Because he reclined at banquet above the powerful men of Jerusalem. They said of Nicodemus ben Gurion that he had three bushels of flour to feed each and every inhabitant of Jerusalem. About Ben Kalba Savua they said that he had a house of four acres of gardens overlaid with gold.

They said to Rabbi Yohanan, "Look, here comes Rabbi Eliezer's father."

He said, "Make a place for him"; so they made a place, sitting him next to Rabbi Yohanan. Yohanan looked over at Rabbi Eliezer and asked him, "Say a word of Torah for us."

He replied, "Rabbi, let me give you an analogy for what this is like. It's like a cistern from which one cannot draw more water than what has been put into it. So I cannot say any more Torah but that which I have learned from you."

Rabbi Yohanan replied, "Let me give *you* an analogy for what this is like. It's like a wellspring that gushes water and has the power to give forth more than has been stored in the well. So you can say more Torah than what they received at Sinai."

Rabbi Yohanan said to Eliezer, "Maybe you are shy in my presence? Allow me to stand away from you."

Rabbi Yohanan stood and went outside, so that Rabbi Eliezer could sit and expound. His face beamed like sunlight, rays of light emanating like those that shone from Moses's face, until one could not tell if it were day or night. Rabbi Yohanan came back in behind Eliezer and kissed him on the head. He said, "Happy are you Abraham, Isaac, and Jacob, that this one is your offspring!"

Hyrcanus asked, "To whom do you say this?"

They told him, "To Eliezer, your son!"

He replied, "He should not have said this; but happy am *I* that he is my offspring!"

Rabbi Eliezer was sitting and expounding while his father was standing. When Eliezer noticed his father there, he was nonplussed. He said, "Father, sit, for I cannot speak words of Torah while you are standing!"

Hyrcanus replied, "Son, I did not come to hear you preach, but to disown you from my properties. But now that I've come to see you and observed all this praise, your brothers are disowned from the property, and they are given over to you as a gift!"

Eliezer said, "But I am not as worthy as they are. Furthermore, if I were to desire real estate, it would be up to God to provide me, as it is said, 'The earth is the Lord's, and all the fullness thereof, the world and all who dwell there' [Psalm 24:1]. And were I to desire silver and gold, it would be up to God to provide me, as it is said, 'Mine is the silver and the gold, declares the Lord of Hosts' [Haggai 2:8]. All I wish from God is Torah, as it is said, 'Thus I love Your commandments more than gold, even fine gold' [Psalm 119:127]."

(Pirke Rabbi Eliezer 2)

8 / ח Road Trip with Fireworks

The story is told that Rabbi Yohanan ben Zakkai was riding his donkey on a journey. Rabbi Elazar was driving the donkey, walking behind it. Elazar asked, "Rabbi, would you recite a chapter of the works of the Chariot for me?"

Yohanan replied, "Did I not teach you the mishnah that 'one may not explore the works of the Chariot with any other person, unless he is a sage who can understand it through his own knowledge'?"

Elazar countered, "Rabbi, permit me to say one thing that you taught me."

Rabbi Yohanan replied, "Speak." At that, Rabbi Yohanan immediately got down off the donkey, wrapped himself in his cloak, and sat upon a rock beneath an olive tree.

Elazar asked him, "Rabbi, why did you get off of your donkey?"

Yohanan replied, "Is it right that I should remain on my donkey while you explore the works of the Chariot? God's Presence will be among us, and the ministering angels will accompany us!"

Elazar immediately opened the works of the Chariot and expounded. Fire came down from heaven and surrounded all of the trees in the field. They all burst into song. What did they sing? "Praise God from the earth, sea monsters and all the depths ... fruit trees and all the cedars say ... 'Hallelujah!' (Psalm 148)."

An angel answered from amidst the flames, "These, yes, yes, these are the works of the Chariot!"

Rabbi Yohanan stood and kissed Elazar on the head. Yohanan said, "Blessed is God, the Lord of Israel, who gave such a son to Abraham our father; for he knows how to understand, and investigate, and expound upon the works of the Chariot. There are those who preach well, yet they do not practice. There are those who practice well, but they cannot preach. You practice what you preach! Happy are you, Abraham our father, that Elazar ben Arakh is your offspring!"

(BABYLONIAN TALMUD, HAGIGAH 14B)

9/ט Anything He Can Do, I Can Do, Too

When these things were reported to Rabbi Yehoshua, he and Rabbi José the Priest were on a journey. They said, "Let us also investigate the works of the Chariot."

Rabbi Yehoshua opened and expounded. Now that day was midsummer, yet the sky became knotted with clouds and something like a rainbow appeared in the clouds. The ministering angels came a-mustering to hear, like folks who come to watch the entertainment of a bride and groom.

(BABYLONIAN TALMUD, HAGIGAH 14B)

10/י I Had a Dream ... I've Been to the Mountaintop

Rabbi José the Priest went and spoke of these matters to Rabbi Yohanan. To which Rabbi Yohanan said, "Happy are you and happy are they who gave birth to you! Happy are my eyes that have seen such! I had a dream. Indeed, I and you were reclining at a banquet on Mount Sinai. A voice, an echo came from heaven and said, 'Come up here! Come up here! There are great banquet tables spread with delicate foods for you. You, and your students, and your students' students are invited up to first class!'"

(BABYLONIAN TALMUD, HAGIGAH 14B)

11 / ב Paradise Ain't All It's Cracked Up to Be

It was recited by our rabbis: Four entered paradise.

They are Ben Azzai, and Ben Zoma, the Other, and Rabbi Akiva.

Rabbi Akiva said to them, "When you arrive at the pure marble stones, do not say, 'Water, water!' for it is said, 'He who speaks falsehoods will not stand before My eyes' [Psalm 101:7]."

Ben Azzai glimpsed and died. Scripture says of him, "The death of God's beloved is grievous in the eyes of the Lord" (Psalm 116:15).

Ben Zoma glimpsed and was smitten. Scripture says of him, "Did you find honey? Eat only what you need, lest you grow too full and vomit it" (Proverbs 25:16).

The Other chopped the sprouts.

Rabbi Akiva went out in peace.

(Babylonian Talmud, *Hagigah* 14b)

Once Shimeon ben Zoma was standing bewildered. Rabbi Yehoshua passed by and asked after his health, once, then again, but he did not reply. On the third attempt, Ben Zoma replied in confusion. Yehoshua asked him, "What is this Ben Zoma? Where are your feet?"

He replied, "Nothing from nothing, Rabbi."

Yehoshua said, "I swear by heaven and earth, I am not moving from here until you tell me where your feet are."

Ben Zoma explained, "I was speculating on the works of Creation, and it seemed to me that there is no more than two or three fingersbreadth between the upper and lower waters. Further, Genesis does not say, 'And God's wind blows,' but rather, 'God's spirit hovers' [Genesis 1:2]—which is to say it hovers like a bird hovers just over its nest as it lands, flapping its wings. And the wings do not quite touch the nest as it hovers."

Rabbi Yehoshua turned and said to his students, "Ben Zoma has gone!"

In but a few days, Ben Zoma had left the world.

(*Genesis Rabbah* 2:4)

12 / ל The Siege

Our House [the Temple] was destroyed, our Sanctuary was burned; we were exiled from our land. He sent the caesar Nero against them. As he came, Nero shot an arrow to the east; it landed on Jerusalem. To the west; it landed on Jerusalem. To all four points of the compass; it landed on Jerusalem.

Nero asked a child, "Tell me the verse of Scripture you are studying." The child said, "I will wreak My vengeance upon Edom, through the hand of My people Israel" (Ezekiel 25:14).

Nero reasoned, "The Blessed Holy One seeks to destroy His house and then wipe His hands on that man."

So he fled and went and converted to Judaism. His descendant was Rabbi Meir.

He sent the caesar Vespasian against them. He came and besieged them for three years. Within Jerusalem there were three rich men: Nicodemus ben Gurion, Ben Kalba Savua, and Ben Tzitzit HaKeset.

Nicodemus ben Gurion, for the sun broke through [nakdah] on his behalf. Ben Kalba Savua, for all who enter his house as hungry as a dog [keleb] leave sated [savua]. Ben Tzitzit HaKeset, whose ritual fringes [tzitzit] dragged upon throw pillows [kesatot]. There are those who say that his cushion for reclining at a banquet [kisato] was placed among those of the great men of Rome.

One of the rich men told the besieged Jerusalemites, "I will provide you all with wheat and barley." Another said, "Wine, and salt, and oil." Yet another said, "Kindling." The sages praised the one who offered kindling, for Rav Hisda used to give over all the keys of his estate to his servant except for the key to the woodshed, for Rav Hisda used to say that every storeroom of wheat required sixty storerooms of kindling. They had enough provision to feed the besieged Jerusalemites for twenty-one years!

Among them there were thugs. The rabbis said to them, "Let us go out and make peace with the Romans." But those thugs did not permit them to do so. The thugs said, "We will go out and make war upon them." The rabbis said, "The matter will not have support (from heaven).” So those thugs arose and burned the storehouses of wheat and barley, and famine ensued.

(Babylonian Talmud, Gittin 56a)

13 / מ Comic Relief

Martha bat Boethius, the rich woman of Jerusalem, sent for her messenger and told him, “Go, bring me fine flour.” By the time he went, it was sold out.

He came and told her, “There is no fine flour, but there is white flour.” She told him, “Go, bring it to me.” By the time he went, it was sold out.

He came and told her, “There is no white flour, but there is whole wheat flour.” She told him, “Go, bring it to me.” By the time he went, it was sold out.

He came and told her, “There is no whole wheat flour, but there is barley flour.” She told him, “Go, bring it to me.” By the time he went, it was sold out.

She removed her shoes and said, “I will go out and see if I can find anything to eat.”

A piece of something stuck to her foot and she died!

Rabbi Yohanan ben Zakkai read as her eulogy, “The most tender and delicate of women, who would not allow the sole of her foot to touch the ground” (Deuteronomy 28:56).

(Babylonian Talmud, Gittin 56a)

14 / נ The Rabbi Confronts Caesar, or the Three Wishes

Abba Sikra, the head of the gang of thugs in Jerusalem, was the son of Rabbi Yohanan ben Zakkai’s sister. Yohanan sent him the message, “Come to me in secret.” When he arrived, Yohanan asked, “How long will you continue doing this, killing everyone with famine?”

He replied, “What can I do? If I say anything to them they will kill *me*!”

Yohanan said, "Let's see if there is a way for me to leave Jerusalem. It might be possible that I can save a small bit."

He said, "Pretend that you are ill, and have everyone come and ask after you. Then put something smelly nearby and have them say your soul has gone to its rest. Let your disciples enter—and do not let anyone else do it, lest they feel that you are too light—for everyone knows that a living person feels lighter than a corpse."

They did so. Rabbi Eliezer entered on one side and Rabbi Yehoshua on the other side. When they came to the gate with the "corpse," the guards sought to stab the body to be sure it was really dead. The disciples protested, "Do you want people to say that you desecrated the body of our master by stabbing him!" So they thought to just shove him. The disciples again protested, "Do you want people to say that you desecrated the body of our master by shoving him!" They relented and opened the gate. They went out.

When Rabbi Yohanan got there, he said to Vespasian, "Peace be upon you, O King; peace be upon you, O King!"

Vespasian replied, "You have condemned yourself twice over. First, I am not emperor and yet you have committed lèse-majesté by hailing me as emperor! Further, if I were emperor, what took you so long to come?"

Rabbi Yohanan responded, "As for your saying that you are not emperor, surely you are an emperor; otherwise Jerusalem would not be given into your hands. As it is written, 'The Lebanon trees shall fall by a majesty' [Isaiah 10:34].... And as for your asking why I did not come sooner, those thugs among us would not permit it."

Vespasian said, "If you had a barrel of honey with a serpent coiled around it, would you not destroy the barrel for the sake of the serpent?"

Rabbi Yohanan was silent.

Rabbi Yosef, and some say it was Rabbi Akiva, recited the verse, "It is I, the Lord, who turns sages back and makes nonsense of their knowledge" (Isaiah 44:25). What he should have said to him was, "Take a pair of tongs, remove the serpent, and leave the honey barrel intact."

Just then a military attaché arrived from Rome and said, "Arise, for Caesar has died, and the nobles of Rome wish to seat you as their head."

Vespasian had just put on one boot; but when he tried to put on the second, it would not go on. So he tried to remove the first boot but could not. He asked, "What's this?"

Rabbi Yohanan explained, "Don't worry, it's just the good news you've received, as it is said, 'Good tidings fatten the bone' [Proverbs 15:30]. What is the remedy? Bring someone with whom you are unhappy and have him pass before you, as it is said, 'Despondency dries up the bones' [Proverbs 17:22]."

He did so and his boot went on!... Vespasian said, "I must leave now and will send someone in my stead. But ask of me some boon that I may grant it."

He said, "Give me Yavneh and its sages, and the Gamalielite line, and a physician to heal Rabbi Tzadok."

Rabbi Yosef, and some say it was Rabbi Akiva, recited the verse, "It is I, the Lord, who turns sages back and makes nonsense of their knowledge" (Isaiah 44:25). What he should have said to him was, "Let Jerusalem go this time." But Yohanan had worried that he would not do that much, and then he would not have saved even a small bit.

As for the physician to heal Rabbi Tzadok (for Rabbi Tzadok had fasted for forty years trying to prevent the destruction of Jerusalem; he became so thin that when he ate something, you could watch it go down his gullet from outside him!), the physician fed him fruit juice on the first day, on the next day broth, and then gruel, until little by little his innards healed.

(BABYLONIAN TALMUD, *GITTIN* 56A–B)

15 / ס The Gnat's Revenge

Vespasian went and sent Titus. "And he said, 'Where is their God, the Rock in whom they sought refuge' (Deuteronomy 32:37)?" This verse refers to Titus, that evil one, who blasphemed against heaven. What did he do? He took a prostitute by the hand, entered into the Holy of Holies, spread forth a Torah scroll, and committed a transgression upon it. Then he took his sword, penetrated the veil of the Temple, and a miracle occurred and blood spurted forth. Titus thought he had killed Himself, as it is said, "Your foes roar in the midst of Your meeting place, they place their standards as ensigns" (Psalm 74:4).

Abba Hanan said, "'Who is mighty like You, O Lord?' [Psalm 89:9]. Who is so mighty hard as You, that You witness the curses and blasphemy of that evil one and yet are silent?" Among the school of Rabbi Ishmael they taught, "'Who is like You among the mighty [ba'elim], O Lord?' [Exodus 15:11]. Who is like you among the mute [ba'elmim]?"

What did Titus do? He took the veil of the Temple and used it like a basket in which he put all of the vessels of the Sanctuary. He loaded them on a ship and went to celebrate a triumph in his city of Rome....

A storm arose on the sea and threatened to capsize him. Titus reasoned, "It seems to me that their god only has power upon water. When Pharaoh came, he drowned him in water. When Sisera came, he drowned him in water. Now he wants to drown me in water! If the god of the Jews really has power, let him make war with me upon dry land!"

A voice came forth and said to him, "Evil one, son of an evil one, offspring of the evil Esau! I have a simple creature in My world named a gnat." *Why is it called "a simple creature"? For it has a mouth but has no rectum.* "Get up on dry land and make war with it!"

When Titus arrived at dry land, a gnat flew up his nose and drilled into his brain for seven years.

One day when he was passing the gate of a blacksmith's shop, he heard the sound of the hammer hitting the anvil and the gnat was silenced. Titus thought, "There's a solution!"

Each day he brought a smith who hammered in his presence. He paid a gentile four *zuz* to hammer, but to a Jewish smith he said, "It's enough that you have seen your enemy so." This worked for thirty days, but then the sound of the hammering no longer availed to silence the gnat.

It is taught: Rabbi Pinchas ben Aroba said, "I was among the great men of Rome; and when Titus died they split open his head and found that the gnat had grown to the size of a free-range bird weighing two kilos."

As it is taught in the Mishnah: Like a one-year-old pigeon weigh-ing two kilos.

(BABYLONIAN TALMUD, GITTIN 56B)

16 / ע Rainmaker

The rabbis recited: Once upon a time all of Israel had gone up on pil-grimage to Jerusalem to celebrate the festival, but they had no water to drink. Nicodemus ben Gurion approached a local grandee and asked, "Loan me twelve wells worth of water for the pilgrims and I shall repay you those twelve wells. But if I cannot repay you on time, I pledge to give you twelve talents of silver."

He agreed and set a time for repayment. When the time came and it had still not rained, he sent this message in the morning, "Remit to me the water or the money that you owe me."

Nicodemus replied, "I still have time. The entire day is mine."

At noontime he sent this message, "Remit to me either the water or my money that is in your hands."

He replied, "I still have waiting time in the day."

In the afternoon he sent, "Remit to me either the water or my money that is in your hands."

He replied, "I still have waiting time in the day."

That grandee sneered at Nicodemus, "All year long it has not rained. Do you think it will rain now?" He entered the bathhouse in joy.

While the grandee was going to the bathhouse in his delight, Nicodemus entered the Jerusalem Temple in his sorrow. Nicodemus wrapped himself in his cloak and stood in prayer. He said to God, "Master of the Universe, it is revealed and known before You that I did this not for my own glory, nor for the glory of my father's house. I did this for Your glory, that there might be water for the pilgrims to drink!"

Immediately the sky became knotted with clouds and rain fell until the twelve wells were filled with water and there was even more in addition.

As the grandee left the bathhouse, Nicodemus left the Jerusalem Temple. When they confronted one another Nicodemus said, "Give me the value of my extra water that is in your hands!"

He replied, "I realize that the Blessed Holy One disturbed the world on your behalf, yet I still have an opening to extract my money from you. The sun has already set, so the rains actually fell in my dominion!"

Nicodemus went back into the Jerusalem Temple, wrapped himself in his cloak, and stood once more in prayer. He said to God, "Master of the Universe! Make it known that You have beloved ones in Your world."

Immediately, the clouds dispersed and the sun shone. At that moment, the grandee said, "Had the sun not broken through [*nikdarah*], I would have had an opening to extract my money from you."

It was taught that his name was not Nicodemus, but rather Buni. So why was he called Nicodemus? For the sun broke through [*nikdarah*] on his behalf.

(BABYLONIAN TALMUD, *TAANIT* 19B–20A)

17 / נ Nicodemus and Buni—Uncensored!

MISHNAH: If he is found innocent [following sentencing], they release him. If not, he goes forth to execution. The herald goes before him saying: "So-and-so is being executed for such-and-such a sin. So-and-so and so-and-so are the witnesses. Anyone who has testimony to his innocence, come and testify."

TALMUD: Abbaye said, "And the herald must say, 'On such-and-such a day, at such-and-such an hour, at such-and-such a place,' in case there are those who have information; so that they can come to impugn the false witnesses." *The herald goes before him*: "before him" physically, but not "before him" temporally.

But it is taught: They hung up Jesus of Nazareth on the eve of Passover. And the herald went before him by forty days, saying: "Jesus of Nazareth is going out to be executed for practicing sorcery, and he enticed and misled the Jews. Anyone who has exculpatory evidence come forth and testify." Yet they found no evidence of innocence and they hung him up on the eve of Passover.

Ulla said, "Does this make sense? Jesus of Nazareth was a man of overturned merit! He was an enticer! The Merciful One said, 'Show him no pity or compassion' [Deuteronomy 13:9]. But the case of Jesus is an exception as he was close to the government."

The rabbis taught: Jesus of Nazareth had five disciples: Mattai, Niccai, Netzer, Buni, and Thoda.

(Babylonian Talmud, *Sanhedrin* 43a)

18 / צ Rainmaker—The Sequel

The rabbis taught: Once most of the month of Adar had passed but it had not rained. They sent a message to Honi the *Me`Aggel*: "Pray that the rain may fall!" He prayed but the rains did not fall.

He made a circle and stood within, the way that the prophet Habakkuk did, as it is said, "I will stand upon my watch, take my place along the tower" (Habakkuk 2:1).

Honi said to God, "Master of the Universe, your children look to me, for I am like a member of Your household. I vow by Your great name that I shall not stir from here until You have mercy upon Your children."

It began to drizzle.

His disciples said to him, "Rabbi, we look to you that we may not die! It seems to us that these rains are only falling to release you from your vow!"

Honi said, "I did not ask for thus, but for rains to fill cisterns, irrigation ditches, and wells!" So the rain came down in force, so that each drop could fill the mouth of a barrel. The sages measured that no drop was smaller than a liter.

His disciples said, "Rabbi, we look to you that we may not die! It seems to us that these rains are only falling to destroy the world!"

Honi said to God, "I did not ask for thus, but for rains of bounty, blessing, and beneficence." Then the rain fell normally, continuing until everyone had to go to the Temple Mount because of the rain.

They said, "Rabbi, just as you prayed that the rains would fall, now pray that they may go away."

He replied, "I have received a tradition that one does not pray about too much of a good thing! Nevertheless, bring me a bullock for a thanksgiving offering."

Honi laid his two hands upon the bullock and said to God, "Master of the Universe, Your people Israel whom You have brought forth from Egypt cannot endure too much good or too much punishment. When You were angry at them, they could not endure. When You suffused them with good, they could not endure. May it be Your will that the rains may cease and there be relief for the world." Immediately, the wind blew, the clouds dispersed, and the sun shone. And everyone went out to the fields to gather mushrooms and truffles.

Shimeon ben Shetah sent Honi the following message: "Were you not Honi, I would have decreed a ban upon you! For if these years had been like those of the prophet Elijah—who had the keys to rain in his hand—would you not have profaned God's name? Yet what shall I do? You offend God and God still does what you ask for! You are like a spoiled child who offends his father and that father does what the child asks anyway. He says, 'Daddy, take me to the hot baths, rinse me in the cold pool, gimme peanuts, almonds, peaches, pomegranates'—and the father gives it to him! It is about you that Scripture says, 'May your father rejoice, and the mother who bore you delight' (Proverbs 23:25)."

(BABYLONIAN TALMUD, *TAANIT* 23A)

19 / ק The Rabbis' Rip Van Winkle

That righteous man was troubled all his days by this verse: "A Song of Ascents. We were like dreamers when God returned the captivity of Zion" (Psalm 126:1). He asked, "Who can nap for seventy years?"

One day he was traveling on the road and saw a man planting a carob tree. He asked him, "How long will it take for that tree to bear fruit?"

The man answered, "Up to seventy years."

Honi asked, "Are you sure you will live for seventy years?"

He replied, "This man found the world with carob trees. Just as my forefathers planted for me, I too plant for those who come after me."

Honi sat and ate a sandwich. Then asleep overcame him. He napped. While he was sleeping, a stony outcropping surrounded him, hiding him from view. He napped for seventy years. When he awoke, he saw that man collecting carobs from the tree. He asked, "Are you the one who planted it?"

He said, "I am his son's son."

Honi reasoned, "I infer from this that I had a seventy-year nap!"

And he saw that his donkey had given birth to many offspring.

Honi went to his home. He asked them, "Is the son of Honi the *Me'Aggel* still alive?"

They said, "His son is not; his grandson is."

He told them, "I am Honi the *Me'Aggel!*" But they did not believe him.

So he went to the study house. He overheard the rabbis saying, "The law is as clear as in the days of Honi the *Me'Aggel*. For when he entered the study house, he would resolve any difficulties that the rabbis had."

He announced to them, "I am he!" Not only did they not believe him, but they did not pay him the respect he deserved.

His spirit became weak. He prayed for God's mercy and died.

Rava said, "It's what folks say: 'Either companionship or death.'"

(Babylonian Talmud, *Taanit* 23a)

20 / ר Pretty Woman 1 and 2

"If you know not, O fairest of women" (Song of Songs 1:8).

"Because you would not serve the Lord your God ... you shall have to serve your enemies" (Deuteronomy 28:47–48).

Once, when Rabbi Yohanan ben Zakkai was going up to Maon Yehuda, he saw a young woman collecting barleycorns from horse dung. Rabbi Yohanan ben Zakkai asked them, "Did you see that young woman? What is she?"

His disciples replied, "Jewish."

He asked, "Who owns the horse?"

They replied, "An Arabian traveler."

Rabbi Yohanan ben Zakkai said to his disciples, "All my life I was troubled by this verse. I would read it and not understand it: 'If you know not, O fairest of women' [Song of Songs 1:8]."

Because you did not want to serve Heaven, behold you now serve the lowest of the Arabian gentiles. Because you did not want to pay a *beka* as the head tax to heaven, behold you now pay fifteen *shekels* to the government of your enemy.

(MEKHILTA DERABBI ISHMAEL, YITRO 1)

A story is told about Rabbi Yohanan ben Zakkai, who was riding a donkey and his disciples were following behind him. He saw a young woman collecting barley from beneath the hooves of the cattle of Arabians. When she saw Rabbi Yohanan ben Zakkai, she wrapped herself in her hair and stood before him. She said, "Rabbi, sustain me."

He asked, "Whose daughter are you?"

She replied, "I am the daughter of Nicodemus ben Gurion. Rabbi, do you remember when you signed my marriage agreement?"

Rabbi Yohanan ben Zakkai said to his disciples, "I signed her marriage agreement and read therein a million gold dinars promised by her in-laws as a bride price. As for this young woman's family, they would not go to worship in the Temple Mount until woolen carpets were laid beneath their feet. Then they would enter, worship, and return to their homes in joy. All my life I have searched for the meaning of this verse, and now I have found it, 'If you know not, O fairest of women, follow the tracks of the sheep and graze your kids among the shepherds' tents' [Song of Songs 1:8]."

Do not read the verse as saying "your kids" [*gediyotayikh*], but as though it says "your corpses" [*geviyotayikh*].

For so long as the Jews do the will of the Omnipresent, no nation or government can rule them. But when the Jews do not do the will of the Omnipresent, they are given into the hands of a lowly nation. And not just into the hands of a lowly nation, but beneath the feet of the cattle of a lowly nation.

(SIFRE DEUTERONOMY 305)

21 / ש Pretty Woman 3, 4, 5

A case is cited regarding Martha bat Boethius. The sages ruled that she could receive two barrels of wine as a daily maintenance allowance. This proves that the sages have the right to rule on wine allowances....

Rabbi Hezekiah quoted Rabbi Abbahu in the name of Rabbi Yohanan, "They also ruled about a daily cooked-food allowance."

Despite this, she cursed the court, saying, "You should only give this to your own daughters!"

Rabbi Akhah said, "We all replied to her, 'Amen!'"

Rabbi Elazar ben Tzadok said, "May I never see consolation if what I say is not true. I saw her collecting barleycorns from between the hooves of horses in Acre. I recited the following verse about her: 'The most tender and delicate of women, who would not allow the sole of her foot to touch the ground' [Deuteronomy 28:56]. 'If you know not, O fairest of women, follow the tracks of the sheep' [Song of Songs 1:8].

A story is told about Miriam, daughter of Shimeon ben Gurion. The sages ruled that she should have a five hundred dinar per diem perfume allowance, although she was only waiting for her brother-in-law to do his levirate duty.

Despite this, she cursed the court, saying, "You should only give this to your own daughters!"

Rabbi Akhah said, "We all replied to her, 'Amen!'"

Rabbi Elazar ben Tzadok said, "May I never see consolation if what I say is not true. I saw her tied by her hair to the tail of a horse in Acre. I recited the following verse about her, 'The most tender and delicate of women, who would not allow the sole of her foot to touch the ground' [Deuteronomy 28:56]."

(PALESTINIAN TALMUD, *KETUBOT* 5:7)

22 / ת The End: We Hope

Rabbi Ishmael said, "From the day the Temple was destroyed, by rights we Jews should no longer eat meat nor drink wine, as an expression of mourning for our lost Sanctuary. Yet it is our principle that the rabbinic court should not enact decrees upon the Jews that they will not observe."

He also said, "Since the Romans have uprooted Torah from amongst us through their decrees, we no longer have a raison d'être. So we should decree an end to Judaism! Let no man marry a wife or bear children! Let there no longer be circumcision ceremonies, until the very seed of Abraham run its course and is no more!"

They said to him, "It is better that the Jews continue in error, than that you make such decrees and they continue in defiance of rabbinic law."

When the last Temple was destroyed, separatists multiplied among the Jews, who would not eat meat or drink wine. Rabbi Yehoshua dealt with them.

He said, "My children, why do you not eat meat?"

They replied, "Shall we eat meat, which was offered daily as a perpetual sacrifice upon the altar, but it is no more!"

He said, "Fine, we shall not eat meat. But why do you not drink wine?"

They replied, "Shall we drink wine, which was daily poured as a libation upon the altar; but it is no more!"

He said to them, "Fine, we shall not drink it. But if so, perhaps we should not eat bread, for they brought two ceremonial loaves and the showbread in the Temple. And perhaps we should not drink water, which was also poured as a libation upon the altar. And then we should not eat figs or grapes, which were brought as first fruit offerings at Pentecost."

They were silenced.

He said to them, "My children, it is not permissible to mourn excessively. Yet neither is it permissible to not mourn at all. Rather, this is what our sages suggest: 'You should paint your house with lime, but leave a small patch unpainted, as a remembrance of Jerusalem. You should prepare all the dishes for a banquet, yet refrain from serving one, as a remembrance of Jerusalem. And a woman should put on her jewelry, yet remove a piece, as a remembrance of Jerusalem.' As it is said, 'If I forget you Jerusalem, may my right hand wither; may my tongue stick to my palate if I do not remember you, if I do not place Jerusalem above my highest joy' [Psalm 137:5–6]. For all who mourn Jerusalem will merit seeing her joy, as it is said, 'Rejoice with Jerusalem and be glad for her, all who love her; all who mourned her will rejoice with her!' [Isaiah 66:10]."

(*TOSEFTA SOTA* 15:10–15)

Appendix 2

Who's Who

(Unless otherwise noted, rabbis are from the Land of Israel and centuries are in the Common Era.)

Abba Hanan: Second-century rabbi.

Abba Saul: Second-century rabbi.

Abba Sikra: A renegade leader of revolt in Jerusalem, 66–70 CE.

(Rabbi) Abbahu: Fourth-century rabbi.

Abbaye: Fourth-century Babylonian rabbinic leader.

(Rabbi) Akhah: Fourth-century rabbi.

(Rabbi) Akiva: Second-century rabbi.

al-Bukhari: Ninth-century compiler of Muslim Hadith traditions.

Anas ibn Malik: Seventh-century companion of the Prophet Muhammad.

Antigonus of Sokho: Third-century-BCE proto-rabbinic leader.

Aristotle: Fourth-century-BCE Greek philosopher.

(Saint) Augustine: Fourth- to fifth-century church father.

Ben Azzai (Shimeon ben Azzai): Second-century rabbi.

Ben-Gurion, David: Born David Grün, first prime minister of the modern State of Israel.

Ben Kalba Savua: First-century rich man of Jerusalem.

Ben Tzitzit HaKeset: First-century rich man of Jerusalem.

Ben Zoma (Shimeon ben Zoma): Second-century rabbi.

Beruriah: Second-century wife of Rabbi Meir and Jewish leader/thinker.

Buni: A first-century Jew, either a nickname for Nicodemus or a disciple of Jesus.

(Rabbi) Elazar ben Arakh: First-century rabbi.

(Rabbi) Elazar ben Tzadok: Late-first-century rabbi.

(Rabbi) Eliezer ben Hyrcanus: First-century rabbi.

Elijah: Biblical prophet.

(Rabbi) Elijah Gaon of Vilna: 1720–1797, leader of the intellectual anti-Hasidic movement, renown Talmudic authority in Vilnius, Lithuania.

(Rabbi) Elisha ben Avuyah: Second-century rabbi who became an apostate.

Epicurus: Fourth- to third-century-BCE Greek philosopher.

Flavius Josephus: First-century Jewish historian.

(Rabbi) Gamaliel: The Elder lived in the early first century; the latter was his grandson who lived in the second century. Each was reputed to be a rabbinic leader of the Palestinian Jewish community.

Gamalielites: The descendants of Rabbi Gamaliel, each a dynastic Jewish leader.

Hadrian: Emperor of Rome during the Bar Kokhba rebellion (132–135 CE).

Hai ben Sherira Gaon: Eleventh-century Babylonian rabbinic leader.

(Rabbi) Hannina: First-century rabbi.

(Rabbi) Hezekiah: Late-fourth-century rabbi.

Hillel (the Elder): First-century-BCE to first-century-CE proto-rabbinic leader.

(Father) Hippolyte Delehaye: Nineteenth-century Bollandist monk and scholar.

(Rav) Hisda: Fourth-century Babylonian rabbi.

Homer: Ninth-century-BCE Greek epic poet, author of *Iliad* and *Odyssey*.

Honi the *Me`Aggel*: Second-century-BCE Jewish charismatic and rainmaker.

(Rabbi) Ishmael: Second-century rabbi.

(Saint) Jerome: Fourth- to fifth-century church father.

Jesus: First-century rabbi, believed by Christians to be the Messiah and son of God.

Jeter, Derek: Twentieth- to twenty-first-century New York Yankee shortstop.

(Rabbi) José the Priest: First-century rabbi.

(Rabbi) Judah: Third- to fourth-century Babylonian rabbi.

(Rabbi) Judah the Patriarch: Second- to third-century rabbinic leader of the Jewish community; compiler of the Mishnah.

(Rabbi) Kahana: Third-century Babylonian rabbi.

Lazar Wolf (the butcher): Twentieth-century character in *Fiddler on the Roof*.

Lazarus: First-century Jewish corpse, raised from the dead by Jesus.

Maccabees: Second- to first-century-BCE rebels and priestly leaders of Jewish revival.

Maimonides: Rabbi Moses ben Maimon, twelfth-century CE rabbinic authority, courtier, and physician.

Martha bat Boethius: First-century rich woman.

Mattai: Reported by Talmud as a disciple of Jesus.

(Rabbi) Meir: Second-century rabbinic leader.

Muhammad: Seventh-century prophet of Islam.

Muslim ibn al-Hajjaj: Ninth-century compiler of Muslim Hadith traditions.

Nahum of Gimzo: Second-century Jewish charismatic.

(Rabbi) Nathan: Second-century rabbi who moved from Babylonia to Palestine.

Nebuchadnezzar: King of Babylonian Empire who forced exile upon Judea in 586 BCE.

(Rabbi) Nehemiah: Second-century rabbi.

Nero: First-century Roman emperor.

Nestor: Character in Homer's *Odyssey*.

Netzer: Reported by Talmud as a disciple of Jesus.

Niccai: Reported by Talmud as a disciple of Jesus.

Nicodemus (Nakdimon) ben Gurion: First-century rich man of Jerusalem.

The Other (see Elisha ben Avuyah): Second-century rabbi who became an apostate.

Otto Rudolph: Nineteenth- to twentieth-century German theologian.

(Rabbi) Pinchas ben Aroba: First-century rabbi.

Plato: Fifth- to fourth-century-BCE Greek philosopher.

Rashi (Solomon ben Isaac): Eleventh-century rabbi and commentator.

Rav: Third-century Babylonian rabbinic leader.

(Rabbi) Rava bar Yosef: Fourth-century Babylonian rabbinic leader.

Raymundo Martini: Thirteenth-century Dominican friar and medieval inquisitor.

Shammai (the Elder): First-century-BCE to first-century-CE proto-rabbinic leader.

(Rabbi) Shimeon ben Azzai: Second-century rabbi.

Shimeon ben Gurion: Character mentioned in Palestinian Talmud.

(Rabbi) Shimeon ben Netanel: First-century rabbi.

Shimeon ben Shetah: Second-century-BCE proto-rabbinic leader.

(Rabbi) Shimeon ben Yohai: Second-century rabbi.

(Rabbi) Shimeon ben Zoma: Second-century rabbi.

Shimeon the Righteous: Third-century-BCE proto-rabbinic leader.

(Rabbi) Tarphon: First-century rabbi.

Thoda: Reported by Talmud as a disciple of Jesus.

Titus: First-century Roman emperor who destroyed Jerusalem and its Temple.

(Rabbi) Tzadok: First-century rabbi.

Ulla: Fourth-century rabbi who moved from Palestine to Babylonia.

Vespasian: First-century Roman emperor; father of Titus.

(Rabbi) Yehoshua ben Hananiah: First-century rabbi.

(Rabbi) Yermiah: Fourth-century rabbi.

(Rabbi) Yohanan: Third-century rabbinic leader.

(Rabbi) Yohanan ben Zakkai: First-century rabbinic leader.

Yosé ben Yoezer: Second-century-BCE proto-rabbinic leader.

Yosé ben Yohanan: Second-century-BCE proto-rabbinic leader.

(Rabbi) Yosef: Third- and fourth-century Babylonian rabbi.

Zeno: Fourth- to third-century-BCE Greek philosopher; founder of the Stoic school.

Glossary

Abba: An early title of pre-rabbinic Jewish authority.

Acre: City of northern Galilee.

agoranomos: Roman government market supervisor; set fair prices.

Avot DeRabbi Nathan: Early commentary on Mishnah tractate *Pirke Avot*, edited in eighth and ninth centuries CE.

Babylonia: Modern Iraq, home of a major Jewish community for twenty-five hundred years.

Babylonian Talmud: See Talmud.

BCE: Before the Common Era, equivalent to the Christian usage of BC.

beka: Weight used in monetary measure.

Ben Sira (book of Apocrypha): Jewish wisdom work, found in church Bible but not Hebrew Bible.

Beth Ezuba: Town in Galilee mentioned by Josephus.

Blessing after Meals: Recited by observant Jews, thanking God for a meal.

CE: Common Era, equivalent to the Christian usage of AD.

circumcision: Rite performed on the eighth day of baby boy's life to initiate him into Jewish community.

Damasit: A town with public baths of natural hot springs.

daughter of a voice: Postbiblical mode of heavenly revelation.

Dead Sea Scrolls: Found in 1948 in Judean desert, a group of biblical and extra-biblical documents from second century BCE through first century CE.

Deus absconditus: The absent God, a theological construct.

dinar: An Eastern Roman coin.

Ecclesiasticus: See Ben Sira.

elders: The communal council. Members held the title "elder" no matter their actual age.

Emmaus: A town name. Usually the town had hot springs. In Christian Scripture, Emmaus was the site where Jesus first appeared to his disciples after the resurrection.

Epicurean(ism): Roman-era Greek philosophy that denied providence of the gods.

Epicurus: See Epicurean(ism).

Essene: An ascetic from the late First Temple period, often associated with the Dead Sea Scroll community.

First Temple: Solomon's Jerusalem Temple, destroyed by Babylonians in 586 BCE.

fisc: Imperial Roman treasury.

Gelt: Literally, "gold." Lucre, cash, money.

Genesis Rabbah: Rabbinic Midrash on the biblical book of Genesis, edited in Galilee ca. fifth century CE.

Great Assembly, Men of the: A group mentioned in *Pirke Avot* presumed to rule the Jewish community in the postbiblical period.

gushkara: A type of coarse wheat flour.

Hadith: A Muslim tradition about the prophet Muhammad.

hagiography: Literally, "sacred writing." The "lives" of the saints.

hammam: Hot springs.

hasid: A pious one. Sometimes associated with Essenes.

Hasidei Ashkenaz: German pietists of the twelfth to thirteenth century.

Haver: A pre- and early rabbinic title for a person trustworthy in tithing. Also a Hebrew term for study partner and friend.

Iliad: Homeric epic poem.

Iudea Capta: Literally, "Judea captured." Inscription on Roman coins.

Jamnia: Roman garrison town that became the center for Rabbi Yohanan ben Zakkai's disciples following the destruction of Jerusalem and became known as Yavneh.

Jumaah: Arabic for Friday, time of weekly major Muslim gathering for prayer.

Ketuvim: Literally, "writings." Third major section of Hebrew Bible.

Khirbet Qumran: Place of Dead Sea Scroll community in Judean desert.

kohen: A Jewish priest, of the biblical tribe of Aaron.

kosher: Fit for eating according to biblical and rabbinic law.

levirate: A law of Deuteronomy providing for the marriage of a widow in a childless marriage to the deceased husband's brother in order to carry on the family name.

mammon: Money.

Maon Yehuda: A place-name, locale unknown.

Melchilta DeRabbi Ishmael: Earliest rabbinic commentary on biblical book of Exodus. Edited in Land of Israel early third century CE.

Mensch: Yiddish and German; literally "human being." A stand-up guy.

Merkaba Shelaymah: A collection of medieval Jewish mystical texts.

Mesopotamia: The fertile crescent between the Tigris and Euphrates Rivers; modern Iraq.

midrash: Rabbinic biblical interpretation.

Midrash Mishle: Ninth-century rabbinic midrash/commentary on biblical book of Proverbs.

Minor Prophets: Twelve shorter books of biblical prophecy found in the Prophetic section of the Hebrew Bible.

Mishnah: A late-second-century compendium of rabbinic legal opinions.

Neptune: Roman god of the sea.

nomos: Greek; law and legal system.

Odyssey: Homeric epic poem.

Oral Torah: Rabbinic law and teaching.

Palestinian (Jerusalem) Talmud: Commentary on the Mishnah compiled in the Land of Israel, edited in the early fifth century CE. See also Talmud.

Pharisees: Group of late Second Temple pietists, often seen as forebears to the rabbis

Pirke Avot: Tractate of the Mishnah devoted to wisdom sayings of the early rabbis.

Pirke Rabbi Eliezer: A ninth-century-CE midrash on Bible from Creation through death of Miriam, edited under Islam.

Prayer, the: Eighteen/nineteen benedictions composed by the rabbis for daily liturgy.

prophets: Israel's intercessors with God.

Prophets: Second major section of Hebrew Bible.

Pugio Fidei: Work by thirteenth-century Dominican monk Raymundo Martini, used to debate Jews during Inquisition.

Pumbedita: Babylonian town, location of major Talmudic academy.

rabbi: Literally, "master." A teacher of Torah to disciples.

reductio ad absurdum: A mode of rhetoric by which the faulty argument of an opponent is unmasked by following it to its logical, yet absurd, conclusion.

Rosh HaShanah: Jewish New Year.

sanctum sanctorum: Holy of Holies, the inner Sanctuary of Jerusalem Temple.

Second Temple: The rebuilt Jerusalem Temple, lasting from sixth century BCE through 70 CE when it was destroyed by Roman army.

Seder: Literally, "order." Passover night liturgy for Jewish home celebration.

Sefer HaRazim: Jewish mystical work.

shalem: Hebrew; intact, whole, at peace.

shalom: Hebrew; peace, hello, goodbye.

Shalom aleichem: Hebrew greeting, "Peace unto you!"

shekels: Biblical Hebrew; coins, money.

Shema: Deuteronomy: 6:4–9, recited twice daily in Jewish liturgy.

Sicarii: Rebels and/or terrorists during the war against Rome 66–70 CE. Named for the daggers (*sicarii*) they carried to murder both their Roman as well as their Jewish enemies.

Sifre Deuteronomy: Earliest rabbinic commentary on biblical book of Deuteronomy, edited early third century CE.

Sisera: Enemy of biblical Israel; see Judges 4–5.

Stoic(ism): Greco-Roman philosophy akin to rabbinic Judaism.

Sukkot: Literally, "booths." Biblical harvest festival.

Talmud: Compendium of commentary on the Mishnah, compiled in Babylonia in the sixth century. See also Palestinian (Jerusalem) Talmud.

Tosefta: Third-century companion to the Mishnah, compendium of rabbinic legal opinion.

triclinium: Greco-Roman dining table; also, dining room.

tzuris: Yiddish; troubles.

World to Come: In rabbinic eschatology, this is what comes after history ends. The equivalent to the Messianic era.

yarmulke: Yiddish; skullcap worn by observant Jews.

Yavneh: Place of Yohanan ben Zakkai's disciples. See also Jamnia.

yetzer ra: Hebrew; the inclination to do evil; libido.

yetzer tov: Hebrew; the inclination to do good; superego.

Yiddish: European Jewish folk dialect.

yod: Smallest letter of the Hebrew alphabet.

Yom Kippur: Biblical and rabbinic holiday; Day of Atonement.

Zoroastrian: Religion of Sasanian Empire in third- to seventh-century Babylonia.

Suggestions for Further Reading

Alter, Robert. *The Art of Biblical Narrative*. New York: Basic Books, 1983.

Holtz, Barry, ed. *Back to the Sources: Reading the Classic Jewish Texts*. New York: Simon and Schuster, 1986.

Rubenstein, Jeffrey L. *Rabbinic Stories*. Mahwah, NJ: Paulist Press, 2002.

———. *Talmudic Stories: Narrative Art, Composition, and Culture*. Baltimore: Johns Hopkins University Press, 2003.

Schafer, Peter. *Jesus in the Talmud*. Princeton, NJ: Princeton University Press, 2009.

Shapiro, Rami. *Ethics of the Sages:* Pirke Avot—*Annotated & Explained*. Woodstock, VT: SkyLight Paths, 2006.

Visotzky, Burton L. *Reading the Book: Making the Bible a Timeless Text*. Philadelphia: Jewish Publication Society, 2005.

Visotzky, Burton L., and David Fishman, eds. *From Mesopotamia to Modernity: Ten Introductions to Jewish History and Literature*. Boulder, CO: Westview Press, 1999.

Bible Study/Midrash

Sage Tales: Wisdom and Wonder from the Rabbis of the Talmud
By Rabbi Burton L. Visotzky Illustrates how the stories of the Rabbis who lived in the first generations following the destruction of the Jerusalem Temple illuminate modern life's most pressing issues. 6 x 9, 256 pp, HC, 978-1-58023-456-6 **$24.99**

The Modern Men's Torah Commentary: New Insights from Jewish Men on the 54 Weekly Torah Portions *Edited by Rabbi Jeffrey K. Salkin*
A major contribution to modern biblical commentary. Addresses the most important concerns of modern men by opening them up to the messages of Torah.
6 x 9, 368 pp, HC, 978-1-58023-395-8 **$24.99**

The Genesis of Leadership: What the Bible Teaches Us about Vision, Values and Leading Change *By Rabbi Nathan Laufer; Foreword by Senator Joseph I. Lieberman*
6 x 9, 288 pp, Quality PB, 978-1-58023-352-1 **$18.99**

Hineini in Our Lives: Learning How to Respond to Others through 14 Biblical Texts and Personal Stories *By Rabbi Norman J. Cohen, PhD* 6 x 9, 240 pp, Quality PB, 978-1-58023-274-6 **$16.99**

A Man's Responsibility: A Jewish Guide to Being a Son, a Partner in Marriage, a Father and a Community Leader *By Rabbi Joseph B. Meszler*
6 x 9, 192 pp, Quality PB, 978-1-58023-435-1 **$16.99**

Moses and the Journey to Leadership: Timeless Lessons of Effective Management from the Bible and Today's Leaders *By Rabbi Norman J. Cohen, PhD*
6 x 9, 240 pp, Quality PB, 978-1-58023-351-4 **$18.99**; HC, 978-1-58023-227-2 **$21.99**

Righteous Gentiles in the Hebrew Bible: Ancient Role Models for Sacred Relationships *By Rabbi Jeffrey K. Salkin; Foreword by Rabbi Harold M. Schulweis; Preface by Phyllis Tickle* 6 x 9, 192 pp, Quality PB, 978-1-58023-364-4 **$18.99**

The Wisdom of Judaism: An Introduction to the Values of the Talmud
By Rabbi Dov Peretz Elkins 6 x 9, 192 pp, Quality PB, 978-1-58023-327-9 **$16.99**

The Wisdom of Judaism Teacher's Guide 8½ x 11, 18 pp, PB, 978-1-58023-350-7 **$8.99**

Congregation Resources

Empowered Judaism: What Independent Minyanim Can Teach Us about Building Vibrant Jewish Communities
By Rabbi Elie Kaunfer; Foreword by Prof. Jonathan D. Sarna
Examines the independent minyan movement and the lessons these grassroots communities can provide. 6 x 9, 224 pp, Quality PB, 978-1-58023-412-2 **$18.99**

Spiritual Boredom: Rediscovering the Wonder of Judaism *By Dr. Erica Brown*
Breaks through the surface of spiritual boredom to find the reservoir of meaning within. 6 x 9, 208 pp, HC, 978-1-58023-405-4 **$21.99**

Building a Successful Volunteer Culture
Finding Meaning in Service in the Jewish Community
By Rabbi Charles Simon; Foreword by Shelley Lindauer; Preface by Dr. Ron Wolfson
Shows you how to develop and maintain the volunteers who are essential to the vitality of your organization and community. 6 x 9, 192 pp, Quality PB, 978-1-58023-408-5 **$16.99**

The Case for Jewish Peoplehood: Can We Be One?
By Dr. Erica Brown and Dr. Misha Galperin; Foreword by Rabbi Joseph Telushkin
6 x 9, 224 pp, HC, 978-1-58023-401-6 **$21.99**

Inspired Jewish Leadership: Practical Approaches to Building Strong Communities
By Dr. Erica Brown 6 x 9, 256 pp, HC, 978-1-58023-361-3 **$24.99**

Jewish Pastoral Care, 2nd Edition: A Practical Handbook from Traditional & Contemporary Sources *Edited by Rabbi Dayle A. Friedman, MSW, MAJCS, BCC*
6 x 9, 528 pp, Quality PB, 978-1-58023-427-6 **$30.00**

Rethinking Synagogues: A New Vocabulary for Congregational Life
By Rabbi Lawrence A. Hoffman, PhD 6 x 9, 240 pp, Quality PB, 978-1-58023-248-7 **$19.99**

The Spirituality of Welcoming: How to Transform Your Congregation into a Sacred Community *By Dr. Ron Wolfson* 6 x 9, 224 pp, Quality PB, 978-1-58023-244-9 **$19.99**

Holidays/Holy Days

Who by Fire, Who by Water—Un'taneh Tokef
Edited by Rabbi Lawrence A. Hoffman, PhD
Examines the prayer's theology, authorship and poetry through a set of lively essays, all written in accessible language.
6 x 9, 272 pp, HC, 978-1-58023-424-5 **$24.99**

All These Vows—Kol Nidre
Edited by Rabbi Lawrence A. Hoffman, PhD
The most memorable prayer of the Jewish New Year—what it means, why we sing it, and the secret of its magical appeal.
6 x 9, 300 pp (est), HC, 978-1-58023-430-6 **$24.99**

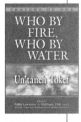

Rosh Hashanah Readings: Inspiration, Information and Contemplation
Yom Kippur Readings: Inspiration, Information and Contemplation
Edited by Rabbi Dov Peretz Elkins; Section Introductions from Arthur Green's These Are the Words
Rosh Hashanah: 6 x 9, 400 pp, Quality PB, 978-1-58023-437-5 **$19.99**; HC, 978-1-58023-239-5 **$24.99**
Yom Kippur: 6 x 9, 368 pp, Quality PB, 978-1-58023-438-2 **$19.99**; HC, 978-1-58023-271-5 **$24.99**

Jewish Holidays: A Brief Introduction for Christians
By Rabbi Kerry M. Olitzky and Rabbi Daniel Judson
5½ x 8½, 176 pp, Quality PB, 978-1-58023-302-6 **$16.99**

Reclaiming Judaism as a Spiritual Practice: Holy Days and Shabbat
By Rabbi Goldie Milgram 7 x 9, 272 pp, Quality PB, 978-1-58023-205-0 **$19.99**

Shabbat, 2nd Edition: The Family Guide to Preparing for and Celebrating the Sabbath
By Dr. Ron Wolfson 7 x 9, 320 pp, Illus., Quality PB, 978-1-58023-164-0 **$19.99**

Hanukkah, 2nd Edition: The Family Guide to Spiritual Celebration
By Dr. Ron Wolfson 7 x 9, 240 pp, Illus., Quality PB, 978-1-58023-122-0 **$18.95**

The Jewish Family Fun Book, 2nd Edition
Holiday Projects, Everyday Activities, and Travel Ideas with Jewish Themes
By Danielle Dardashti and Roni Sarig; Illus. by Avi Katz
6 x 9, 304 pp, 70+ b/w illus. & diagrams, Quality PB, 978-1-58023-333-0 **$18.99**

Passover

My People's Passover Haggadah
Traditional Texts, Modern Commentaries
Edited by Rabbi Lawrence A. Hoffman, PhD, and David Arnow, PhD
A diverse and exciting collection of commentaries on the traditional Passover Haggadah—in two volumes!
Vol. 1: 7 x 10, 304 pp, HC, 978-1-58023-354-5 **$24.99**
Vol. 2: 7 x 10, 320 pp, HC, 978-1-58023-346-0 **$24.99**

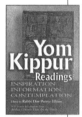

Freedom Journeys: The Tale of Exodus and Wilderness across Millennia
By Rabbi Arthur O. Waskow and Rabbi Phyllis O. Berman
Explores how the story of Exodus echoes in our own time, calling us to relearn and rethink the Passover story through social-justice, ecological, feminist and interfaith perspectives. 6 x 9, 288 pp, HC, 978-1-58023-445-0 **$24.99**

Leading the Passover Journey: The Seder's Meaning Revealed,
the Haggadah's Story Retold *By Rabbi Nathan Laufer*
Uncovers the hidden meaning of the Seder's rituals and customs.
6 x 9, 224 pp, Quality PB, 978-1-58023-399-6 **$18.99**; HC, 978-1-58023-211-1 **$24.99**

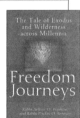

Creating Lively Passover Seders, 2nd Edition: A Sourcebook of Engaging Tales,
Texts & Activities *By David Arnow, PhD* 7 x 9, 464 pp, Quality PB, 978-1-58023-444-3 **$24.99**

Passover, 2nd Edition: The Family Guide to Spiritual Celebration
By Dr. Ron Wolfson with Joel Lurie Grishaver 7 x 9, 416 pp, Quality PB, 978-1-58023-174-9 **$19.95**

The Women's Passover Companion: Women's Reflections on the Festival of Freedom
Edited by Rabbi Sharon Cohen Anisfeld, Tara Mohr and Catherine Spector; Foreword by Paula E. Hyman
6 x 9, 352 pp, Quality PB, 978-1-58023-231-9 **$19.99**; HC, 978-1-58023-128-2 **$24.95**

The Women's Seder Sourcebook: Rituals & Readings for Use at the Passover Seder
Edited by Rabbi Sharon Cohen Anisfeld, Tara Mohr and Catherine Spector
6 x 9, 384 pp, Quality PB, 978-1-58023-232-6 **$19.99**

Social Justice

Confronting Scandal
How Jews Can Respond When Jews Do Bad Things
By Dr. Erica Brown
A framework to transform our sense of shame over reports of Jews committing crime into actions that inspire and sustain a moral culture.
6 x 9, 192 pp, HC, 978-1-58023-440-5 **$24.99**

There Shall Be No Needy
Pursuing Social Justice through Jewish Law and Tradition
By Rabbi Jill Jacobs; Foreword by Rabbi Elliot N. Dorff, PhD; Preface by Simon Greer
Confronts the most pressing issues of twenty-first-century America from a deeply Jewish perspective. 6 x 9, 288 pp, Quality PB, 978-1-58023-425-2 **$16.99**
There Shall Be No Needy Teacher's Guide 8½ x 11, 56 pp, PB, 978-1-58023-429-0 **$8.99**

Conscience
The Duty to Obey and the Duty to Disobey
By Rabbi Harold M. Schulweis
Examines the idea of conscience and the role conscience plays in our relationships to government, law, ethics, religion, human nature, God—and to each other.
6 x 9, 160 pp, Quality PB, 978-1-58023-419-1 **$16.99**; HC, 978-1-58023-375-0 **$19.99**

Judaism and Justice
The Jewish Passion to Repair the World
By Rabbi Sidney Schwarz; Foreword by Ruth Messinger
Explores the relationship between Judaism, social justice and the Jewish identity of American Jews. 6 x 9, 352 pp, Quality PB, 978-1-58023-353-8 **$19.99**

Spirituality/Women's Interest

New Jewish Feminism
Probing the Past, Forging the Future
Edited by Rabbi Elyse Goldstein; Foreword by Anita Diamant
Looks at the growth and accomplishments of Jewish feminism and what they mean for Jewish women today and tomorrow.
6 x 9, 480 pp, Quality PB, 978-1-58023-448-1 **$19.99**; HC, 978-1-58023-359-0 **$24.99**

The Divine Feminine in Biblical Wisdom Literature
Selections Annotated & Explained
Translation & Annotation by Rabbi Rami Shapiro
5½ x 8½, 240 pp, Quality PB, 978-1-59473-109-9 **$16.99**
(A book from SkyLight Paths, Jewish Lights' sister imprint)

The Quotable Jewish Woman
Wisdom, Inspiration & Humor from the Mind & Heart
Edited by Elaine Bernstein Partnow
6 x 9, 496 pp, Quality PB, 978-1-58023-236-4 **$19.99**

The Women's Haftarah Commentary
New Insights from Women Rabbis on the 54 Weekly Haftarah Portions, the 5 Megillot & Special Shabbatot
Edited by Rabbi Elyse Goldstein
Illuminates the historical significance of female portrayals in the Haftarah and the Five Megillot. 6 x 9, 560 pp, Quality PB, 978-1-58023-371-2 **$19.99**

The Women's Torah Commentary
New Insights from Women Rabbis on the 54 Weekly Torah Portions
Edited by Rabbi Elyse Goldstein
Over fifty women rabbis offer inspiring insights on the Torah, in a week-by-week format.
6 x 9, 496 pp, Quality PB, 978-1-58023-370-5 **$19.99**; HC, 978-1-58023-076-6 **$34.95**

See Passover for *The Women's Passover Companion: Women's Reflections on the Festival of Freedom* and *The Women's Seder Sourcebook: Rituals & Readings for Use at the Passover Seder.*

Inspiration

God of Me: Imagining God throughout Your Lifetime
By Rabbi David Lyon Helps you cut through preconceived ideas of God and dogmas that stifle your creativity when thinking about your personal relationship with God. 6 x 9, 176 pp, Quality PB, 978-1-58023-452-8 **$16.99**

The God Upgrade: Finding Your 21st-Century Spirituality in Judaism's 5,000-Year-Old Tradition *By Rabbi Jamie Korngold; Foreword by Rabbi Harold M. Schulweis* A provocative look at how our changing God concepts have shaped every aspect of Judaism. 6 x 9, 240 pp (est), Quality PB, 978-1-58023-443-6 **$15.99**

The Seven Questions You're Asked in Heaven: Reviewing and Renewing Your Life on Earth *By Dr. Ron Wolfson* An intriguing and entertaining resource for living a life that matters. 6 x 9, 176 pp, Quality PB, 978-1-58023-407-8 **$16.99**

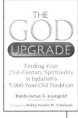

Happiness and the Human Spirit: The Spirituality of Becoming the Best You Can Be *By Rabbi Abraham J. Twerski, MD* Shows you that true happiness is attainable once you stop looking outside yourself for the source. 6 x 9, 176 pp, Quality PB, 978-1-58023-404-7 **$16.99**; HC, 978-1-58023-343-9 **$19.99**

A Formula for Proper Living: Practical Lessons from Life and Torah *By Rabbi Abraham J. Twerski, MD* 6 x 9, 144 pp, HC, 978-1-58023-402-3 **$19.99**

The Bridge to Forgiveness: Stories and Prayers for Finding God and Restoring Wholeness *By Rabbi Karyn D. Kedar* 6 x 9, 176 pp, Quality PB, 978-1-58023-451-1 **$16.99**

The Empty Chair: Finding Hope and Joy—Timeless Wisdom from a Hasidic Master, Rebbe Nachman of Breslov *Adapted by Moshe Mykoff and the Breslov Research Institute* 4 x 6, 128 pp, Deluxe PB w/ flaps, 978-1-879045-67-5 **$9.99**

The Gentle Weapon: Prayers for Everyday and Not-So-Everyday Moments— Timeless Wisdom from the Teachings of the Hasidic Master, Rebbe Nachman of Breslov *Adapted by Moshe Mykoff and S. C. Mizrahi, together with the Breslov Research Institute* 4 x 6, 144 pp, Deluxe PB w/ flaps, 978-1-58023-022-3 **$9.99**

God Whispers: Stories of the Soul, Lessons of the Heart *By Rabbi Karyn D. Kedar* 6 x 9, 176 pp, Quality PB, 978-1-58023-088-9 **$15.95**

God's To-Do List: 103 Ways to Be an Angel and Do God's Work on Earth *By Dr. Ron Wolfson* 6 x 9, 144 pp, Quality PB, 978-1-58023-301-9 **$16.99**

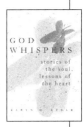

Jewish Stories from Heaven and Earth: Inspiring Tales to Nourish the Heart and Soul *Edited by Rabbi Dov Peretz Elkins* 6 x 9, 304 pp, Quality PB, 978-1-58023-363-7 **$16.99**

Life's Daily Blessings: Inspiring Reflections on Gratitude and Joy for Every Day, Based on Jewish Wisdom *By Rabbi Kerry M. Olitzky* 4½ x 6½, 368 pp, Quality PB, 978-1-58023-396-5 **$16.99**

Restful Reflections: Nighttime Inspiration to Calm the Soul, Based on Jewish Wisdom *By Rabbi Kerry M. Olitzky and Rabbi Lori Forman* 4½ x 6½, 448 pp, Quality PB, 978-1-58023-091-9 **$15.95**

Sacred Intentions: Daily Inspiration to Strengthen the Spirit, Based on Jewish Wisdom *By Rabbi Kerry M. Olitzky and Rabbi Lori Forman* 4½ x 6½, 448 pp, Quality PB, 978-1-58023-061-2 **$15.95**

Kabbalah/Mysticism

Jewish Mysticism and the Spiritual Life: Classical Texts, Contemporary Reflections *Edited by Dr. Lawrence Fine, Dr. Eitan Fishbane and Rabbi Or N. Rose* Inspirational and thought-provoking materials for contemplation, discussion and action. 6 x 9, 256 pp, HC, 978-1-58023-434-4 **$24.99**

Ehyeh: A Kabbalah for Tomorrow *By Rabbi Arthur Green, PhD* 6 x 9, 224 pp, Quality PB, 978-1-58023-213-5 **$18.99**

The Gift of Kabbalah: Discovering the Secrets of Heaven, Renewing Your Life on Earth *By Tamar Frankiel, PhD* 6 x 9, 256 pp, Quality PB, 978-1-58023-141-1 **$16.95**

Seek My Face: A Jewish Mystical Theology *By Rabbi Arthur Green, PhD* 6 x 9, 304 pp, Quality PB, 978-1-58023-130-5 **$19.95**

Zohar: Annotated & Explained *Translation & Annotation by Dr. Daniel C. Matt; Foreword by Andrew Harvey* 5½ x 8½, 176 pp, Quality PB, 978-1-893361-51-5 **$15.99**
(A book from SkyLight Paths, Jewish Lights' sister imprint)

See also *The Way Into Jewish Mystical Tradition* in The Way Into... Series.

Spirituality

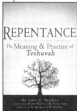

Repentance: The Meaning and Practice of *Teshuvah*
By Dr. Louis E. Newman; Foreword by Rabbi Harold M. Schulweis; Preface by Rabbi Karyn D. Kedar
Examines both the practical and philosophical dimensions of *teshuvah*, Judaism's core religious-moral teaching on repentance, and its value for us—Jews and non-Jews alike—today. 6 x 9, 256 pp, HC, 978-1-58023-426-9 **$24.99**

Tanya, the Masterpiece of Hasidic Wisdom
Selections Annotated & Explained
Translation & Annotation by Rabbi Rami Shapiro; Foreword by Rabbi Zalman M. Schachter-Shalomi
Brings the genius of *Tanya*, one of the most powerful books of Jewish wisdom, to anyone seeking to deepen their understanding of the soul.
5½ x 8½, 240 pp, Quality PB, 978-1-59473-275-1 **$16.99**
(A book from SkyLight Paths, Jewish Lights' sister imprint)

Aleph-Bet Yoga: Embodying the Hebrew Letters for Physical and Spiritual Well-Being
By Steven A. Rapp; Foreword by Tamar Frankiel, PhD, and Judy Greenfeld; Preface by Hart Lazer
7 x 10, 128 pp, b/w photos, Quality PB, Lay-flat binding, 978-1-58023-162-6 **$16.95**

A Book of Life: Embracing Judaism as a Spiritual Practice
By Rabbi Michael Strassfeld 6 x 9, 544 pp, Quality PB, 978-1-58023-247-0 **$19.99**

Bringing the Psalms to Life: How to Understand and Use the Book of Psalms
By Rabbi Daniel F. Polish, PhD 6 x 9, 208 pp, Quality PB, 978-1-58023-157-2 **$16.95**

Does the Soul Survive? A Jewish Journey to Belief in Afterlife, Past Lives & Living with Purpose *By Rabbi Elie Kaplan Spitz; Foreword by Brian L. Weiss, MD*
6 x 9, 288 pp, Quality PB, 978-1-58023-165-7 **$16.99**

First Steps to a New Jewish Spirit: Reb Zalman's Guide to Recapturing the Intimacy & Ecstasy in Your Relationship with God *By Rabbi Zalman M. Schachter-Shalomi with Donald Gropman* 6 x 9, 144 pp, Quality PB, 978-1-58023-182-4 **$16.95**

Foundations of Sephardic Spirituality: The Inner Life of Jews of the Ottoman Empire
By Rabbi Marc D. Angel, PhD 6 x 9, 224 pp, Quality PB, 978-1-58023-341-5 **$18.99**

God & the Big Bang: Discovering Harmony between Science & Spirituality
By Dr. Daniel C. Matt 6 x 9, 216 pp, Quality PB, 978-1-879045-89-7 **$16.99**

God in Our Relationships: Spirituality between People from the Teachings of Martin Buber *By Rabbi Dennis S. Ross* 5½ x 8½, 160 pp, Quality PB, 978-1-58023-147-3 **$16.95**

The Jewish Lights Spirituality Handbook: A Guide to Understanding, Exploring & Living a Spiritual Life *Edited by Stuart M. Matlins*
What exactly is "Jewish" about spirituality? How do I make it a part of my life? Fifty of today's foremost spiritual leaders share their ideas and experience with us.
6 x 9, 456 pp, Quality PB, 978-1-58023-093-3 **$19.99**

Judaism, Physics and God: Searching for Sacred Metaphors in a Post-Einstein World
By Rabbi David W. Nelson 6 x 9, 352 pp, Quality PB, inc. reader's discussion guide,
978-1-58023-306-4 **$18.99**; HC, 352 pp, 978-1-58023-252-4 **$24.99**

Meaning & Mitzvah: Daily Practices for Reclaiming Judaism through Prayer, God, Torah, Hebrew, Mitzvot and Peoplehood *By Rabbi Goldie Milgram*
7 x 9, 336 pp, Quality PB, 978-1-58023-256-2 **$19.99**

Minding the Temple of the Soul: Balancing Body, Mind, and Spirit through Traditional Jewish Prayer, Movement, and Meditation *By Tamar Frankiel, PhD, and Judy Greenfeld*
7 x 10, 184 pp, Illus., Quality PB, 978-1-879045-64-4 **$18.99**

One God Clapping: The Spiritual Path of a Zen Rabbi *By Rabbi Alan Lew with Sherril Jaffe*
5½ x 8½, 336 pp, Quality PB, 978-1-58023-115-2 **$16.95**

The Soul of the Story: Meetings with Remarkable People
By Rabbi David Zeller 6 x 9, 288 pp, HC, 978-1-58023-272-2 **$21.99**

There Is No Messiah ... and You're It: The Stunning Transformation of Judaism's Most Provocative Idea *By Rabbi Robert N. Levine, DD*
6 x 9, 192 pp, Quality PB, 978-1-58023-255-5 **$16.99**

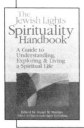

These Are the Words: A Vocabulary of Jewish Spiritual Life
By Rabbi Arthur Green, PhD 6 x 9, 304 pp, Quality PB, 978-1-58023-107-7 **$18.95**

Spirituality/Prayer

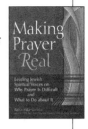

Making Prayer Real: Leading Jewish Spiritual Voices on Why Prayer Is Difficult and What to Do about It *By Rabbi Mike Comins*
A new and different response to the challenges of Jewish prayer, with "best prayer practices" from Jewish spiritual leaders of all denominations.
6 x 9, 320 pp, Quality PB, 978-1-58023-417-7 **$18.99**

Witnesses to the One: The Spiritual History of the *Sh'ma*
By Rabbi Joseph B. Meszler; Foreword by Rabbi Elyse Goldstein
6 x 9, 176 pp, Quality PB, 978-1-58023-400-9 **$16.99**; HC, 978-1-58023-309-5 **$19.99**

My People's Prayer Book Series: Traditional Prayers, Modern Commentaries *Edited by Rabbi Lawrence A. Hoffman, PhD*
Provides diverse and exciting commentary to the traditional liturgy. Will help you find new wisdom in Jewish prayer, and bring liturgy into your life. Each book includes Hebrew text, modern translations and commentaries from all perspectives of the Jewish world.

Vol. 1—The *Sh'ma* and Its Blessings
  7 x 10, 168 pp, HC, 978-1-879045-79-8 **$29.99**
Vol. 2—The *Amidah* 7 x 10, 240 pp, HC, 978-1-879045-80-4 **$24.95**
Vol. 3—*P'sukei D'zimrah* (Morning Psalms)
  7 x 10, 240 pp, HC, 978-1-879045-81-1 **$29.99**
Vol. 4—*Seder K'riat Hatorah* (The Torah Service)
  7 x 10, 264 pp, HC, 978-1-879045-82-8 **$29.99**
Vol. 5—*Birkhot Hashachar* (Morning Blessings)
  7 x 10, 240 pp, HC, 978-1-879045-83-5 **$24.95**
Vol. 6—*Tachanun* and Concluding Prayers
  7 x 10, 240 pp, HC, 978-1-879045-84-2 **$24.95**
Vol. 7—Shabbat at Home 7 x 10, 240 pp, HC, 978-1-879045-85-9 **$24.95**
Vol. 8—*Kabbalat Shabbat* (Welcoming Shabbat in the Synagogue)
  7 x 10, 240 pp, HC, 978-1-58023-121-3 **$24.99**
Vol. 9—Welcoming the Night: *Minchah* and *Ma'ariv* (Afternoon and
  Evening Prayer) 7 x 10, 272 pp, HC, 978-1-58023-262-3 **$24.99**
Vol. 10—Shabbat Morning: *Shacharit* and *Musaf* (Morning and
  Additional Services) 7 x 10, 240 pp, HC, 978-1-58023-240-1 **$29.99**

Spirituality/Lawrence Kushner

I'm God; You're Not: Observations on Organized Religion & Other Disguises of the Ego
6 x 9, 256 pp, HC, 978-1-58023-441-2 **$21.99**

The Book of Letters: A Mystical Hebrew Alphabet
Popular HC Edition, 6 x 9, 80 pp, 2-color text, 978-1-879045-00-2 **$24.95**
Collector's Limited Edition, 9 x 12, 80 pp, gold-foil-embossed pages, w/ limited-edition silkscreened
print, 978-1-879045-04-0 **$349.00**

The Book of Miracles: A Young Person's Guide to Jewish Spiritual Awareness
6 x 9, 96 pp, 2-color illus., HC, 978-1-879045-78-1 **$16.95** *For ages 9–13*

The Book of Words: Talking Spiritual Life, Living Spiritual Talk
6 x 9, 160 pp, Quality PB, 978-1-58023-020-9 **$18.99**

Eyes Remade for Wonder: A Lawrence Kushner Reader *Introduction by Thomas Moore*
6 x 9, 240 pp, Quality PB, 978-1-58023-042-1 **$18.99**

God Was in This Place & I, i Did Not Know: Finding Self, Spirituality and
Ultimate Meaning 6 x 9, 192 pp, Quality PB, 978-1-879045-33-0 **$16.95**

Honey from the Rock: An Introduction to Jewish Mysticism
6 x 9, 176 pp, Quality PB, 978-1-58023-073-5 **$16.95**

Invisible Lines of Connection: Sacred Stories of the Ordinary
5½ x 8½, 160 pp, Quality PB, 978-1-879045-98-9 **$15.95**

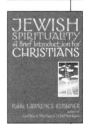

Jewish Spirituality: A Brief Introduction for Christians
5½ x 8½, 112 pp, Quality PB, 978-1-58023-150-3 **$12.95**

The River of Light: Jewish Mystical Awareness
6 x 9, 192 pp, Quality PB, 978-1-58023-096-4 **$16.95**

The Way Into Jewish Mystical Tradition
6 x 9, 224 pp, Quality PB, 978-1-58023-200-5 **$18.99**; HC, 978-1-58023-029-2 **$21.95**

Theology/Philosophy/The Way Into... Series

The Way Into... series offers an accessible and highly usable "guided tour" of the Jewish faith, people, history and beliefs—in total, an introduction to Judaism that will enable you to understand and interact with the sacred texts of the Jewish tradition. Each volume is written by a leading contemporary scholar and teacher, and explores one key aspect of Judaism. The Way Into... series enables all readers to achieve a real sense of Jewish cultural literacy through guided study.

The Way Into Encountering God in Judaism
By Rabbi Neil Gillman, PhD
For everyone who wants to understand how Jews have encountered God throughout history and today.
6 x 9, 240 pp, Quality PB, 978-1-58023-199-2 **$18.99**; HC, 978-1-58023-025-4 **$21.95**
Also Available: **The Jewish Approach to God:** A Brief Introduction for Christians
By Rabbi Neil Gillman, PhD
5½ x 8½, 192 pp, Quality PB, 978-1-58023-190-9 **$16.95**

The Way Into Jewish Mystical Tradition
By Rabbi Lawrence Kushner
Allows readers to interact directly with the sacred mystical texts of the Jewish tradition. An accessible introduction to the concepts of Jewish mysticism, their religious and spiritual significance, and how they relate to life today.
6 x 9, 224 pp, Quality PB, 978-1-58023-200-5 **$18.99**; HC, 978-1-58023-029-2 **$21.95**

The Way Into Jewish Prayer
By Rabbi Lawrence A. Hoffman, PhD
Opens the door to 3,000 years of Jewish prayer, making anyone feel at home in the Jewish way of communicating with God.
6 x 9, 208 pp, Quality PB, 978-1-58023-201-2 **$18.99**

The Way Into Jewish Prayer Teacher's Guide
By Rabbi Jennifer Ossakow Goldsmith
8½ x 11, 42 pp, PB, 978-1-58023-345-3 **$8.99**
Download a free copy at www.jewishlights.com.

The Way Into Judaism and the Environment
By Jeremy Benstein, PhD
Explores the ways in which Judaism contributes to contemporary social-environmental issues, the extent to which Judaism is part of the problem and how it can be part of the solution.
6 x 9, 288 pp, Quality PB, 978-1-58023-368-2 **$18.99**

The Way Into Tikkun Olam (Repairing the World)
By Rabbi Elliot N. Dorff, PhD
An accessible introduction to the Jewish concept of the individual's responsibility to care for others and repair the world.
6 x 9, 304 pp, Quality PB, 978-1-58023-328-6 **$18.99**

The Way Into Torah
By Rabbi Norman J. Cohen, PhD
Helps guide you in the exploration of the origins and development of Torah, explains why it should be studied and how to do it.
6 x 9, 176 pp, Quality PB, 978-1-58023-198-5 **$16.99**

The Way Into the Varieties of Jewishness
By Sylvia Barack Fishman, PhD
Explores the religious and historical understanding of what it has meant to be Jewish from ancient times to the present controversy over "Who is a Jew?"
6 x 9, 288 pp, Quality PB, 978-1-58023-367-5 **$18.99**; HC, 978-1-58023-030-8 **$24.99**

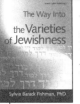

Theology/Philosophy

The God Who Hates Lies: Confronting and Rethinking Jewish Tradition
By Dr. David Hartman with Charlie Buckholtz
The world's leading Modern Orthodox Jewish theologian probes the deepest questions at the heart of what it means to be a human being and a Jew.
6 x 9, 275 pp (est), HC, 978-1-58023-455-9 **$24.99**

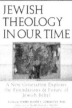

Jewish Theology in Our Time: A New Generation Explores the Foundations and Future of Jewish Belief *Edited by Rabbi Elliot J. Cosgrove, PhD; Foreword by Rabbi David J. Wolpe; Preface by Rabbi Carole B. Balin, PhD*
A powerful and challenging examination of what Jews can believe—by a new generation's most dynamic and innovative thinkers.
6 x 9, 240 pp, HC, 978-1-58023-413-9 **$24.99**

Maimonides, Spinoza and Us: Toward an Intellectually Vibrant Judaism
By Rabbi Marc D. Angel, PhD A challenging look at two great Jewish philosophers and what their thinking means to our understanding of God, truth, revelation and reason. 6 x 9, 224 pp, HC, 978-1-58023-411-5 **$24.99**

The Death of Death: Resurrection and Immortality in Jewish Thought
By Rabbi Neil Gillman, PhD 6 x 9, 336 pp, Quality PB, 978-1-58023-081-0 **$18.95**

Doing Jewish Theology: God, Torah & Israel in Modern Judaism *By Rabbi Neil Gillman, PhD*
6 x 9, 304 pp, Quality PB, 978-1-58023-439-9 **$18.99**

Hasidic Tales: Annotated & Explained *Translation & Annotation by Rabbi Rami Shapiro*
5½ x 8½, 240 pp, Quality PB, 978-1-893361-86-7 **$16.95***

A Heart of Many Rooms: Celebrating the Many Voices within Judaism
By Dr. David Hartman 6 x 9, 352 pp, Quality PB, 978-1-58023-156-5 **$19.95**

The Hebrew Prophets: Selections Annotated & Explained
Translation & Annotation by Rabbi Rami Shapiro; Foreword by Rabbi Zalman M. Schachter-Shalomi
5½ x 8½, 224 pp, Quality PB, 978-1-59473-037-5 **$16.99***

A Jewish Understanding of the New Testament *By Rabbi Samuel Sandmel; Preface by Rabbi David Sandmel* 5½ x 8½, 368 pp, Quality PB, 978-1-59473-048-1 **$19.99***

Jews and Judaism in the 21st Century: Human Responsibility, the Presence of God and the Future of the Covenant *Edited by Rabbi Edward Feinstein; Foreword by Paula E. Hyman*
6 x 9, 192 pp, Quality PB, 978-1-58023-374-3 **$19.99**

A Living Covenant: The Innovative Spirit in Traditional Judaism
By Dr. David Hartman 6 x 9, 368 pp, Quality PB, 978-1-58023-011-7 **$25.00**

Love and Terror in the God Encounter: The Theological Legacy of Rabbi Joseph B. Soloveitchik *By Dr. David Hartman* 6 x 9, 240 pp, Quality PB, 978-1-58023-176-3 **$19.95**

A Touch of the Sacred: A Theologian's Informal Guide to Jewish Belief
By Dr. Eugene B. Borowitz and Frances W. Schwartz
6 x 9, 256 pp, Quality PB, 978-1-58023-416-0 **$16.99**; HC, 978-1-58023-337-8 **$21.99**

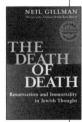

Traces of God: Seeing God in Torah, History and Everyday Life *By Rabbi Neil Gillman, PhD*
6 x 9, 240 pp, Quality PB, 978-1-58023-369-9 **$16.99**

Your Word Is Fire: The Hasidic Masters on Contemplative Prayer
Edited and translated by Rabbi Arthur Green, PhD, and Barry W. Holtz
6 x 9, 160 pp, Quality PB, 978-1-879045-25-5 **$15.95**

I Am Jewish
Personal Reflections Inspired by the Last Words of Daniel Pearl
Almost 150 Jews—both famous and not—from all walks of life, from all around the world, write about many aspects of their Judaism.
Edited by Judea and Ruth Pearl 6 x 9, 304 pp, Deluxe PB w/ flaps, 978-1-58023-259-3 **$18.99**
Download a free copy of the *I Am Jewish Teacher's Guide* at www.jewishlights.com.

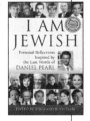

Hannah Senesh: Her Life and Diary, The First Complete Edition
By Hannah Senesh; Foreword by Marge Piercy; Preface by Eitan Senesh; Afterword by Roberta Grossman
6 x 9, 368 pp, b/w photos, Quality PB, 978-1-58023-342-2 **$19.99**

*A book from SkyLight Paths, Jewish Lights' sister imprint

About Jewish Lights

People of all faiths and backgrounds yearn for books that attract, engage, educate, and spiritually inspire.

Our principal goal is to stimulate thought and help all people learn about who the Jewish People are, where they come from, and what the future can be made to hold. While people of our diverse Jewish heritage are the primary audience, our books speak to people in the Christian world as well and will broaden their understanding of Judaism and the roots of their own faith.

We bring to you authors who are at the forefront of spiritual thought and experience. While each has something different to say, they all say it in a voice that you can hear.

Our books are designed to welcome you and then to engage, stimulate, and inspire. We judge our success not only by whether or not our books are beautiful and commercially successful, but by whether or not they make a difference in your life.

For your information and convenience, at the back of this book we have provided a list of other Jewish Lights books you might find interesting and useful. They cover all the categories of your life:

Bar/Bat Mitzvah	Life Cycle
Bible Study / Midrash	Meditation
Children's Books	Men's Interest
Congregation Resources	Parenting
Current Events / History	Prayer / Ritual / Sacred Practice
Ecology / Environment	Social Justice
Fiction: Mystery, Science Fiction	Spirituality
Grief / Healing	Theology / Philosophy
Holidays / Holy Days	Travel
Inspiration	Twelve Steps
Kabbalah / Mysticism / Enneagram	Women's Interest

Stuart M. Matlins, Publisher

Or phone, fax, mail or e-mail to: **JEWISH LIGHTS Publishing**
Sunset Farm Offices, Route 4 • P.O. Box 237 • Woodstock, Vermont 05091
Tel: (802) 457-4000 • Fax: (802) 457-4004 • www.jewishlights.com
Credit card orders: (800) 962-4544 (8:30AM–5:30PM ET Monday–Friday)
Generous discounts on quantity orders. SATISFACTION GUARANTEED. Prices subject to change.